D0793102

Identities on Trial in the United States

CROSSING BORDERS IN A GLOBAL WORLD: APPLYING ANTHROPOLOGY TO MIGRATION, DISPLACEMENT, AND SOCIAL CHANGE

Series Editors: Raúl Sánchez Molina and Nancy Anne Konvalinka

Mission Statement

By crossing political, social, cultural, and identity borders, current migrants, refugees, and travelers meet challenges of globalization in their processes of displacement, incorporation, and adaptation to new settlements. These circumstances open up opportunities for anthropologists and members of related disciplines to work together with migrants, residents, and communities seeking to contribute to knowledge and action. This series addresses these challenges and their intersections with national, ethnic, gender, and generational identities by providing a range of interdisciplinary theoretical and methodological frameworks that outline how scholars and practitioners can approach not only knowledge, but also application. This series provides models of collaboration and interaction in the economy and labor market and in policy, social and physical reproductions, health, education, and other social institutions.

Advisory Board

Maria Eugenia Bozzoli, Adi Bharadwaj, Monica Bonaccorso, Lucy M. Cohen, Yasmine Ergas, Andrés Fábregas Puig, Carles Feixa, Ubaldo Martínez Veiga, Marit Melhuus, Alicia Re Cruz, Amy Speier, Meenakshi Thapan, and María Amelia Viteri

Books in Series

Identities on Trial in the United States: Asylum Seekers from Asia, by ChorSwang Ngin.

Identities on Trial in the United States

Asylum Seekers from Asia

ChorSwang Ngin

LEXINGTON BOOKS
Lanham • Boulder • New York • London

Published by Lexington Books
An imprint of The Rowman & Littlefield Publishing Group, Inc.
4501 Forbes Boulevard, Suite 200, Lanham, Maryland 20706
www.rowman.com

Unit A, Whitacre Mews, 26-34 Stannary Street, London SE11 4AB

Copyright © 2018 by The Rowman & Littlefield Publishing Group, Inc.

All rights reserved. No part of this book may be reproduced in any form or by any electronic or mechanical means, including information storage and retrieval systems, without written permission from the publisher, except by a reviewer who may quote passages in a review.

British Library Cataloguing in Publication Information Available

Library of Congress Cataloging-in-Publication Data Available

ISBN 978-1-4985-7473-0 (cloth : alk. paper)
ISBN 978-1-4985-7475-4 (pbk. : alk. paper)
ISBN 978-1-4985-7474-7 (electronic)

™ The paper used in this publication meets the minimum requirements of American National Standard for Information Sciences—Permanence of Paper for Printed Library Materials, ANSI/NISO Z39.48-1992.

Printed in the United States of America

Contents

Foreword

David W. Haines

Identities on Trial in the United States: Asylum Seekers from Asia takes you inside the courtrooms and lawyers' offices where the fate of asylum applicants is determined, and shows how the complex cultural backgrounds of asylum applicants both help and hinder their cases. It is an exceedingly important book on a vital and convoluted topic, and the author's approach is an ideal blend of personal account and scholarly analysis. ChorSwang Ngin has worked as an expert witness in a wide range of asylum cases over many years involving applicants from different parts of Asia. So she has worked within the system. She is also an established anthropology professor with strong personal, professional, and linguistic grounding in Asia, especially with the many kinds of Chinese who end up seeking asylum from different countries of Asia. She is thus ideally suited to explain to the lawyers and judges—and to her readers here—exactly who these asylum applicants are in cultural terms, what kind of situations in their home countries propelled them out, and exactly why their applications for asylum make sense in terms of their background.

Much of the book reads like an intellectual detective story: what does it take on the ground to navigate and create a successful asylum case? Ngin's recounting of the details of each case is an effective walk-through of an asylum process that is often hard to understand, hard to access, and sometimes hard to believe. Even with her background, she has often found gaps that required the search for yet more information. Her experience is thus that the presumed expert must not only be knowledgeable but also know how to know more. Her experience in that endless quest yields here a volume that is absolutely essential to anyone dealing with refuge and asylum in the United States—or elsewhere for that matter. It would also be a wonderful addition to undergraduate courses on immigration and an invaluable component in graduate ones.

Early on in the book, readers will be faced with the complexities of what asylum is. The legal grounds for asylum—persecution because of race, religion, nationality, political opinion, or social group—are often treated as self-evident and obvious. But they are not. As Professor Ngin ably explains through varied cases, all of those grounds are often unclear and often intermixed. She is particularly attentive to issues of race. Race and nationality, for example, are especially contentious since they overlap with each other and with what we often think of as ethnicity. She recounts how she had to give up her anthropologically-based critique of race and learn to accept race as an unavoidable category in asylum cases. She had to shift from an anthropological critique of the concept of race to an anthropological documentation of who a person is in conventional racial categories. This is a hard lesson for academics: critiques of social constructs—like race—can be detrimental to the very people those academics may be trying to support.

One issue that merits particular attention in this book is the nature of truth. There is a certain kind of truth about identity that has to be supplied to the court. The court insists on knowing not only whether someone is a bona fide refugee but also exactly who that person is in more general terms. For example, are they really "Chinese" if they don't come from China? Even if people aiding the case recognize how difficult that Chinese label may be, they still have to certify it to the court. They also, Ngin believes, must certify it to themselves. The author may in some ways be an advocate, but she is also a truth seeker. When she certifies someone as being some kind of person—like a Chinese—she must herself be convinced that the identifying label is proper. Her careful amassing of cultural detail about asylum applicants is thus both to convince herself and to convince the court about who someone is.

Following the author through the many cases that constitute this book illuminates how complex social and cultural reality can be, and how expert must be the triangulation of social interactions, cultural beliefs, and very specific historical and geographical contexts. The ability of the anthropologist to certify truth, rather than simply advocating or critiquing, is crucial. The last thing an argumentative and adversarial situation like an asylum case needs is yet more argument. That is particularly so given court contexts that, as she describes, often include massive and sometimes truly horrifying misunderstanding and misinformation on the part of attorneys and judges alike. The goal may not be truth in some abstract grand sense, but it is a practical truth that must be sufficient to, and consonant with, the world of asylum cases.

As you read this book, you will recognize the complexity of the asylum process and the mixed motivations, competencies, incompentencies, and occasional venality of those holding forth in the courtroom. Follow carefully this deliberative process of establishing who people are as a matter of actual truth (or close to it) and as a matter of placing them within the categories that rule the granting or withholding of asylum. To ignore the categories of the system, whether right or wrong, is to undermine or even forfeit the possibility of asylum, and thus to damage the asylum seekers' lives in both their physical (life or death; progress or hardship) and more spiritual senses (spirits lifted up, spirits broken).

As you read, also get to know the people that she is getting to know. Piece together your own sense of what is plausible, of what makes people who they are, and of how that identity can be validated both in a humanistic and a legalistic way. And get to know the patient anthropologist interviewer and investigator who is trying to know these people on their terms, on her terms, and on the court's terms, who is trying to keep to the facts and not the emotions, but who is also personally torn by the conflicting information, perceptions, and prejudices that collide in asylum cases.

Acknowledgments

There are many who made this book possible. I owe a debt of gratitude to the asylum seekers and their attorneys and partners, especially Kenneth Goodsell, Dr. St. Elmo Nauman, Jr., Meiji Sopoto, Amanda Sonneborn and Chris Busey who trusted me with the application of anthropology in the asylum process.

I thank the Honorable Judges and Government Counsels in the immigration courts in Los Angeles, Phoenix, and Chicago who questioned and listened to an academic anthropologist in their adjudication of asylum cases. I especially thank attorney Joann Yeh, for her friendship, partnership, and legal insights, and her coauthorship of three chapters that provided the collaboration between law and anthropology.

I thank the Provost's Office at California State University, Los Angeles, for a sabbatical in 2015, which allowed precious uninterrupted time to focus on research and writing.

Over the years, colleagues and friends in the United States and abroad, at conferences and seminars, have provided conversations, discussions, guidance, and support on the asylum cases and in the writing. I cannot mention them all but I wish especially to thank Anthony Good for his critical comments and for reading early chapters of this book. I thank David Haines for his enthusiastic support, his numerous suggestions for revision, and for writing the forward. I thank Reed Malcolm of the University of California Press for his encouragement and his vision, which was pivotal to the book's format. To James Loucky for his inspiration as a pioneer on asylum research; to Lawrence Rosen, Richard Wilson, and Didier Fassin whose pioneering work lighted the way for this work; to Ina Tjandrasuwita for keeping me abreast of conditions in Indonesia; to Mark Hitman for many discussions on both law and religion. Special "thank you" to Bob Miles whose "racialization" saved me from the "race" jam. I also thank Loh Wei Leng, Chan Chee Khoon and Tan Keng Seng for keeping me focused on my work. To my Cal State LA colleagues Cheryl Ney, Lena Chao, James Brady, Catherine Haras, Scott Wells, Raquel Ackerman, Kate Sullivan, Heidi Riggio, and many others for their support and encouragement. My gratitude also goes to librarian colleagues and friends Yongyi Song, and Ying Xu for their collegiality and material on Asia; and to Daniel Tseng of the University of California, Irvine and Fulbright at Hong Kong University for material on asylum research.

My students bear some responsibility for this book: the origin lies in my attempt to demystify refugee and asylum research and the possibility of anthropological contribution. Erin Thomason, Cecilia Salvi, Gregory Urban, Alix Politanoff, Melanie Saldaña, Jose Trinidad Castaneda III, Michelle Dragoo, Jaymee Ng, and Hannah Jacobson have read chapters from earlier drafts and provided comments. Natasha Khana and Lanie Trinh worked on the references. The final appearance of the book was the collective effort of a team of thirteen editors. Students enrolled in my graduate course in 2017—Merissa Craft, Randi Dillard, Gricelda Espinoza, Lynnelle Garcia, Raul Iglesias, Manson Johnson, Neil Kohanski, Wendy Layco, Erika McMullin, Graciela Rodriguez, Valeria Rodriguez, Jack Sukimoto, Nancy Verduzco—updated, prepared references, and meticulously checked for consistency. Special thanks to Neil Kohanski for preparing the bibliography, Valeria Rodriguez for the diagrams, and Wendy Layco for the final editing.

I thank Emerald Publishing Limited for permission to include "Proving 'Race' Identity of Chinese Indonesian Asylum Seekers," in *Special Issue: Cultural Expert Witnessing* (Studies in Law, Politics and Society, Volume 74, 2018, Austin Sarat, Leila Rodriguez (ed.) Emerald Publishing Limited, pp. 133–64).

My sincere thanks go to Kasey Beduhn, Becca Rohde, and Melissa McClellan of Lexington Books who were always available to answer my questions.

Last, but not least, to Elaine Chao Thomas and Stephen Thomas for their years of support, and to Richard, Liana and Phillip who tolerated my absence with love and understanding. Most important of all, to my husband and friend, Eric Chang, who supported me with constant encouragement. In addition, to Archer, Lark, Ethan and Janie who lightened my heart when the going got tough.

Introduction

The Asylum Seeker as the Anthropological Figure of the Twenty-First Century

SEEKING SANCTUARY

In a brightly lit Immigration Office in Anaheim, California, a twenty-nine-year-old woman by the name of Dewi Wisante[1] had applied for asylum protection after entering the United States on a tourist visa. Dewi claimed she was a Chinese from Indonesia who had fled the anti-Chinese civil strife in 1998 where Chinese women were systematically raped and Chinese businesses burnt. The Immigration Officer had denied Dewi's asylum petition, arguing that she had failed to prove she was persecuted on account of her "race"—one of the five grounds of the 1951 Refugee Convention. The Immigration Officer suggested Dewi obtain the help of an anthropologist to verify her "Chinese race."

Anthropology has long been the discipline associated with the concepts of "race" and "culture" in our research and teaching. Dewi requested my help, thinking perhaps, that since I was an anthropologist teaching courses on "race" and Asia, I would be able to help determine her identity. I conducted an oral history on her and submitted the report to her attorney, but it was rejected due to my failure to state Dewi's "race." The rejection in proving Dewi's identity left me in an anthropological dilemma: how does one determine the "race" of a person while acknowledging it as a socially constructed notion? Or how to determine her "Chinese-ness" when she did not even possess a Chinese name and could not communicate in Mandarin or any of the several Chinese dialects I was fluent in? Without proof of Dewi's persecution on account of her "race," she faced deportation and an uncertain future.

Based on a treaty on forced migration created in 1951—the Convention Relating to the Status of Refugee, updated and accepted by the General Assembly in 1967, refugee status or asylum may be granted to people who have been persecuted, or fear they will be persecuted, on account of race, religion, nationality, membership in a particular social group, or political opinion (UNHCR 2016). The United States, as the world's top refugee resettlement country, accepts both refugees and asylum seekers.

Each day, refugees and asylum seekers are driven by violent wars, ethnic strife, a government's expulsion of people, and collapsed economies to cross borders in search of safety. Refugees, often fleeing wars in great numbers, are assisted by humanitarian organizations and governments to determine their status as refugee before they enter the country that agreed to accept them. Unlike the refugees, asylum seekers to the United States do not present a picture of a mass of humanity surging toward a border. Some individual asylum seekers cross the border illegally. Those arrested are detained in prison-like conditions and are deported unless they are given a chance to tell their story in front of an immigration judge. A few fortunate ones, like Dewi, entered the country on a legal temporary visa and then applied for asylum.

To be granted refugee status and receive asylum protection, the asylum seekers must prove that they are who they say they are. In the context of countless millions of refugees and asylum seekers attempting to enter another country, how is their identity determined? How does one know if they are telling the truth? And how does one know that they were persecuted? (Haas 2017). Distinguishing a genuine asylum seeker from a fraudulent economic migrant presents a challenge to the asylum adjudicators, as well as the anthropologists who have been asked to decipher the identities of the asylum seekers. To decipher the identity of an asylum seeker, I have employed Fassin and d'Huillin's (2005) idea of the *asylum seeker* as the *anthropological figure* of the twenty-first century, in comparison to the *refugee* as a figure of the twentieth century. Anthropologically verifying the asylum seeker's identity presents a challenge to both theories and methods. Law requires specificity on the "race" and cultural identity of a person, while anthropology deals with the heterogeneity and hybridity of individuals in a changing world. In the example of verifying persecution on account of "race," how can anthropology designate the asylum seeker with a "race" while arguing humans cannot be divided into a fixed number of races? Verifying the identity of the asylum seekers as an anthropological expert witness also *puts anthropological truth on trial*. Do we really know an asylum seeker is telling the truth when we are only able to gather oral accounts without the opportunity to conduct actual fieldwork or witness their persecution?

CONFRONTING THE *ANTHROPOLOGICAL FIGURE*

Early in the twentieth century, the world witnessed massive numbers of refugees flowing out of Europe. Many people escaping the wars were resettled in the United States. The harrowing experience of war and escape, of statelessness, and of individual rights, became the subject of Hannah Arendt's writings. Arendt, who was born in 1906, in Konigsberg (then part of Germany), was Jewish. She became politicized when she observed and collected evidence of the persecution of German Jews. Her arrest by the Gestapo, her escape, her own statelessness, and her own refugee experience led to some monumental works on totalitarianism, the rights of an individual, and the human condition (Arendt 2004). The refugee experience shapes the lives of many people. The refugee, according to Arendt, is the *historical subject* of the twentieth century (Fassin and d'Halluin 2005). In the twenty-first century, the world is also confronted with massive numbers of people whose identity must be verified. Fassin and d'Halluin (2005) refer to this twenty-first century individual seeking asylum as the *anthropological figure*, when compared to the refugee as the *historical subject* of the twentieth century.

Asylum seekers, like refugees, face similar plight in their homeland. But they are not screened at the border while waiting in refugee camps. Instead, they are examined upon entry on a case-by-case basis for a chance to be recognized as legal subjects of a state. The grounds under which an asylum seeker will be granted asylum—race, religion, nationality, membership in a particular social group, and political opinion—are the staples of our anthropological inquiry. To understand the culture of a people, anthropologists conduct fieldwork and analyze its families and kinship, religion and magic, politics, and how people make a living. For comparison, we examine people in places far and near, big and small, past and present. The grounds of the Refugee Convention within which the adjudicators must decide if the asylum seeker qualifies as a refugee are embedded within anthropological examination of a people's culture. Therefore, to decipher the identity of an asylum seeker is akin to conducting basic anthropological enquiries. This time, the *anthropological figure* is the asylum seeker. In addition, unlike the traditional approach of our anthropological enquiry where we seek out informants to gather information while doing fieldwork, the asylum seeker as an *anthropological figure* comes to us for our expertise on culture to figure out his or her identity for the asylum courts.

CHALLENGING ANTHROPOLOGICAL THEORIES AND METHODS

Deciphering the anthropological figure presents several challenges to anthropology. How should anthropology handle the idea that the persecution against the asylum seeker is due to his or her race and culture, religion and beliefs, gender and sexual orientation, or nationality and political opinion?

First of all, anthropologists have long argued that race is socially constructed, and people cannot be represented by only a few cultural criteria. However, if we are asked to provide anthropological support on asylum cases, we are tested by the requirement of specifying the "race" or "culture" of the asylum seekers. Furthermore, the distinction between race and culture, culture and ethnicity, and ethnicity and nationality, often overlap in everyday and conventional usage.

Second, the gathering of ethnographic data cannot be done in a traditional anthropological fieldwork setting. Without being in the field, there are no actual practices and behaviors to observe, nor the ability to check actual practices against what the asylum seekers have said. The asylum seekers are away from their familiar surroundings. They are also without friends and kin, or the support of a community. Thus, we cannot consult with others to verify the identity of the asylum seeker.

Third, many asylum seekers also come without proof of their persecution. Their abusers, their rapists, and the police who are often their tormentor are not likely to act as their witnesses or to provide a report of their abuse. Yet, to support the asylum seeker and their attorneys, the anthropologist is often required to somehow verify the persecution against them. The lack of both witnesses and physical evidence challenges anthropology to come up with new concepts and ways of gathering data to account for the identities of the anthropological figure, and to suggest plausible reasons for their persecution.

ANTHROPOLOGICAL CREDIBILITY ON TRIAL

At the heart of most asylum cases is the issue of credibility: if the asylum seeker's testimony and representations are found to be credible, then s/he is likely to receive refugee status and protection (Einhorn and Berhold 2015, 30). Today, as millions of potential refugees and asylum seekers are desperate to enter countries accepting refugees—mostly Western democracies—many nations are rethinking their obligations and their hospitality (Fassin 2013). According to Fassin and d'Halluin (2005), until the 1980s, claimants operated within a climate of "trust, in which the applicant was presumed to be telling the truth." Today, however, claimants must represent their concerns within a "climate of suspicion," one "in which the asylum seeker is seen as someone trying to take advantage of the country's hospitality" (Fassin and d'Halluin 2005, 600). Governments are understandably anxious to maintain orderly migration and to increase the protection and defense of their national borders (Pickering 2006; Fassin 2013). The United States, traditionally known for accepting the largest number of refugees, is concerned with terrorists among those admitted after September 11, and must also address the anti-immigrant sentiment in the nation (Lee 2015).

As nations suffer from "compassion fatigue" with increased restrictions on refugees and asylum seekers, more people have resorted to illegal means of entering a country. With the rise in illegal immigration, genuine asylum petitioners who have made it legally through a national border are subjected to increased scrutiny. They have been criminalized in discourse and in practices (Pickering 2006). The authorities typically assume, as a default position, that all stories told to them are lies and therefore subject the asylum seekers to identity analysis (Blommaert 2009). Asylum adjudicators, presuming fraud among the asylum seekers, routinely reject their applications. Christopher Einolf (2001), a former immigrant judge and asylum attorney in Los Angeles, echoed this feeling of deep ambivalence by concluding that "[i]mmigration judges are also more skeptical of asylum seeker's credibility, as a general rule, than asylum officers, and more likely to deny an applicant's claim" (160). The difficulty of the asylum seeker in obtaining asylum is described by Bohmer and Shuman (2008) as "a Kafkaesque parable of homeless stateless aliens who are turned away at every possible point of entry with no place to go. They are given impossible tasks, marked by unfathomable suffering, the most difficult being the job of proving that they are who they say they are" (625). That is, the sum of all the problems encountered by the asylum seekers—from flight to plight—hinges on a single criterion: they are judged solely from the perspective of the adjudicators.

According to the United States Department of Justice Fact Sheet (2007), "asylum cases are judged based upon the law and the facts, and each case is protected by a robust review and appeal process. . . . Asylum adjudication does not lend itself well to statistical analysis. . . . Each asylum application is adjudicated on a case-by-case basis, and each case has many variables that need to be considered by an adjudicator. . . . The burden of proof is on the asylum applicants to credibly establish past persecution or a well-founded fear of future persecution" (1). If asylum cases are decided by the asylum adjudicator on a case-by-case basis, with the burden of proof dependent on the asylum applicant, it is therefore the subjective input of the adjudicator that determines the asylum outcome. In a study conducted in the United States, legal scholars described the chances of obtaining asylum recognition as akin to playing a game of roulette (Ramji-Nogales, Schoenholtz, and Schrag 2009). According to these scholars, the approval rate of asylum applications from the same country, and processed in the same courtroom, can vary as much as 90 percent. Ultimately, gaining asylum is the luck of the draw. A website for data gathering, data research, and data distribution compiled by the University of Syracuse tracks asylum granting rates by judges, also reveals a tremendous difference in the judge's inclination to issue or deny asylum petitions. This suggests that the "luck" of being assigned to one judge or the other may play a role in the outcome of an asylum petition (Transactional Records Access Clearinghouse 2013).

Rather than relying on luck alone, some asylum seekers attempt to maximize their chances of gaining asylum themselves. In France, for instance, while the number of asylum applications have gone up during the last few decades, the country's rate of acceptance has gone down (Fassin 2013). Desparate asylum seekers take additional measures. For example, some asylum seekers have visited doctors, claiming their physical and mental conditions were the result of past persecution, and requested medical certificates to attest to those conditions (Fassin and d'Halluin 2005). The doctors who volunteer to help these asylum seekers are forced to confront an ethical dilemma: should they stretch the truth for the asylum seekers by writing a medical letter attesting that their physical scars are genuine, and their psychological trauma is real? Or, should medical professionals take no action despite the pleas for their help? In the French example, when the truth of the asylum seeker is not believed, the medical certificate becomes the truth-bearer. The truth authority now rests with the medical profession, and the body itself becomes the evidence in asylum cases. In New York City, asylum seekers, too, have sought attorneys willing to listen to their stories and file petitions attesting to their persecution. In 2014, a number of attorneys were arrested for making "fraudulent claims"—claims that the petitioners were indeed asylum seekers when in fact they may have only wanted a way to remain in the United States. The attorneys gave an explanation for their behavior. According to newspaper reports, some of the attorneys said they were motivated by "a compulsion to help Chinese immigrants make a better life for themselves" (Semple, Goldstein, and Singer 2014, 7). They argued those who had worked so hard to flee authoritarian rule in China should be able to stay in the United States and that they acted as a last resort against the inhumanity of a system where people in need are not being believed. That is, they file petitions to help the asylum seekers win asylum by stretching the truth. It was a situation that those in the legal profession wished they did not have to be put into.

When an asylum system makes accepting the credibility of the asylum seekers difficult, the doctors and attorneys have become the "producers of truth" in asylum cases. With the help of doctors and lawyers, the asylum seeker now benefits from these professionals' recognized credibility, improving their chance of winning asylum. The challenge Dewi's case presents to anthropology—if we accept the engagement with asylum work—is enormous. By agreeing to give our opinion on the asylum seeker's identity, unwittingly, we too have been asked to join the precarious business of truth-telling and truth-making for asylum seekers. If the credibility of the asylum seeker is on trial, the validity of anthropological knowledge is being questioned as well.

ADJUDICATING ASYLUM CASES IN A WORLD OF UNCERTAINTIES

In the same brightly-lit office where Dewi applied for asylum, filmmaker Shari Robertson and her colleagues made their documentary, "Well-Founded Fear" (Robertson et al. 2006). The filmmakers invited their audience to imagine the life of an asylum seeker.

> Imagine that your life has fallen apart—something terrible has happened and you've lost every material possession, you've been tortured or seriously hurt, or maybe you've gotten out of jail in time. You've said goodbye to the people you love and now you find yourself faced with the barest possibility of a new start, a glimmer of hope that you can begin a new life in a strange new place in relative safety. Your papers have been submitted, your life is being processed, and now here is your chance. You will enter a small, fluorescent-lit office where you will have one hour to tell your story to a neutral bureaucrat. Two weeks later you will return to pick up a paper. This page will tell you your fate.

The filmmakers then invite the audience to imagine themselves in the shoes of an immigration officer:

> Now imagine yourself on the other side of the desk, in the small bright office. . . . You come to work every morning and you have no idea who you'll meet, because a computer assigns cases at random. You walk out into the waiting room and call someone's name—a name from any one of a hundred countries. Each person comes to tell you a story. Sometimes a lawyer or a translator is there. You have listened to blood-curdling details, you have seen a lot of confusion, and you have heard many lies. In the afternoon you have an additional 90 minutes to research and to write up a defense of your decision. Your job is to convince your supervisor that each person deserves one of two things—to be invited to stay here in safety, or to be deported. There is no recommendation in between.

Bound by international treaties and national protocols on asylum protection, legal mechanisms designed to analyze the eligibility and granting of legal status must distinguish legitimate from illegitimate asylum seekers, and refugees from economic migrants. It involves a bureaucracy of immigration officers, government counsels, and judges who decide on the asylum application. Supporting their work are the interpreters, courtroom staff, and services providing biometric authentication of the asylum petitioner. In adjudicating an asylum case, the crucial task for the immigration officer and other asylum adjudicators is deciding who the asylum petitioner is, based on a name, written content in an application form, his or her oral account, and what the physical presence of the claimant suggests to the adjudicator.

In everyday encounters, whether the person is of one race or culture or another, is often not subjected to intense investigation. If one sees a Chinese, we assume the person is from China. If one sees a person who looks Indian, we assume the person is from India, and so forth. But in an era of globalization and rapid migrations of peoples, it is not always possible to know with certainty the identities of a person indicated by the person's name or appearance—an ethnic Chinese could be a Chinese American or a third generation Indonesian, while an Indian could just as likely be a British Indian or a Tamil-speaking Malaysian. In a globalized world, the old certainties of aligning race with culture, religion, and place, are no longer certain. Cross-cultural competency through an interdisciplinary approach best affords the truthful asylum seeker a fair hearing and a just result (Lawrance and Ruffer 2015, 47). Without taking the possibilities of multiplicities into account, we depend on old assumptions of perceived notions of who the others are. I undertook this book project to examine the challenges in figuring out the identities of the asylum seekers from a number of Asian countries and the persecution they had endured as I assisted attorneys with their asylum cases in the United States.

There are five parts in this book. The first four parts examine cases based on the five grounds of the Refugee Convention: race, nationality, religion, membership in a particular social group, and political opinion. Each chapter consists of different asylum seekers' stories of persecution and escape and the anthropological challenges I encountered in providing the attorneys with reasonable sociocultural explanations when evidentiary proofs of persecution against the asylum seekers were lacking. Three of the fifteen chapters are coauthored with immigration attorney Joann Yeh.

Part I is focused on proving persecution based on the asylum seeker's "race" and nationality identities. In chapter 1, using Dewi Wisante's case as an example, I discussed how ethnicity and culture are bound up with the ground on "race" by examining the history of the idea of race, the United States Census classification based on race, the popular use of the idea of race, and the difficulty of identifying the Indonesian Chinese as belonging to a particular "race." When the concept of "race" failed to identify the Chinese from

Indonesia, in chapter 2, I verified the asylum seekers' "Chinese culture" by excavating the layers of their identity through language, names, and customs relating to honoring the dead. In chapter 3, I employed the innovative idea of racialization and its relationship to racism to meet the legal requirement of persecution on account of "race" (Miles 2003). In chapter 4, in my attempt to verify the nationality of Khun Yaw, I tell the story of a Mandarin-speaking student activist who claimed imprisonment and torture for four years in a Myanmar prison. His fraudulent documents, and his refusal to speak in Burmese complicated the sleuth work necessary to ascertain his identity in his asylum application.

In part II, I explored the difficulty of proving persecution on the grounds of religion. Chapter 5 paves the way by telling the asylum stories from an anthropological perspective of three Indonesian Chinese who applied for asylum protection in the United States because of the 1998 anti-Chinese civil unrest: Ms. Wilan, a devout Catholic woman whose husband was presumed dead when his motor repair shop was burnt; Mr. Budi, a Buddhist monk who possessed four aliases when he petitioned for asylum; and Mr. Yohanan, an Evangelical Christian pastor who withdrew his asylum petition to return to Indonesia "to do God's work." Religion played a role in all their cases, but their attorneys failed to use this fact in their asylum applications. In chapter 6, coauthored with Attorney Joann Yeh, we documented three asylum cases from China to show the painful difficulty of adjudicating cases on persecution of underground Chinese Christian house church members in the case of Mr. Wu and Ms. Liu, and an obscure Chinese *I-Kuan Tao*, as in the case of Ms. Yang. In Joann Yeh's representation of Mr. Wu, Ms. Yang and Ms. Liu's asylum cases in court revealed some important court proceedings rarely observed by the public. We included these cases to ask: Who has the canonical authority on religious cases if the cases are adjudicated without outside expertise? In chapter 7, I tell the story of Mr. Michael Situ Tanjung, a young man from Indonesia who grew up in California. Having followed his heart, and swayed by his Catholic Filipino and Vietnamese girlfriends, he converted from Islam to Catholicism, making him an apostate. His fear of returning to Indonesia and decision to apply for asylum protection also meant working through the difficulties of gaining asylum on the ground of persecution based on religion.

Part III, "Persecution on Account of Membership in a Particular Social Group" documents the stories of two Chinese Indonesian women, Jeni Chuck Smith and Mrs. Harianto, who experienced sexual violence in Indonesia. The difficulty of proving rape is well known. The witnesses are long gone. The physical evidence has disappeared. Due to shame, few women report to the police. The police are also unlikely to produce documents attesting to their abuse. Through detailed anthropological accounts consistent with details of traditional Malay village ritual practices on Jeni Chuck Smith's case in chapter 8, I was able to show with certainty that rape had occurred despite a lack of evidence and witnesses. In chapter 9, I show that through careful mapping of the shame Mrs. Harianto had endured, I was able to help her gain asylum protection even though she had no physical evidence of the rape and had missed the "one-year rule" for asylum applications. In chapter 10, I examine a dowry dispute involving Rani, a Malaysian Indian woman entangled in a conflict between tradition and modernity within her own home, and the Malaysian police's handling of her domestic abuse based on Malaysian Muslim cultural ideas of marriage in a multicultural and multireligious society. Working on the case with pro bono attorneys from Seyfarth Shaw, a major Chicago law firm, which had adopted the case from the National Immigration and Justice Center, suggests that a collaboration between major law firms and nongovernmental organizations could pave the way to engage sociocultural anthropology in doing asylum work.

Part IV, "Persecution on Account of Political Opinion" covers three Kafkaesque scenarios of asylum seekers from China. Chapter 11 is on the story of Ms. Li, who fled persecution because of her practice of Falun Gong, a *qigong* type exercise that the Chinese government had labeled as an "evil cult." Attorney Joanne Yeh's presentation in court of my sociocultural explanation of her application highlights the issues of translating a Chinese cultural idea of "filial piety" in an American courtroom with adjudicators who are unable to distinguish Asians from Asian Americans. The next two chapters include stories of two victims of China's one-child policy and their appeal to the Bureau of Immigration Appeals. Chapter 12 explores the story of Ms. Chun, a Chinese woman who was kidnapped by the Chinese government and forced to have an abortion six months into her pregnancy. The immigration court in the United States denied her asylum because it argued that she had failed to state correctly from which side of the hospital bed she was shown the aborted fetus. Chapter 13 covers the case of Mr. Sung, a doctor from Central China who was publicly humiliated, stripped of his position, and forced to have a vasectomy because his wife had escaped the government's dragnet to successfully have a second child. Working on their stories and appeals, the cases unveil China's one-child policy's terrible destruction of lives and the equally unforgiving US government's "rationales" for denying them asylum. The court denied the Chinese woman's petition based on the argument that she had filed a "frivolous claim." The court denied the Chinese doctor's petition because he was only "embarrassed" by the vasectomy. There was no mention of their opposition toward the Chinese government's policies, which demonstrated persecution on account of political opinion.

Part V is on the collaboration between Law and Anthropology. In chapter 14, Joann Yeh and I delve deeper into the difficulty asylum seekers face. We conducted ethnographic research in a Los Angeles community, which attracts asylum seekers from Asia. Joann Yeh and I asked: How do asylum seekers know where to go for help? In our research, we discovered the use of ethnicity and color by law firms (*lüshilou*) to attract potential asylum seekers, and the use of asylum as an "option" by many who want to remain in the country. We also examined the legal system—the quasi-judicial Article I courts—that contributed to the difficulty of the US government adjudicating asylum cases. In the final chapter, chapter 15, Joann Yeh and I address the fear of asylum fraud and the possibility of gaining asylum in a climate of doubt. We analyzed twenty-seven asylum cases that I had completed; the analysis suggests a 100 percent asylum approval in eleven cases with representation from the same attorney. Based on this result, we suggest that a positive asylum result is possible if an attorney is determined to win the "asylum lawfare" by utilizing various resources available, including the expertise of an anthropologist. I use the story of a woman wearing a burka during a Merit Hearing to highlight the attorney's use of a subtle strategy to bring about a positive asylum outcome. The case is compared with another where asylum was denied. By examining the identities of asylum seekers as if they are the subjects of anthropological enquiry, I have offered my anthropological expertise to help their attorneys, and indirectly, the judges, in adjudicating their statuses. Without major changes in the grounds of the 1951 Refugee Convention, and without the global cooperation to address the humanitarian crisis confronted by refugees and asylum seekers, this fruitful collaboration between law and anthropology deserves duplication to bring about a more humane outcome for the asylum seekers.

NOTE

1. Throughout this book, the names of asylum applicants, the dates of their application, along with any identifying and home country information, have been altered to protect their confidentiality. This is in accordance with the standard anthropological tradition of protecting our interlocutors who have allowed us to learn about their "culture." Related to protecting the confidentiality of the asylum seekers is whether or not I should obtain their individual permission since their stories contain highly personal and sensitive material. My discussions with Attorney Joann Yeh and Attorney Mark Hitman clarified the issue. First of all, the asylum petitioners came to me at the requests of their attorneys. On each case, I submit my signed report to the attorney who either submits it as a document in the client's file, or incorporates my findings into a brief on the client. These reports become a part of the documents in the legal docket, and are in the public records. To access an individual's records, a person may obtain permission from the asylum seekers or from their attorney. An asylum petitioner's information is also protected by attorney-client confidentiality. The names of the attorneys and judges are their real names, unless otherwise stated.

Part I

PERSECUTION ON ACCOUNT OF RACE AND NATIONALITY

Chapter 1

I Don't Need Your Bones to Know Your Race

In the spring of 2003, a woman by the name of Dewi Wisante requested to meet with me. At the appointed time, Dewi and her female companion, Meiji Sopoto, both of indeterminate ethnic and cultural origin, tried to explain the purpose of their visit in a mixture of English and Bahasa Indonesia/Malay, which I knew. Dewi told me that she had survived the horrendous May 1998 anti-Chinese riot in Jakarta, where Chinese homes and businesses were torched and Chinese women were gang raped in public. Too afraid to remain, Dewi joined others to escape the worst civil unrest in recent Indonesian memory. After entering the United States on a tourist visa, she applied for asylum protection with the help of a private immigration service agency. Before I could ask how I could help them, Dewi asked me, "Can you tell I am of the Chinese race?"

The question caught me by surprise. As discussed previously, many of us academics read, write, and teach about race. We tell our students there is no "race," that race is socially constructed, and that human beings cannot be divided into four or five "races." While we ask people to self-identify for the Census, on application forms for college admission, to rent an apartment, or to receive a scholarship, those in tune with local sensibilities do not ask a person's race unless there is a need to know. To ask is to invoke assumptions and profiling.

Dewi told me her application was denied by an immigration officer at the Anaheim Immigration Office in Orange County, California, because he said she had not provided evidence indicating she was persecuted on account of her "Chinese race."

"How do I prove my Chinese race?" Dewi asked the Immigration Officer.

"Go consult an anthropologist."

Over the past decade, judges and adjudicators have become more sensitive to evidence and narrative in their decision-making by incorporating external expertise (Lawrance and Ruffer 2015). Lawrance and Ruffer defined this individual as the *expert witness*, or "a person, who by virtue of education, or profession, or experience, or a combination of all, is believed to have special subject matter knowledge beyond that of the average person sufficient that others rely on him for his opinion" (3). Meiji Sopoto at the immigration service agency helped Dewi track down a forensic anthropologist who told her he could only determine her "race" if she was "DOA" (Dead on Arrival), so he could measure her bones. Undeterred by this inauspicious answer, Dewi and Meji told me they found me at a university because I taught anthropology, with courses on race and Asia. Intrigued by how to tell a person's "Chinese race," I thought of my childhood in multiethnic Malaysia where I learned Mandarin and various dialects of Chinese, as well as Malay, also spoken in neighboring Indonesia. I am also one of the few fortunate individuals who has actually observed a great variety of "Chinese" in different parts of China during several research projects on the "involuntary resettlement" of Chinese minority populations affected by the building of hydroelectric dams. Additionally, I have personally observed the Chinese in their great global diaspora through my travels in Asia, North America, Mexico, and Europe. Yet, during that crucial moment meeting Dewi, I felt uncomfortable making a judgment on her "Chinese race" identity. Based on her physical appearance, Dewi could have come from any one of the many countries and locations I have visited. In the context of Southern California, she could be mistaken as Japanese, Korean, Vietnamese, or Chinese from China or anywhere in the world.

If the Immigration Officer handling Dewi's case was unable to ascertain Dewi's "race" identity, if the forensic anthropologist was unwilling to verify her "race" except through her bones, and if I—possessing both "indigenous knowledge" on the Chinese and learned scholarship on "race" and the Chinese in the diaspora—could not do it either, how would another person with less experience verify Dewi's "Chinese race" identity? When I recognized how my opinion on Dewi may have life and death consequences, a sense of gravity pervaded my research. The pressure to provide every argument possible to ascertain her identity was tremendous. Sitting in front of me was an asylum seeker who feared for her life if she were to return to Indonesia. She had to prove her "Chinese race" to an immigration judge at the next level of the asylum application process, and any mistake I made would be more than a matter of cultural misinterpretation: it could have consequences of deportation, imprisonment, torture, and even death for the asylum applicant. Conducting research on Dewi's "Chinese race" identity, and on later cases from Indonesia and other countries in Asia, forced me to examine the limitations and possibilities of anthropology in my role as an *expert witness* to support the asylum seeker.

In part I, "Persecution on Account of Race and Nationality," I document the difficult process of attempting to provide evidentiary proofs of persecution on the ground of "Chinese race" by including four major ideas: a) "proving" Dewi's "race" without reifying the idea of "race," b) attempting to identify Dewi through her culture without essentializing "Chinese-ness," c) doing ethnography to reveal the asylum seeker's cultural identity under a condition of cultural erasure, and d) demonstrating persecution through the idea of racialization.

My approach in communicating my argument on the asylum seeker's identity to the asylum adjudicators was to sketch out the following questions and to provide a response to each one.

First—could I distinguish Dewi from other ethnic groups, including a dozen "races" under the Census categories of Asian in the United States? The response to this question is covered in the sections addressing the social construction of "race" in this chapter.

Second—what "Chinese" cultural attributes should I provide to support Dewi's claims of her "Chinese-ness" without using the idea of "race" or essentializing the notion of culture? The response to this question is covered in chapter 2, "How Much Chinese Should a Chinese Be?"

Third—could I support the contention that an asylum seeker was persecuted on account of "race"—as stipulated by the Refugee Convention—without using the notion of race? To accomplish this task, in chapter 3, I clarified the idea of race from racialization and race from racism. By using the concept of racialization, I argued Dewi suffered persecution as a Chinese in Indonesia, without employing the idea of race.

DEWI'S STORY

Dewi told me that, on that fateful day in May 1998, she was at work in a foreign-owned company in Jakarta. After hearing about the rioting in the city, the manager gave his employees permission to go home early. Dewi's Malay *pribumi* (native) colleagues left for home as usual; glad to have the day off. But the half-dozen employees of Chinese descent were afraid they might run into an angry *pribumi* mob on the street. They hid in their office while mobs banged on their office gates and buildings burned around them. Dewi and her colleagues in hiding were lucky. The flames changed directions, and the mobs moved on. Dewi hid in her office for two days. After she managed to get home through side streets and back alleys, attackers attempted to break into the apartment Dewi shared with her sister and aunt, which was located in a segregated Chinese neighborhood in Jakarta. Too terrified to remain in Indonesia, she joined a hundred thousand others, many of them Chinese, in fleeing Indonesia.

Dewi's ancestors had migrated from China several generations ago. She grew up with her twin sister in the extended household of her grandparents, parents, and paternal uncles and aunts. They observed various Chinese customs and festivals. The family spoke a mixture of the Hokkien dialect, Mandarin, and Bahasa Indonesia. Dewi acquired her current name under former president Suharto's rule when he forced the Chinese to change their names to "non-Chinese-sounding names." In a policy of forced assimilation, he also banned the learning of Chinese by closing all Chinese schools and Chinese language newspapers. As a result, Dewi never learned to speak, read, or write Chinese.

Based on my interview with Dewi, I wrote a report on Dewi's "Indonesian Chinese" cultural and ethnic identity for her attorney. I was aware that, according to the 1951 Refugee Convention, a person seeking asylum protection from harm must first prove a well-founded fear of persecution on account of race, religion, nationality, membership in a particular social group, or political opinion. The person must also apply within a year and show that the persecution was not random, but targeted on the stipulated grounds.

Given my anthropological understanding on "race," I could not simply declare a person as belonging to a particular "race." Instead, I included a discussion on its relative unimportance for verifying a person's identity and emphasized instead the sociocultural aspects of her origin. I also suggested a more common social science convention of referring to individuals in ethnic and cultural terms in recognition of the confusion and overlapping use of race with ethnicity and culture. To my surprise, Dewi's attorney returned the report, saying that I had failed to include my expert opinion on Dewi's "Chinese race." Unaccustomed to this anachronistic request, I asked for clarification. The attorney suggested an official inclusion of Dewi's "race," so I rewrote the report and submitted a final copy to Judge Gembacz, who heard Dewi's case.

THE "RACE" DILEMMA

The Immigration Officer and Dewi's attorney, who expected me to provide an opinion on Dewi's race, had forced me to deal with one of the most intellectually challenging subjects. How do we determine Dewi's "race" when the overwhelming opinion of social scientists has declared "race" as a social construct? Contemporary students of anthropology will also immediately recognize that the human population cannot be reduced to a number of races, much less a "Chinese race."

The Immigration Officer and Dewi's attorney, in their attempt to verify if Dewi was persecuted on account of her "race," were following an idea of "race" enshrined in the 1951 Refugee Convention—an idea created during the middle of the last century before the emergence of recent scholarship on "race." To argue that "race" is a socially constructed idea, and that Dewi's identity could not be determined "racially," was to ask the Immigration Officer and Dewi's attorney to abandon a key component of their legal toolkit. Indeed, the Immigration Officer, the forensic anthropologist, and the attorney for Dewi all expected Dewi to be judged according to a racialized framework of understanding so that her particular "Chinese race" could be understood.

To verify Dewi's "race" in accordance with the expectations of the asylum adjudicators, I would have to retain the idea of "race" in the verification. That is, I was forced to suspend my subscription to the social constructivist idea of "race" and attempt to understand Dewi within the framework based on "race" as it is commonly understood. If I were to temporarily suspend my thinking of "race" as a social construct, would I be able to verify Dewi's "race"?

ANTHROPOLOGY AND THE BIOLOGY OF "RACE"

Humans vary biologically, but our visually observable features led early scientists to conclude that those who share similar features must be closely related by common descent from a particular "line" or "race" of mankind. In the late eighteenth and early nineteenth centuries, during the peak of European colonial expansion to different parts of the world, Carolus Linnaeus, the Swedish naturalist who created the taxonomic classification system in *Systema Naturae* (1758) divided humanity into four distinct groups; each group is based on geography and physical features (skin color) and linked with temperament, customs and habits (Buettner-Janusch 1966; Pfeiffer 1969):

> *Americanus or red:* Tenacious, contented, free, ruled by custom
> *Europeanus or white:* Light, lively, inventive, ruled by rites
> *Asiaticus or yellow:* Stern, haughty, stingy, ruled by opinion
> *Africanus or black:* Cunning, slow, negligent, ruled by caprice

In 1795, Johann Friedrich Blumenbach, a German professor of medicine and anthropology, expanded on the work of Carolus Linnaeus, and divided mankind into five races to reflect their physical appearance (American Anthropological Association 2007):

> Caucasian, or the white race
> Mongolian, or the yellow race
> Ethiopian, or the black race
> American, or the red race
> Malayan, or the brown race

This idea of "race," whether conceived of as separate divine creation or divergent products of natural history, came to be accepted as the existence of biologically distinct groups. Some social scientists refer to this science of "race" as the *theory of racialism*, i.e., the belief that human types are manifested in biological and behavioral characteristics (Sanjek and Gregory 1994; Bauman 2009). The *theory of racialism* and anthropology's association with the study of human origins and human variation also marked the emergence of "anthropology" as a field (Goodman 2001).

As a study of human beings, most anthropological "classics" begin with a description of the people, from morphological characteristics to "racial" types, followed by the economy, language, kinship, marriage customs, magic, and witchcraft (Firth 1968; Lessa 1966; Williams 1965). According to anthropologist Alan Goodman (2001), this seamless description from morphology ("racial types") to ethnic character, to language and culture, helps to entrench anthropology with the earlier idea of the *theory of racialism*.

If we were to follow the logic proposed by this *theory of racialism* according to Linnaeus' taxonomy, Dewi would be Asiaticus, or "yellow;" and according to Blumenbach's expanded scheme, Dewi could be Mongolian or "the yellow race."

By the end of the nineteenth century, a growing body of scientific evidence began to undermine the idea of "races" as natural, discrete, and fixed subdivisions of the human species (Goodman, Moses, and Jones 2012). Modern biologists and genetic scientists' rejection of the biological meaning of "race" was based on the recognition of the greater heterogeneity within the so-called "races." What we view as differences between "races" were in fact a few phenotypes—the genes that are expressed as skin color, eye color, hair texture, body shapes, etc. Invisible to us are the genes that determine blood type, color blindness, our susceptibility to diseases and a host of other features.

Today, many anthropologists recognize that all the "races" of humanity interbreed and can produce perfectly viable human offspring; we are all members of the same species. Human variations in physical characteristics are the result of adaptations to the environment and genetic drift—the random changes of genes across interbreeding populations. As a species, we show a tremendous plasticity in adaptation to the environment (PBS 2003). A difference in skin color between groups, formerly ascribed to "biological" differences between "races," can now be explained by the environmental conditions alone.

With the idea of "race" proven false by the weight of science, many anthropologists, such as Franz Boas, have tried to critique and deconstruct the idea of "race." They argued that the concept of "race" was unnecessary, just another "four-letter word" (Brace 2005), fiction, "man's most dangerous myth" (Montagu 1997), and "shamefully obsolete and potentially harmful" (Goodman 2001, 31). In 1989, the American Anthropological Association (AAA) issued a statement on race after years of membership input and initiated "RACE: A Public Education Project." Then in 2010, the American Anthropological Association hosted a national dialogue on "race" in conjunction with the Black Congressional Caucus in Washington, D.C. Recently, a book and website, "Race: Are We So Different?" continued with the early mission of the AAA to engage the public in order to debunk the *theory of racialism* (Goodman, Moses, and Jones 2012).

Other scholars have contributed to public education by addressing the erroneous idea of "race." A particularly significant one is *Race: The Power of an Illusion*, which scrutinizes "race" as both a biological myth and a social invention (PBS 2003). In a NOVA Online program, "Does Race Exist?" two leading anthropologists from different sides of the debate gave their opinions on whether "race" exists in biological terms. One position, given by Dr. C. Loring Brace, stated there is no biological entity that warrants the term "race." A second position, represented by Dr. George W. Gill, is taken mostly among physical anthropologists working with law enforcement, who retains the idea of "race" to assess "race" as a material reality from skeletal remains (Brace and Gill 2000).

Given anthropology's long association with the study of "race," it is not surprising that the Immigration Officer would ask Dewi to find an anthropologist to "prove" her "race." It also explains her attorney's request that I provide a description of Dewi's physical characteristics to satisfy the Refugee Convention's requirement of persecution on account of "race." That is, in the language of the Refugee Convention, the word "race" was used as if "race" tangibly existed.

This interpretation of the biological idea of "race" would account for the Immigration Officer's rejection of Dewi's asylum application for having failed to prove her "Chinese race" and her attorney's request that I provide a description of Dewi's physical characteristics to satisfy the Refugee Convention's requirement of persecution on account of "race." That is, the Immigration Officer and the attorney for Dewi are following the biological concept of "race" and a *theory of racialism*—a belief that human beings can be divided into a few "races" and that an individual belongs to one "race" or the other.

Despite the "race" language of the Refugee Convention, a nuanced reading of the meaning of "race," according to the *International Handbook on Refugees*, also suggests it can be broadly defined and "understood in its widest sense to include all kinds of ethnic groups that are referred to as 'races' in common usage" (quoted in Musalo, Moore, and Boswell 2007, 491).

If this broader legal interpretation that an asylum petitioner may belong to any of the "ethnic groups that are referred to as 'races' in common usage" is accepted as the working definition, it opens up an opportunity for my research to ascertain if Dewi is ethnically Chinese in "common usage" in Indonesia as well as in the United States, rather than defining her identity exclusively in racialist terms. By what criteria do we judge a person's "Chinese-ness?" Is it skin complexion, physical features, language, ancestry, religion, ethnicity, or culture? Do we judge a Chinese person in Indonesian with the same yardstick as a Chinese person in the United States? In the context of Southern California, Dewi could be confused with a person from China, Japan, Korea, and any country in Southeast Asia or anywhere in the Chinese diaspora. My job to determine Dewi's identity would have to include distinguishing her not only from other Asians, but also from other Chinese, both in Indonesia and in the United States.

THE SOCIAL CONSTRUCTION AND REIFICATION OF RACE

To distinguish Dewi from "all kinds of ethnic groups and races" under the categories of Asians in the United States, I must first show the distinction between "race" and "ethnicity" by presenting the emergence of the two concepts in the United States.

While many in anthropology have moved away from using the idea of "race," and although the idea of "race" as a biological concept has been proven false by the weight of scientific evidence, it continues its grip on the American psyche. To anthropologist Audrey Smedley, "race" in North America is a social reality and a worldview shared by politicians, the media and the public alike (Smedley and Smedley 2012). Prominent scholar Andrew Hacker (2003) speaks of "America's two principal races" as "Black and White, Separate, Hostile, Unequal." Carl Rowan (1996), the late journalist, warns against an impending "race war." While some claim there is decreasing significance of the idea of race (Wilson 1980), references to "race" in the American daily newspaper are headlines, such as "Race and Policing,"

"Racial Problems" and "Are Race Relations Getting Better or Worse?" are ubiquitous. The United States Census Bureau specifically asks Americans about their "race" and "ethnicity." Individuals are expected to know their race and ethnicity. Potential employers, doctors, landlords, credit card companies and universities all require individuals to identify their race. The police shooting of young black youths are framed around the importance of race. In all these common usages, there is tremendous overlap and mindless interpenetration of the issues of race with ethnicity. Also, the specific idea of race required by the immigration office and Dewi's attorney are not the same as the idea of race as employed by the United States Census and as understood by the general public.

Three major institutions that continue to structure and influence the use of the idea of "race" are the United States Census Bureau (Anderson and Feinberg 1999), the United States legal institutions (Hing 1993), and popular discourse by both scholars and the public (Sanjek and Gregory 1994). Each institution reaffirms the use of the idea of "race" by another institution, in turn securing and entrenching the idea of "race" in the context of a growing United States as a nation professing the ideals of freedom and democracy while faced with increasing ethnic and cultural diversity.

THE SOCIAL CONSTRUCTION OF BLACKS IN THE UNITED STATES

A discussion of "race" in the United States must begin with the first United States Census in 1790 when the fledgling federal government attempted to create a representative democracy to apportion political power among a set of constituencies. It had to count the people within its boundary for the purposes of allocating political representation and tax responsibility among the states. The United States was the first nation in the world to institute a regular population count to apportion political power (Anderson and Feinberg 1999, 14). Given the demographic diversity of the United States, a difficult issue arose when the government had to consider "the question of defining exactly who was part of the 'population' deserving the right to political participation in the society and owing responsibility to pay taxes to the state" (13). That is, how to count the enslaved Africans and the Indians in the decennial Census.

The solution to these dilemmas of counting the enslaved Africans and Indians was to hedge the universal rule of counting the population for apportionment with the proviso of adding to the general population (a) "three fifths of all other Persons," and (b) "Indians not taxed" (Anderson and Fienberg 1999, 14). At the time, Southerners in the United States considered enslaved Africans property for purposes of tax assessments, not for political representation, and therefore they were counted as "three-fifths" of a free person. Indians were considered members of foreign states and therefore they were "Indians not taxed" and only "civilized Indians" were to be included in the decennial census. Anderson and Fienberg also noted that while civil categories were initially used to classify populations into free, "other persons" (that is, slaves), and "Indians not taxed," they also contended that "nowhere did the Constitution mention a racial classification, and in fact, the framers used the ambiguous 'other persons' to define slaves" (14). Similarly, reflecting the greater importance of religious or national difference, early colonial laws refer to "whites" as "Christians" and "Englishmen" rather than "whites" (PBS 2003).

However, the preexisting racial terminologies of "white," "black," and "red," quickly supplanted the civil statuses. That is, in a growing nation, as would-be citizens come from all over the world, laws also emerged to specify who belongs and who does not. Besides taxing and figuring out how to count "irregular" persons such as enslaved Africans and the native peoples, color was also used to allocate benefits. The first law to use color to sort the multitude of people was the Naturalization Act of 1790, which reserved naturalized citizenship for "white persons" only (Lopez 2006). Questions of "who is white" and "why is someone white" came to dominate American political discussion, and exclusions based on skin color followed. For example, by the 1890 Census, children of descendants between Europeans and Africans came to be designated as "mulattoes," those having "from three-eighths to five-eighths black blood"; "quadroons," those having "one-fourth black blood"; "octoroons," those having one-eighth or any trace of "black blood" and "black" any person with "three-fourths or more black blood" (Goldberg 1990). Many states, however, declared anyone with at least one-thirty-second "Negro blood" to be legally black. This was the one drop blood rule, regardless of the color of the skin. The categories of "mulatto," "quadroon" and "octoroon" were eventually dropped altogether by the 1900 Census and the children of these mixed parentage came to be subsumed under the category Negro or black. Later groups of European immigrants—the Armenians, the Sicilians, and many other darker-skinned people designated as "races" according to the common ethnological classification of the period—became identified as "white," while fair-skinned Americans with "one drop" of "African" blood came to be designated as black. In anthropology, this practice has come to be known as the *rule of hypodescent*.

THE SOCIAL CONSTRUCTION OF THE CHINESE IN THE UNITED STATES

As the first largest Asian group to arrive in the United States, the Chinese were welcomed for their labor, yet denied citizenship, and soon bore the brunt of the nativist cry and racialized exclusions under many laws specifically targeting the Chinese (Hing 1993). In the years before the Chinese Exclusion Act of 1882, racialized qualities previously assigned to blacks also became Chinese characteristics. The *San Francisco Alta* newspaper warned, "Every reason that exists against the toleration of free blacks in Illinois may be argued against that of the Chinese here," and magazine cartoons referred to the Chinese as *nagurs*, and "a slight removal from the African race" (Takaki 1989, 101). That is, based on the classification of that era, Dewi would be considered "black."

The importance of "whiteness" has tremendous implications because without citizenship, nonwhites are denied the right to vote, own property, file suit, and testify in court. For example, fifty thousand Armenians fleeing genocide in their homelands had come to the United States in the early twentieth century. The 1909 federal authorities classified Armenians as "Asiatics" and denied them naturalized citizenship. On behalf of an Armenian applicant, anthropologist Franz Boas argued he was "white" (Takaki 1989, 15; Lopez 2006, 5). Boas' expert witness opinion was to have tremendous economic consequences for the Armenians. Because they were "white," they were able to acquire citizenship and then farmland in California, while the Japanese, who had been farmers in California longer, were denied the right to acquire farmland because, under the Alien Land Law of 1913, they were not citizens (Takaki 1989, 5). It would be tempting to speculate on Boas' dilemma if he had been asked to testify on the Japanese's "race" classification at the time he was asked to testify on the Armenians'.

The designation and construction of people in the United States was based on more than mere differences in "blood" and "pigmentation," it was an attempt to maintain "racial" purity by the formal "racial classification furnished by the history of census taking" (Goldberg 1990, 239). The "race" of a person was constructed to serve this legal purpose. When the "race" did not fit, laws were changed. According to Takaki (1989), at the California State Constitutional Convention of 1878, John F. Miller warned: "Were the Chinese to amalgamate at all with our people, it would be the lowest, most vile and degraded of our race, and the result of the amalgamation would be a hybrid of the most despicable, a mongrel of the most detestable that has ever afflicted the earth" (101). Two years later, California lawmakers enacted legislation to prohibit the issuance of a license authorizing marriage of a white person with a "negro, mulatto, or Mongolian." In 1879, the State of California prohibited marriages between whites and "Mongolians," which was the term used to designate the large number of Chinese immigrants and their descendants present in the state. When Salvador Roldan, a Filipino who wanted to marry a white woman in California, was denied a marriage license because of the prevailing anti-miscegenation law, Roldan argued to the courts that he was not Mongolian, but Malay, according to the ethnological classification of the period. Due to the Roldan case, the law in California was changed to include Malays as Mongolian (Takaki 1989). Thus, we see how "racial" groupings came to be constructed by the government's deliberate changes in the classification of populations. When existing law prohibits marriage between a Mongolian and a white, and when a Malay wants to marry a white, the government changed a Malay into a Mongolian so that he could not marry a white as well. In the process of the Census counting of its people, and laws enacted and revised to maintain its "racial purity," a nation with a heterogeneous population—the result of immigration, enslavement, conquest, labor recruitment and natural procreation—came to be classified socially and legally into two principal races of whites and blacks.

RACE AND ETHNICITY IN THE UNITED STATES CENSUS

While the word "race" continued to be used to refer to "blacks" regardless of "proportion of blood," the word "ethnicity" became the central focus of scholars everywhere after the publication of Barth's (1969) *Ethnic Groups and Boundaries* and Cohen's (1969) *Customs and Politics in Urban Africa.* In the United States, "race" and "racial differences" came to be used in regard to differences between blacks and whites, as noted in Warner's (1941) *Yankee City* studies in the 1940s; and "ethnicity" was used to make sense of cultural differences among Poles, Greeks and other European immigrant groups. As a result, the label "ethnic" came to be associated with European immigrants and their assimilation into American society after one or two generations. Black equals "race" and white equals "ethnic." By the 1960s, a black/white dichotomy became the dominant American sociological paradigm.

Within the sociological tradition, a major subfield is devoted to the study of "race" and "ethnic relation" with a principal purpose of analyzing the "racial tensions" and the "racial frictions" in the modern world (Banton 1998). In this approach, social theorists analyze social groups based on "race and ethnicities" and their functional equivalents of black, white, Asian, and Latino. The writings of social scientists on "race" and "ethnic studies" in the United States draw on the U.S. Census Bureau's (2017) categories of its people within its boundaries. It has contributed to the image of whites, blacks,

Asian Americans and Latinos as separate "races" within the United States. It is crucial that I address this history of racialized (mis)representation of the use of "race" and "ethnicities" as analytical categories. That is, in many social science writings, "race" and "ethnicity" are correlated with various conditions: privileges, crimes, poverty, intelligence, housing ownership, graduation rate, and so on. The large body of sociological literature on "race" and "ethnicity" paradigms has an enormous influence on scholars and the general public alike. "Race" and "ethnicity" became the designations in the description and categorization of populations in the United States. It is within this contemporary classificatory system that Dewi must be understood, that is, the commonsense understanding of "race" and "ethnicity" in the United States when an asylum seeker's identity is being questioned.

Today, the U.S. Census' classification of America's populations is guided by the 1997 Office of Management and Budget (OMB) standards on "race and ethnicity categories" based on responses to the "race" question collected from Census surveys. According to this classification of America's populations, the great diversity of people are grouped into five "races": White, Black, American Indian or Alaskan Native, Asian, Native Hawaiian or other Pacific Islander, and "People who identify their origin as Hispanic, Latino, or Spanish may be of any 'race'":

> White—A person having origins in any of the original peoples of Europe, the Middle East, or North Africa.
>
> Black or African American—A person having origins in any of the Black racial groups of Africa.
>
> American Indians or Alaska Native—A person having origins in any of the original peoples of North and South America (including Central America) and who maintains tribal affiliation or community attachment.
>
> Asian—A person having origins in any of the original peoples of the Far East, Southeast Asia, or the Indian subcontinent including, for example, China, India, Japan, Korea, Malaysia, Pakistan, the Philippines Islands, Thailand, and Vietnam.
>
> Native Hawaiian or Other Pacific Islander—A person having origins in any of the original peoples of Hawaii, Guam, Samoa, or other Pacific Islands.

The 1997 OMB standards permit the reporting of more than one race. It notes in its guidelines that the racial categories included in the Census questionnaire generally reflect a social definition of race recognized in this country and not an attempt to define race biologically, anthropologically, or genetically. In addition, it is recognized that the categories of the race item include racial and national origin or sociocultural origin. People may choose to report more than one race to indicate their racial mixture, such as "American Indian" and "white." People who identify their origin as Hispanic, Latino, or Spanish may be of any race (Whitehouse 1997).

As a result of the government's practice of legalizing, legitimizing, and shaping of the "racial" classification of its populations through the manipulations of courts and the Census Bureau, the concept of "race" is retained, and ethnicity is used interchangeably with "race." Both terms are used without clarity and remain confusing. Thus, the idea of "race," which emerged in the seventeenth century, persists today, but is muddled, and full of contradictions.

IDENTIFYING DEWI ACCORDING TO CATEGORIES OF THE UNITED STATES CENSUS

In an attempt to identify Dewi according to the United States Census Bureau (2017, under "Asian"), she would have to be placed within the Asian "race" category, as a "person having origins in any of the original peoples of the Far East, Southeast Asia, or the Indian subcontinent including, for example, China, India, Japan, Korea, Malaysia, Pakistan, the Philippines Islands, Thailand, and Vietnam." By labeling her as an Asian, we are not any closer to identifying Dewi and differentiating her from other Chinese Indonesians, or from other Chinese asylum seekers from the Chinese diaspora. Labeling her as Asian would only indicate her origin from the standpoints of the United States within an experience generated by the categorization of populations by the Census, the analysis of "race and ethnicity" by social scientists, the discourses on "race" by the public, representations, and laws within the history of a nation.

But, in order to comply with Dewi's attorney's request, I had to give my position as to the nature of Dewi's "race" within the context of the requirement of the Refugee Convention and the commonsense assumption of a person's race generated by the United States Census.

To get around the requirement to identify her by a type of "race," I describe Dewi as having a "light complexion," with features resembling people from the eastern part of China. That is, I framed Dewi's physical features within Indonesia's understanding of the looks most associated with the Chinese who had migrated to Indonesia. In other words, it is a local Indonesian description of what might constitute a Chinese. The Chinese in China in fact comprise a whole spectrum of looks, from tall individuals with "blonde hair" of the mummies of the Tarim Basin to the looks of Chinese from the emigrant communities of Guangzhou and Fujian provinces Americans are familiar with in the United States.

In this anthropological challenge to prove Dewi's "race," I have briefly looked at the emergence of the idea of "race" as a biological concept and the anthropologists' rejection of the idea of "race." The contradiction between the anthropological rejection of the idea of "race" and the legal requirement to prove Dewi's "race" does not provide a solution that would help the asylum claimant prove her identity. Neither does the United States Census' system of classifying populations based on "race" and ethnicity provide a clear and indisputable place for Dewi's identity.

As an expert witness testifying on other Indonesian Chinese asylum seekers, I have been asked bluntly by the attorney, the counsel for the government, and the judge, "Professor Ngin, can you be certain the person standing in front of you is of the "Chinese race"? I have been instructed by the attorney, on the one hand, to state my answers concisely without trailing into areas in which government counsels could pounce and redirect their questioning into areas that I was not qualified to answer, which would then lead to my disqualification as an expert. On the other hand, by answering that the Chinese Indonesian asylum seekers were not of "Chinese race," could the court deny them asylum because their "race" had nothing to do with the persecution they had endured?

On one occasion, I boldly mentioned my "no-race" position. I stated my contention that the asylum seeker in front of me in court *was of Chinese origin but she was not of the Chinese race.* The presiding judge paused, looked at me, turned off the tape-recording machine, and engaged in a sidebar conversation with me: "Do you mean that we must remove one of five grounds of the Refugee Convention?" I believe the adjudicators in court were not interested in the theoretical development on the idea of race, and its relationship to ethnicity and nationality. I also doubted that the asylum court was the place to present a sketch of my argument on my "no-race" position. I kept quiet. There was no easy answer to the question of Dewi's "Chinese race" identity because of the confusion regarding the idea of "race" with a number of related ideas. From a sociocultural constructionist standpoint, it was futile to use the idea of "race" to identify a person for asylum application or for other purposes, even though the use of the idea of "race" as a physical reality has been used to categorize the diverse peoples of the nation, define entitlements, and enact policies of social exclusion. Unable to verify Dewi's identity by her "race," I examined the use of culture to serve as a proxy for "race."

Chapter 2

How Much Chinese Should a Chinese Be?

If I was unable to verify Dewi's "Chinese race" identity based on her "race," could culture serve as a proxy for "race"?

Behavior and practices associated with a particular culture are not required in the asylum application form. On the application, the asylum petitioner is asked to identify the person's "race"—an inborn feature; not a person's cultural practice, which is acquired through learning. So there exists a "tension" between this expression of culture as something a person is, synonymous with "race," and something one practices, which could be the person's "culture." But given the Immigration Officer's inability to identify Dewi's "race," I had to look into her "culture."

Anthropologists write about culture. In our study of culture, we examine the patterns and meanings of human activity that come into existence through art, language, literature, customs, rituals, and religion. We also examine the beliefs and values of a people and observe the learning and transmission of culture. In the discipline's relationship to knowledge, we inscribe, for the public, the cultures of peoples far and near, big and small, through our production of ethnographies. There are few groups around the world untouched by the discipline's inquiring probe. We become the ethnographic authority of the culture we study. But our representation of culture has also been criticized as totalizing, unchanging, exoticizing, Orientalizing, essentializing, valorizing, and reifying the "Other." In this crisis of representation, studying culture is a terrain few anthropologists are willing to tread. Despite this concern, Dewi's request forced me to consider her "culture" for the purpose of providing evidentiary proof of the Chinese Indonesian asylum seekers' "Chinese" cultural identity.

The challenge for me was how to write about Dewi's culture without making the same mistake as Professor Burton Pasternak. The challenge, discussed by

Anthropologist Kristin Koptiuch (1996) of Professor Pasternak's role as an expert witness, is a lesson worth our attention lest we fall into the same cultural trap. Koptiuch discusses the anthropological concerns of essentializing, totalizing, and freezing culture in time.

Professor Burton Pasternak of Hunter College had served as an expert witness on a cultural defense case in which Mr. Chen, a Chinese immigrant employed as a dishwasher and garment worker, had murdered his Chinese wife for adultery in New York City. Professor Pasternak testified that Mr. Chen was driven by "traditional" Chinese notions about shame and infidelity. Professor Pasternak argued that Mr. Chen could not escape his "originary cultural formation" (Koptiuch 1996, 215), and hence his actions were excusable. Anthropologist Koptiuch argued that Professor Pasternak had failed to take into account the cultural norms on wife-beating of the large Chinese population in New York. That is, Professor Pasternak had disregarded the heterogeneity of the "Chinese" population and their diverse opinions on the acceptability of wife-beating. Without taking the diverse views into consideration, Professor Pasternak's approach was erred by essentializing wife-beating as an acceptable Chinese cultural value. Understandably, Professor Pasternak was making a point for the defense when he served as an expert witness. Nevertheless, his expertise was called into question by other anthropologists for homogenizing Chinese cultures from the homeland and the diaspora into a single, fossilized, cultural formation: that wife-beating and killing is acceptable to the Chinese community. Professor Pasternak won the case for Mr. Chen but lost his credibility in the eyes of his anthropological colleagues. Indeed, Professor Pasternak could have also lost the case for Mr. Chen if the plaintiff had called their own anthropological expert who would undoubtedly testify on the points delineated by Anthropologist Kristin Koptiuch.

The case points to the precariousness of interpreting culture across time and space. It serves as a cautionary tale in attributing characteristics to a culture without critically taking into account theories of globalization, migration, assimilation, localized cultural specificities, and a host of other issues. That is, it points to the problems of ethnographic representation when encountering the postmodern condition (Coombe 1991).

Postmodernism, according to Coombe (1991), helps us "reconceive the concept of culture in terms that integrate it into a study of power, to consider meaning in terms of relations of struggle embodied in everyday practices, and it demands that we view these cultural practices in local contexts, related in specific ways to historical conjunctions in a multinational global economy" (189). This analysis of the discourse about postmodernism helps anthropologists understand our shortcomings and suggests new avenues of departure for critical analysis.

That is, in order to understand Dewi's "Chinese culture" without making the mistake of Professor Pasternak, I must take into account the globalized forces on the representation of her culture in a postmodern condition. Dewi and her family, as well as other Chinese Indonesians, are descendants of Chinese who migrated to Indonesia, some of them before the Dutch colonial era in the seventeenth century. They are referred to as *huaqiao*, literally "Chinese who lived abroad" or "Overseas Chinese." Some of these "Overseas Chinese" sojourners adapted locally, married local women, and created a creolized community of *peranakan*. Those who retained a greater orientation toward their Chinese origin are referred to as *totok*, producing a great degree of internal differentiation based on different adaptation.

During the building of the Indonesian nation, despite a national motto, *Bhinneka Tunggal Ika*, or "Unity in Diversity," suggesting a multicultural unity appropriate for a nation comprising of over three hundred ethnic groups, the Chinese were the only group singled out and classified as people of foreign descent (*keturunan asing*), rather than as an ethnic group (*sukubangsa*) (Coppel 2005). When defined in terms of being foreign (*asing*) instead of indigene (*asli*), even as citizens, they were the foreigners.

Under Suharto, the second president, the Chinese, as foreigners, were excluded from the "moral community" of the nation (Aguilar 2001). Suharto's anti-Chinese policy included some seventy-two laws against the Chinese. He banned everything Chinese from Indonesia: he forced them to change their names to "non-Chinese-sounding names," closed the Chinese schools and newspapers, and forbade even the importation of Chinese medicine, presumably because there was Chinese writing on the packaging or because taking Chinese herbal medicine was associated with the practice of Chinese culture. Universities built by the Chinese communities were nationalized without compensation. The only way for the Chinese in Indonesia to survive was to become merchants. Under state-sponsored anti-Chinese policies of complete cultural genocide, the Chinese were also the scapegoats and targeted for arson and murder in times of social unrest (Aguilar 2001). As an unwanted minority group, they suffered periodic killings that resulted in the anti-Chinese riots of May 1998, which led to Dewi fleeing Indonesia.

When Indonesian Chinese culture was no longer considered legal or legitimate, there was no advantage for Dewi and other Chinese Indonesians to be culturally Chinese. Under Suharto's rule, Chinese cultural attributes were to be discarded, buried, and forgotten. When Dewi first met with the Immigration Officer to apply for asylum protection, it was unlikely that the Immigration Officer had taken this contextual information on Indonesia's exclusion and persecution of its Chinese minority into consideration. If the Immigration Officer was familiar with the experience of Indonesian Chinese and their exodus from the events in May of 1998, he would have focused on the persecution against her, rather than on her Chinese "race" identity. In other words, the Immigration Officer's main concern was how to sort out Dewi's identity, if not by "race," then at least by her Chinese culture. Therefore, my job in helping Dewi with her asylum application was to also understand what constitutes "Chinese-ness" within the context in Los Angeles where Dewi had applied for asylum.

"CULTURES" IN CONTEMPORARY LOS ANGELES

In a modern contemporary metropolis such as today's Los Angeles, with a long history of extraordinary mixes of faiths, ethnicities, and nationalities, school principals, city councilmen, and local politicians all proudly proclaim the number of cultures they represent or serve in their constituencies. The Los Angeles School District claims that it serves ninety-six cultures. People are thought to possess this culture or that culture. If you are Chinese, then you must know about Chinese culture, and if you are Mexican, Mexican culture. City elders and politicians stress the advantages of celebrating each other's culture in a multicultural society. Schools and cities host multicultural celebrations of heritages and faiths from Lunar New Year to Cinco de Mayo to Kwanzaa.

In this popular and liberal discourse on diversity, immigrants and every individual are culturally visible. Every person belongs to a culture—a culture that can be seen through its material and artistic expressions, heard through its languages, songs and music, and tasted through its foods. Celebrating cultures in forms that can be seen, heard, and tasted have become the de facto modes of getting along with others in America as these cultures bump into each other. In this culturally liberal climate, individuals are supposed to possess some semblance of their "original" culture, be it in the form of names, or other accoutrements of culture, to show authenticity. Culture is our social lubricant (Ngin and Torres 2001). No culture is left behind.

The contemporary popular conception of culture is that each of these cultures is bounded. One culture is different from the other culture. Each culture is internally homogeneous; internal differences within each culture are ignored. In the increasingly globalized world, individuals, having lost a sense of their own cultural identity, are seeking cultural authenticity (Cheng 2004, 3) and a cultural connection to their roots. Therefore, many are happy to partake in the cultural opportunities encouraged and provided by a culturally inclusive cosmopolitan metropolis. Ethnic towns proliferate, viewed by city councilmen as potential tourist attractions, and viewed by their ethnic inhabitants as a fountain of their culture (Baker and Ngin 2017).

Due to our multicultural diversity, many denizens of the City of the Angels think we know about each other's culture because we can differentiate one culture from another. As a global city, we are culturally in step with the times. Therefore, we ought to be able to identify a Chinese if we see one based on those visible cultural expressions familiar to us.

Assimilation may take away a person's language ability, but, in the case of Dewi, and other Chinese Indonesians like her, they did not even possess some popular "objective" symbolic markers such as a Chinese name or a westernized Chinese name typical of other Chinese in America that signify them as Chinese for the average American. As a result, American asylum adjudicators are not likely to recognize Chinese Indonesians as Chinese because they are different from the Chinese they are familiar with in the United States.

That is, Dewi's uncommon combination of a familiar appearance as Asian with an unfamiliar name signifies irregularity when she needs to prove credibility as an asylum seeker. Thus, I must conclude that the Immigration Officer's rejection of her application was due to Dewi's *cultural invisibility*, in addition to the Immigration officer's inability to determine her "Chinese race."

Therefore, the task to ascertain Dewi "Chinese-ness" remained.

"CHINESE CULTURE" IN CONTEMPORARY LOS ANGELES

The Chinese in contemporary Los Angeles must be contrasted with those who came to America, circa 1850—mostly men from the Canton area who worked in the gold mines, built the transcontinental railroad, and were pioneers in developing agriculture on the West Coast. They were wanted for their labor but later suffered discrimination that culminated in the Chinese Exclusion Act of 1882. The Act permitted the entry of only students, merchants, diplomats, and ministers. With few Chinese to replenish the Chinese laboring population, and even fewer Chinese women to set up families for the next generation in the community, the old Chinese men huddled in the "bachelor societies" of the Chinatowns.

Even with the repeal of the Chinese Exclusion Act in 1882, Chinese immigration was severely restricted. It was not until after the Immigration and Naturalization Services Act of 1965 that restrictions on emigration from the Eastern Hemisphere was lifted. Migration started with the Chinese students from Taiwan who had remained behind and then brought over their families. Other Chinese, mostly students from the People's Republic of China who were stranded in the United States during the Tiananmen Square incident in

1989, were allowed to remain in the United States by a Congressional Act. In 1990, ahead of the handover of Hong Kong to China, another anxious group of Chinese migrated to Canada and to the United States. During the last two decades, with greater affluence in China, more Chinese from all over China have also arrived in the United States as students, investors, and immigrants. Added to the Chinese from the Greater China of the People's Republic of China, Taiwan, and Hong Kong, are the ethnic Chinese from Vietnam, who comprise about one-third of the Vietnamese Boat People and refugees. Along the way are the Chinese from the diaspora who had migrated to the United States after their initial migrations to Central and South America and elsewhere in the world.

Today's Los Angeles is the new Ellis Island for immigrants. Most immigration officers, like most other Angelenos, would at least be familiar with a typical Chinese surname such as Lee, Wang, Zhang, Lin, Chen, and the usual two-character first names such as Mei Li, Wen Ho, and Xiao Ping. Even if a Chinese had adopted common, westernized first names such as Bruce, Jackie, Nancy, or Jeremy, the Chinese person's name is recognizable through the Chinese surname: Bruce Lee, Jackie Chan, Nancy Kwan or Jeremy Lin. In other words, in the popular discourse of Chinese immigrants in America, the Chinese must have some visible expressions of their native or ancestral culture, such as a Chinese name (or the ability to read or speak Chinese). However, Dewi and other Chinese Indonesians like her, lack the symbolic markers that would conform to the average American's expectation of what constitute a Chinese, therefore signifying them as Chinese. Without them, their identity is questioned.

Angelenos are not the only ones who expect some congruence between a person's ethnicity and their possession of some fundamental, commonly understood cultural attributes. The expectation that a Chinese ought to have a Chinese name occurs even among academics in Asia. Professor Aimee Dawis (2008), a Chinese Indonesian, published an article in the *Jakarta Post* about her experience in Singapore. When her Chinese academic host in Singapore picked her up at the airport, he asked her to explain the lack of fit between her "Chinese looks" and her "non-Chinese" name. The Chinese academic's expectation that there should be a "cultural fit" between a presumed "Chinese look" and a Chinese name is no different from the Immigration Officer's expectation that, if Dewi claims she is Chinese, there must be some evidence of her ethnic claim.

In my informal consultation with colleagues, scholars, and persons of Chinese origin in the United States and in Asia on what constitutes a Chinese, the commonsense criteria never advanced beyond the person's name, ability to speak Chinese, and claim of Chinese ancestry. Most argue that if the person does not have a Chinese name and does not speak Chinese, they are not Chinese. The older generation of Cantonese-speaking Chinese in the San Francisco and Sacramento areas refers disapprovingly to their assimilated American-born children as *jook sum*, (literally "bamboo heart") a pithy reference to the cellular mess inside the bamboo plant despite its hard exterior. That is, they may appear Chinese physically, but they do not "possess" Chinese culture. Therefore, their opinions are often discounted, unless they demonstrate proper expected etiquette in their interactions with the older population. Then, they are considered worthy of being a Chinese, despite their assimilation in America.

"CHINESE CULTURE" OF THE SERVICE INDUSTRIES

This expectation of demonstrable "cultural" visibility is also confounded by those in the multicultural service industry that profess the importance of "cultural competency" in managing a diverse denizen population.

In response to an increasingly diverse workforce, training workshops in cultural competency and multiculturalism are now common in many Western nations. They try to help service providers with a better understanding of the diverse cultures they encounter, sort out the entitlements and rights accorded by law and demanded by minority groups, or by commercial enterprises eager to tap into a new ethnic market.

A superb example of this "cultural management industry" is an article published in *Cross Cultural Management* attempting to help non-Chinese identify what constitutes a Chinese. The author, Ying Fan (2000), posits that "it is still possible to identify certain core cultural values that are held in common by the Chinese people, no matter where they live: mainland China, Hong Kong, Taiwan or by the overseas Chinese." The author continues, "Chinese culture gives the Chinese people their basic identity. These core values are unique and consistent, shaped by a tradition of four thousand years of history and maintained by the same language," which "is uniquely Chinese that distinguish[es] itself not only from Western cultures, but also from other Eastern cultures (for example, Japanese culture)" (4). The list of "core values" assembled by Ying Fan consisted of seventy-one "cultural values," based on an original forty key items from the Chinese Culture Collection compiled by other scholars. These "core values" are grouped under national traits, interpersonal relations, family/social orientation, work attitude, personal traits, time orientation, and relationship with nature. Examples of some of the seventy-one core Chinese cultural values are "patriotism," "embodies Confucian teaching," and "harmony with nature."

In applying this theory of an essentialized list of seventy-one "core values" to Dewi, how Chinese must Dewi be in order to be recognized as Chinese?

If Dewi's adjudicators had judged Dewi against the article by Ying Fan or a similar one on Chinese culture, she would not have qualified as a Chinese from the perspective of these cultural experts.

The invisibility of Dewi's Chinese culture that came from Suharto's legal targeting forbade the purchase and consumption of Chinese culture (importing Chinese medicine), the production of Chinese culture (Chinese-language schools, media, and political organizations), and the distribution of Chinese culture (newspapers and Chinese-language schools). When Indonesian Chinese culture was no longer considered legal or legitimate, the Chinese discarded and buried visible aspects of their culture.

Given the cultural heterogeneity of the Chinese in Los Angeles, it was important to have some sort of cultural yardstick to determine the Chinese-ness of the Chinese asylum seekers. Yet, the "cultural traits" of our popular understanding and the "core values" of the Chinese published by the cultural management industry remain unworkable because Dewi's supposedly Chinese cultural characteristics were already erased under Suharto's regime. Fully cognizant of the contested meanings of "Chinese culture" in different contexts, I could not argue from theory or from received wisdom of what constitutes a Chinese identity, much less that of an Indonesian Chinese. Dewi's Chinese identity remains terra incognita to an American asylum adjudicator.

In uncovering Dewi's cultural identity, it was not sufficient for the anthropologist to assert to the adjudicators that the Indonesian government had banned Chinese culture. The ethnographic authority based on our research is not automatic. To win asylum, the petitioner must be credible. To be credible, there must be evidentiary proof that the petitioner is persecuted on account of her "Chinese" identity. In addition, the petitioner must explain the nonrandom nature of the persecution on account of her Chinese-ness. Thus, the task that remains is to establish the asylum applicant's identity with irrefutable evidence that Chinese Indonesian petitioners are who they say they are.

REVISITING THEORIES AND METHOD

While those in the service industries must respond to the challenges of diversity by "managing culture" through a simplification of complexity, and speak with certainty about cultures, few anthropologists, influenced by the constructivist and postmodern currents dare venture into such simplification lest we encounter the hazards of reducing culture to a list. Nonetheless, the requirement to produce evidentiary proofs on Dewi's identity remains.

Culture, in the words of cultural critic, Raymond Williams, is one of the two most difficult words in the English language. In anthropology, there are over one hundred definitions of culture, from British anthropologist Edward B. Tylor's 1871 definition of culture as a "complex whole which includes knowledge, beliefs, arts, morals, law, customs, and any other capabilities and habits acquired by [a human] as a member of society," to culture as something we learn, is symbolic, and is shared (Bailey and Peoples 2013; Ember and Ember 2009; Kottak 1996). Some define culture as a "software," or a "road map" that determines human behavior. Which, among this plethora of definitions of culture, would point to a clear path to solving the identity of asylum seekers?

In applying anthropological insights to asylum cases, an issue I had to confront was the absence of a concept within our own profession to label the hidden Chinese Indonesian culture. We have high culture and folk culture; culture as a whole and subculture; culture in the singular and culture in the plural (De Certeau 1997). In ethnic studies in the United States, we speak of mainstream culture and culture in the margins. Among Chinese Indonesians, their practices may be of the folk variety in relation to the high culture studied by the Sinologist, or may be considered a subculture among the Indonesian culture as a whole. However, because they were not even recognized during the times of Suharto, practices among Chinese Indonesians did not possess even the status of a "subculture" and may not even be in the margins of the Indonesian consciousness.

Recalling Indonesia as the home of Clifford Geertz's anthropological career, I re-read his *Interpretation of Culture* for inspiration. Geertz (1973) defines culture as a system of signs, meanings, symbols and worldview of a particular group of human beings. Geertz wrote, "Believing, with Max Weber, that man is an animal suspended in webs of significance he himself has spun, I take culture to be those webs, and the analysis of it to be therefore not an experimental science in search of law but an interpretive one in search of meaning. It is explication I am after, construing social expressions on their surface enigmatical" (5). To explicate what culture is, Geertz recommends turning to the practice of social anthropology, or more precisely, doing ethnography. Doing ethnography, he said, is more than establishing rapport, mapping fields, etcetera—it involves thick description. He provides an example of the twitching of an eye—the movement of the upper and lower eyelids. First the twitching can be due to an involuntary eye movement, which we refer to as a "twitch." It can also be distinguished from a wink, which could signify communicating in precise way, or sending a message with a gesture made by the eyelid movement. Or it could include a third meaning where the winker is winking to parody someone's wink, or someone's involuntary twitch (6–7).

Geertz's explication of doing ethnography is important because I needed to ascertain whether the asylum seeker was telling the truth about who she says she was, or a fraud pretending to be someone else in order to gain asylum.

In using basic ethnographic interviews of asking and listening to establish the identity of Dewi, I usually begin with the person's name, family history of migration, the regions of China their family came from, and the Chinese dialects they knew. Among the sixteen Indonesian Chinese I had interviewed, most of the petitioners were able to mention the dialects of their parents or grandparents—Hokkien, Hokchiu, Hakka, and Teochew—but they were unable to relate these Chinese dialects to the regions in Southeastern China, nor could they speak the dialects themselves. When asked specifically about the language they knew, the response was always "Bahasa Indonesia."

My uncovering of Dewi's Chinese identity happened by chance. She had already told me she did not have a Chinese name, and she did not speak Chinese. I persisted. I was curious about the everyday practices of the Chinese Indonesian. So I asked her again about her name and how she addressed her relatives, and foods her family used for celebrating and honoring the dead. It was by conducting careful ethnographic interviews that I was able produce documentable evidence of her Chinese identity.

DEWI RECALLING HER CHINESE NAME

Even though Dewi had already told me her name was Dewi Wisante, I asked again, without suggesting a hint of doubt of her honesty.

"Please tell me your name?"

"Dewi Wisante."

"Do you have a Chinese name?"

"No."

"Did your parents give you a Chinese name?"

She thought, trying to remember.

"Yes but I don't know how to write it."

"Do you know what your name means?"

"Something like a flower. . . ."

"Do you know how to write your name in Chinese?"

"I don't know." But I offered her a pen and a piece of paper anyway.

She tried to put down a stroke or two, but shook her head.

"What does your Mom call you?"

"Ah Mei." (again, a pseudonym)

"If I wrote it for you would you recognize it?" Dewi did not reply me.

"Is this how you write your name in Chinese?" I wrote her a Chinese character for plum blossom.

"Yes."

With Dewi's affirmative response to my last question, I was able to write in the report to her attorney attesting to her possession of a Chinese name given by her family.

Under Suharto's rule, the Chinese were forced to change their name to a "non-Chinese sounding name." According to my Indonesian consultant, they were given thirty days to carry out the name change. In my interviews with other Chinese Indonesians in the Greater Los Angeles community, many had found creative ways to come up with new names.

Alan Soo, a Chinese Indonesian businessman I met in Los Angeles, borrowed a name from his Jewish business partner to become Alan Soleman. Maria Cecilia's father, simply compressed his whole Chinese name, "Chan Thio Tan" into Chandrathiotanta. Others simply adopted existing names common in Indonesia. Given that 85 percent of the Indonesian population are Muslim, many end up with Muslim names. Dr. Ibrahim Irawan, a dentist by profession in Los Angeles, and the founder of *Indonesia Media*, told me his Indonesian assistant, a Muslim, chose a Muslim name for him. In changing his name to a Muslim name, he was thinking of his Chinese family name, "Yee," which he wanted to preserve. So, he advised his assistant to choose Muslim names with the "Yee" sound. As a result, hidden in the word Ibrahim is the "Yee" of his Chinese surname from the "I" sound in Ibrahim. To keep the same Chinese tradition, all of his siblings have chosen Muslim names with the "I" sound found in names such as Idris, Ishak, and Iskandar. After Dr. Ibrahim migrated to the United States, he said he helped his American-born children connect with Chinese culture by sending them to Kung Fu classes in Los Angeles' Chinatown.

The most creative name change came from a business owner in suburban Los Angeles whose made-up name contains the letters KARN. "K" stands for *Kerturangan* or "descended from"; "A" for *Asli* or "origin"; "R" for *Raja* or "royal" and an "N" for *Naga* or "dragon." Thus, unbeknownst to outsiders, her name means "descended from the royal dragon," dragon being the symbol of Chinese-ness. So, despite Suharto's collective erasure of their Chinese identity, through their names, Mr. Soleman, Mr. Chandrathiotanta, Dr. Ibrahim, Ms. Karn, and many others have resisted state domination by hiding their culture within state-sanctioned names. With state prohibition, their Chinese culture became private and invisible but survives publicly in names such as Ibrahim (from the Yee family), Karn (a Chinese descended from the royal dragon), Chandra (from the Chan family), and Soleman (from the Soo family). Thus, among the asylum seekers and the Chinese Indonesians I have interviewed, their public cultural expression may be Indonesian, but their private identity is Chinese.

KINSHIP TERMS OF ADDRESS

Besides asking Dewi about her name and how her family refers to her, I asked how she addressed her parents and her relatives. If she is indeed Chinese, her "Chinese-ness" might be reflected in the terms she uses to address her relatives. In the kinship system commonly practiced among those from Southeast China, they make distinctions based on age, generation, and between those related by marriage (affine relatives) and by blood (consanguine relatives).

For example, in English there is only one term for "aunt" for all of one's parents' sisters, regardless of whether the aunt is older or younger than the parent; and whether she is one's father's sister or mother's sister. In Chinese, on the other hand, there are separate terms to address one's mother's older sister, mother's younger sister, father's older sister, and father's younger sister. In the Hokkien dialect commonly spoken by the Chinese in Indonesia, they would be referred to as *Yee Ma* and *Ah Yee* on the maternal side and *Gho Ma* and *Ah Gho* on the paternal side, making a distinction based on marriage and age. There are further variations to the term of address based on the birth order of the aunt among her siblings. *Yee Ma* and *Gho Ma* command more respect: their positions are recognized in all ritual occasions, such as weddings and funerals. In a wedding ceremony when tea is served to the elders by the new bride and groom, kinship relations and age matter: *Yee Ma*, who is older, is served before *Ah Yee*; and the paternal before the maternal. In everyday practices, as a sign of respect, they are the first to be offered a seat or food before the younger ones. Young children who are taught to address these relatives may not know that each term of address carries with it a relationship based on generation, age, marriage and descent: they often think these are the names of the individuals.

Assisted by a kinship diagram I had constructed for Dewi, I was able to note Dewi's ability to make a distinction between maternal and paternal kin, between generations, and observe the rule based on age in the Hokkien dialect. So, despite not speaking Chinese, Dewi was able to address her relatives in the dialect, providing me with an irrefutable fact that her terms of kinship address resemble those from the Chinese Fujian communities in Southeastern China, and serve as evidence of her Chinese cultural identity.

In contrast, in the Malay-based populations in the region, no distinction is made between relatives on the paternal or the maternal side. For instance, according to my interlocutor and Kamus, the Web's Largest Dictionary (2017), *tante* is used to address the younger or older sister of one's father or mother.

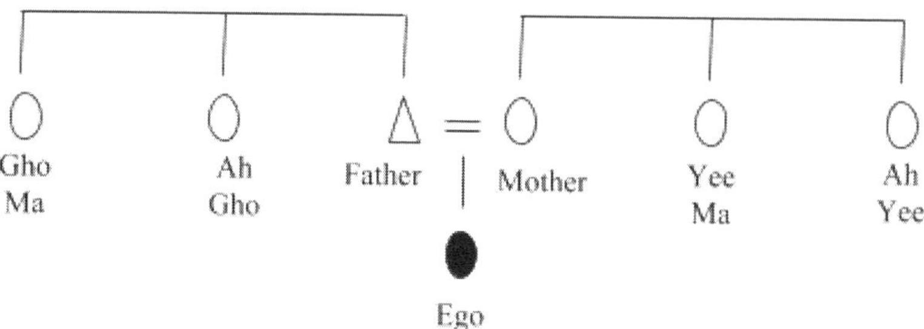

Figure 2.1 Kinship Chart

Without an intimate knowledge of growing up in a Chinese household where children are required to address their relatives by the proper terms customary in Chinese culture, Dewi and other Chinese Indonesian asylees from Indonesia would not have known this. Therefore, knowledge of kinship terms may be one of the means of differentiating "Chinese" Indonesians from other Indonesians.

It is important to note that Chinese American children who speak English may only use the English words "aunt" and "uncle" in addressing their relatives. Migration reduces the chances of having a critical mass and a variety of relatives. Additionally, linguistic assimilation takes away the proper kin terms of address that differentiate maternal and paternal relations. I noted this difference between Chinese and Chinese American kinship terms of addressing kin in anticipation of the adjudicators' knowledge (or lack of knowledge) regarding Chinese in America. If an American asylum adjudicator should presume Chinese American children address all their parents' siblings only as "aunts" and "uncles," as is the common practice in the United States, and presumed it as a universal practice for all Chinese, my report would have provided an explanation of the difference and served to preemptively eliminate any doubts in the mind of the adjudicator.

CLAIMS OF CHINESE-NESS: EATING, CELEBRATING, AND HONORING THE DEAD

One of the strengths of an ethnographic approach is the ability to probe deeply into the meaning of our observations and the stories we hear that may not be obvious during the first pass. In talking with the Indonesian Chinese about their everyday practices, I learned about their Chinese customs and traditions through the food they eat, especially when celebrating special days, and in honoring their ancestors.

Growing up in the household of her grandparents, one of the many foods Dewi remembered was *bahtzaan*, seasoned glutinous rice which is wrapped in bamboo leaves, stuffed with meat, beans, peanuts, and salted eggs, and then tied into a conical-shaped bundle with a long string. The end of the strings are then tied into a cluster, and the whole cluster is cooked by boiling in water. The making of *zaan* involves many women in the family as large numbers of *zaan* are made in one sitting. After the ritual of offering to the deities, the *zaan* are distributed to close relatives. *Zaan* are traditionally made during the fifth day of the fifth month of the lunar calendar to commemorate a patriotic poet in ancient China who jumped into a lake to protest against an unjust government. The villagers, as the story goes, prepared *zaan* and threw them into the water to prevent the fish from eating their beloved poet. In Mandarin Chinese, *zaan* are known as *zongzi*, eaten during *Duanwu* festival.

Another practice Dewi recalled was the eating of mooncake during the Mid-Autumn Festival that occurs on the fifteenth day of the eighth month according to the lunar calendar. Mooncakes are pastries made with various traditional Chinese sweet fillings such as pastes made from lotus seed, red bean, and jujube. Some mooncakes are made from small molds with Chinese characters, flowers, and birds symbolizing harmony. Because of the complicated process of making mooncake, most people buy them from commercial bakeries or restaurants. The practice of eating *zaan* and mooncake is quite common among the Chinese in Southeast Asia and in the United States in communities with a significant Chinese population. It is unclear if people who ate *bahtzaan* or mooncake knew of the cultural significance of the festivals. My interviews with the Chinese asylum seekers did not cover these interesting cultural details.

Among the food items several Chinese Indonesian asylum seekers mentioned as something they ate was pig's trotter (*dter kar* in the Hokkien dialect). At first, I filed it as another Chinese culinary item, like chicken feet, a popular item in dim sum restaurants. But if chicken feet and pig's trotter had equal symbolic value, why were chicken feet not mentioned at all but pig's trotter was mentioned several times? On further research, the special significance of pig's trotters is found in the symbolic meaning of a fanciful name given to the dish, prepared with seaweed and dried oyster, and served during Chinese New Year. The pig's trotter dish is *Huer Cai Soon Chiu* loosely translated as "Grabbing the windfall as it comes along." The addition of seaweed (*fa cai*), or "to explode in wealth," and dried oyster (*hou see*), "great deeds" are said to represent good fortune, health and wealth if one eats them during the New Year. There are no special meanings attached to chicken feet as a dish except that it is delicious.

Another unique food mentioned was "red turtle cake" (*ang ku kueh*), a little two-inch turtle shaped sticky red pastry filled with mung bean eaten during New Year and often used as an offering during the annual Ching Ming Festival when families gather to clean the graves of their ancestors. The turtle is a symbol of longevity. I found this custom even among the Catholic Chinese Indonesians whose ancestors were non-Christians. It is unclear if the Catholics and the younger generation who honor their dead in the traditional ways at Ching Ming with *ang ku kueh* are aware of the symbolic meanings of their practices. But I did not have to share these anthropological concerns in my reports or with the adjudicators. In these everyday practices of eating, celebrating and honoring the dead, Dewi and other Indonesian Chinese had provided more than sufficient evidence to confirm their Chinese origin for the adjudicators.

My line of reasoning in asking Dewi about her dietary practice was that if Dewi had been a Muslim (the majority of Indonesians are Muslim), her diet would not have included pork. Dewi told me the native Indonesians—the *pribumi*—will not eat *zaan* and mooncake because they contain pork.

These special food items are available commercially in communities with a large enough Chinese population. Therefore, an individual purchasing any of these particular cultural items could be of any ethnicity and religion. Eating these foods by themselves do not make them Chinese. But in the context of the Chinese in Indonesia, and by a process of elimination, the person most likely to purchase these items are of non-Muslim origin. In Islam, the pig is *haram*. Haram is an Arabic term meaning sinful and refers to anything that is forbidden. Pork is haram and forbidden. The pig in Chinese culture, on the other hand, is a part of the word that forms the character for family, *jia*, 家. The word for family in Chinese comprises a roof over a pig, indicating the early domestication of the pig at the time of the invention of the word for family. In China today, pork is the most ubiquitous form of meat and the word for meat is the same word for pork (Chang 1977).

As a persecuted people, many have forgotten their culture, and what remains may be hidden. However, through gentle encouragement and meticulous recording of their taken-for-granted everyday practices, I was able to determine to my own satisfaction that Dewi, and other asylum seekers in similar circumstances, are indeed Indonesian of Chinese origin. So when the attorney asked me in court, under oath, if I was able state with certainty the Chinese Indonesian in front of me was indeed of Chinese origin, I was able to answer with confidence.

Chapter 3

Racialization and Persecution

In helping Dewi establish her asylum claims, I was asked to verify her "Chinese race" identity.

It was only through an in-depth oral history of Dewi's everyday practices such as naming children, addressing relatives, eating, celebrating, and honoring the dead, that I was able to reveal, without a doubt, her Chinese origin. These hidden and private aspects of the identities of Dewi and other Chinese Indonesian may be a necessary condition in proving their "Chineseness" but it is not sufficient to account for the persecution against them based on "race." According to the Refugee Convention, the asylum seekers must verify that the attack against them was not random, but they were targeted because they possess characteristics corresponding to one of the five categories identified in the Convention's definition of a refugee (Aleinikoff 1991). Having to prove persecution based on "race" is to return to the conundrum on "race" or "no-race." To state that Dewi belongs to the "Chinese race" is to use an antiquated idea of "race." To state that Dewi was not of the "Chinese race" was to risk failing to "prove" her "Chinese race" in asylum protection as required by the Refugee Convention.

RACIALIZATION AND PERSECUTION

To extract myself from this molasses of the "race/no race" position, I applied the idea of racialization (Miles 2003) to disarticulate the idea of "race" from "racism" and to consider persecution, as similar to racism, as the end product of a racialization process. This racialization process allows one to examine the dynamics beneath why "race" matters to the local Indonesian population. In Miles' theoretical construct, "race" represents the superficial human physical differences such as skin color, bone structure, or eye shapes. He clarified that when we "racialize," we give meaning to those features and cultural attributes that have come to represent a certain population. Thus, racialization is a representational process of signifying and magnifying mostly physical and increasingly cultural features for the purpose of inclusion and exclusion. By emphasizing real or perceived characteristics as elements of inclusion or exclusion, entire social collectives are in effect included or discriminated against. That is, "race" may not matter, but it has significance to the local population.

An examination of this racialization process brings into focus the "racializers" and the "racialized." Through everyday encounters, individuals construct a representation of others and make decisions that affect those racialized. In this theoretical construct, racism is the end result of racialized exclusion. Based on this understanding, the perpetrators and the victims of racism can include people of any "race." This distinction is important because in the dominant American discourse, only "whites" can be the perpetrators of racism. Minorities, such as blacks, Latinos and Native Americans, are the victims of racism and therefore cannot be racist. By expanding the idea that a nonwhite person can be a racist, and that racism can occur between people of the same supposed "race," this theoretical construct opens up the possibility of examining persecution on account of "race" as a ground of the Refugee Convention without invoking the biological concept of "race."

Within the American context of looking at "race" through the United States Census, both Chinese Indonesians and non-Chinese Indonesians would be categorized as "Asian," a term that also lumps together into a single group Chinese and other Asian immigrants to the United States. These multiplicities of Asians are contrasted with blacks, whites, Latinos and Native Americans. The term "Asian" is only useful as a description of the geographical origin of migrants, which is to say, they are all from Asia. Its use would have the same homogenizing effect as the idea of "race" in reducing the Asians into a few characteristics. This homogenizing of diverse groups from Asia for analyzing persecution would only lead us down the path toward the cultural trap suffered by Pasternak described in chapter 2. However, if we view Chinese Indonesian and non-Chinese Indonesian as separate entities, it is then possible to view the dynamics below the surface about what is meant by "Chinese Indonesians."

In arguing that Chinese Indonesians were persecuted on account of their "race," I must demonstrate that they were subjected to a racialization process and were victims of racist exclusion. The process of racialization and racialized exclusion against the Chinese Indonesian is an empirical question that must be documented to show that persecution against them was not random, but that they were targeted on account of their physical features ("race"). In addition, it must be shown that their government was unwilling or unable to protect them. In documenting persecution, I examined the transcripts of my interviews with the asylum seekers against published material to verify the truthfulness of the asylum seekers.

RACIALIZING CHINESE INDONESIANS

As a persecuted and deracinated people, cultural visibility becomes an invitation for unwanted attention and persecution. As a result, Chinese Indonesians have consciously avoided ethnic cultural markers. Without these Chinese cultural markers, as Dewi's Immigration Officer had discovered, he could not determine her identity. Faced with the requirement to ascertain their "Chinese race" identity—without using the simplistic idea of "race" and without common cultural cues to ascertain a Chinese—I began with their personal experiences of persecution where the perpetrator had specifically mentioned "Chinese" as the object of their target. These examples are grouped under textbox 3.1: *Epithets and Slogans Against the "Chinese."* The Chinese Indonesian asylum seekers themselves also noted the difference in their experiences of racialization from that of their *pribumi* peers, as seen in the examples in textbox 3.2: *Indonesian Chinese as Targets*. This differentiation produces two distinct groups of people: Chinese Indonesian and non-Chinese Indonesian. As a persecuted people, the Chinese Indonesians have developed strategies for survival by passing and hiding (textbox 3.3: *Strategies for Survival: Passing, Hiding Ethnic, Gender, and Religious Markers*). With survival in mind, the Chinese Indonesians have also developed a relationship with the Indonesian government structured by avoidance and withdrawal from normal civic engagements (textbox 3.4: *Relationship with the Government and the Pribumi*).

EPITHETS AND SLOGANS AGAINST THE CHINESE

In looking for evidence of persecution against the Chinese, I found epithets and slogans, which included the word "Chinese" as the clearest examples of targeting based on their ethnicity.

In the stories of more than a dozen Chinese Indonesian asylum seekers I found "*balek cina!*" (Go back to China!) to be the most common everyday anti-Chinese epithet. Telling the Chinese to go back to where they came from is to disregard the generations they have been in Indonesia, and to question their loyalty and contribution to the Indonesian nation.

More specific were the "*Cina! Cina! Bunuh Cina! Ambil! Cepat ambil!*" ("Chinese! Chinese! Kill the Chinese! Take! Quickly take!") shouted at the Chinese Indonesians during the course of looting, as told to me by several asylum seekers, including Ms. Beatrice Wilan, whose story is told in Part II on Religion, and "*Diam, Ah Moi!*" (Shut up, little girl!) which was said to one of the asylum seekers when she pleaded a rapist to stop his violence against her. *Ah Moi* was a pejorative use of a Chinese word meaning "little sister."

These explicit references to "China" or "Chinese" in the quotes above and others not listed here, indicate the attackers' obvious regard of the Chinese Indonesians as foreigners and that they were unwanted regardless of their history in Indonesia. The attackers' "objective" identification of their victim is based on their "Chinese" appearance, rather than the Chinese's self-identification. Therefore, the basis of the persecution against the Chinese Indonesian is their imputed "Chinese race." To regard attacks that specifically use the word "Chinese" and its equivalent would be similar to regarding the use of the "N" word as instances of racist hate crimes in the United States against African Americans. If attacks invoking the Chinese-ness of the targets are racist, they are then clear examples of persecution on account of "race."

Textbox 3.1: ***Epithets and Slogans against the "Chinese"***

"*Balek Cina!*" ("Go back to China!")
"*Dasar Cina, Orang Putih, ta boleh ada di-Indonesia*" ("Chinese people, White people, cannot be in Indonesia!)
"*Cina! Cina! Bunuh Cina! Ambil! Cepat ambil!*" ("Chinese! Chinese! Kill the Chinese! Take! Quickly take!") (Shouted during the robbery and arson of an appliance store owned by an asylee of Chinese Indonesian origin.)
"*Cina ta tau di-untung. Diam, kau amoi.*" ("You Chinese never appreciate what you have. You shut up, you Chink.") (Words said during a gang rape.)
"*Bangsat Cina!*" ("You Chinese bastard!")

DIFFERENTIATING AN AWARENESS OF CHINESE (SELF) FROM *PRIBUMI* (OTHER)

Many Chinese Indonesian asylum seekers are fully aware that they are a people who have been persecuted on a daily basis. Despite this, many regard themselves as Indonesian rather than as ethnic Chinese, and have made a conscious attempt to assimilate into Indonesia. The May 1998 anti-Chinese riot was a rude awakening, making them realize that they have been singled out based on their "Chinese-ness" vis-à-vis other Indonesians.

Keni, a twenty-two-year-old asylum seeker, became acutely aware of his identity during the May 1998 riot. A college student at the time, he was returning home after class on that fateful day when he came upon a crowd ripping the clothes off of a Chinese woman. Keni said he was so terrified, he could not help. He stood there helplessly. He said he thought the world was coming to an end for the Chinese. Upon returning to his sister's appliance shop where he helps after school, he discovered that a group of people had started a fire at a shop nearby. He said the police stood by and did nothing. When Keni tried to help his sister save their merchandise, he said the police arrested him for looting. His sister had to pay a bribe to get him out of jail. After a weeklong curfew that kept the violence from erupting, Keni returned to the classroom of the technical college where he was taking classes. Keni said his awareness of being a Chinese was heightened by the shock of the silence among his professors and classmates. No one in his class mentioned anything about the biggest riot to hit Indonesia in recent memory or how it affected them. It was as if his experience of trauma had never happened. He felt as if he was living in a separate world: a world of a persecuted Chinese minority.

The experiences of other Chinese Indonesian asylum seekers, as shown in textbox 3.2, included experiencing arson in their neighborhood and business areas while the non-Chinese did not. Chinese Indonesian women felt they could not use public transportation safely while the non-Chinese could; and they were targeted with violence, whether in the form of sexual abuse by their teachers, or by being forced from their cars after being pulled over on the highway. That is, their Chinese neighborhood, their places of business, and their physical features, are characteristics that can be objectified and differentiated from the other Indonesian collectivities. The Chinese Indonesians were judged by these objective indicators of their Chinese-ness rather than by the invisible "content of their character."

Textbox 3.2: *Indonesian Chinese as the Target*

"My *pribumi* co-workers left for home. But we had to stay back afraid to be attacked."
"The Muslim teacher did not do it to the Muslim girls but he did it to me."
"We thought we would be killed because our skin was of a different color."
"A group of native men ripped the clothes off a Chinese woman until she was totally naked . . ."
"They would pull out Chinese drivers from the road . . ."
"One of the young men on the train, sitting across from me, said to his friends, 'there was a fair skin Chinese girl. I opened her clothes and I touch her here and there . . ."
"Your skin is so smooth, so white. . . . It is ok to talk like that because it is not forbidden by law."
"They were targeting the Chinese-owned electronic stores."
"The rioters were burning the Chinese shop-houses."

STRATEGIES FOR SURVIVAL

The majority of the people in Indonesia are Muslim. Besides Islam, Indonesia also recognizes Hinduism, Buddhism, Catholicism and Christianity. To survive as a persecuted Chinese minority, it is safer to assume an identity that is not being persecuted. With the Muslim being the largest population, one asylum seeker said she keeps a scarf in her car so as to pass as a Muslim when stopped. Another said her family painted a Muslim sign on their door to escape arsonists setting fire to Chinese homes in the neighborhood.

Chinese Indonesian women asylees are especially vulnerable, due not only to their ethnicity, but also to their gender. To reduce their visibility as women, and as "Chinese," they tried to pass as men, as someone poorer, older, and/or uglier. One asylum seeker wears a bandana while riding a motorbike, so that, at a glance, under a helmet and behind a bandana, she does not attract attention as a woman or as a Chinese.

Another young woman rode a motorbike to school before her legal age, instead of walking, to lessen victimization by sexual predators that are often "idle men on a sidewalk." Families with means will chauffeur their daughters, hire a nanny, or request an aunt or a friend to accompany them even for routines such as going to school or to work. Those without means travel in groups for protection and to avoid public transportation. Most disheartening to the women is that no one would come to their assistance when they were groped on a crowded bus, robbed at knifepoint in public, or sexually harassed by male motorbike riders when stopped at a traffic light.

This self-imposed invisibility is most noted among Christians who spoke of avoiding all signs of religiosity. To minimize their vulnerability, they do not carry a bible or wear a cross. They do not show festive Christmas decorations, or hold communal prayers during heightened tension in the community. And when their churches are bombed or attacked, they would change churches (see the detailed discussion in Part II on religion). A Buddhist asylum seeker also mentioned not wearing a jade pendant of a Buddha to avoid identifying herself as Chinese.

Textbox 3.3: *Strategies for Survival: Passing, Hiding Ethnic, Gender, and Religious Markers*

"I keep a scarf in my car in case I am stopped."
"We painted a Muslim sign on the door of our house (to escape arson)."
"We use a Javanese name on our store and we kept our door closed all the time."
"We threw money out of our car window so that we could get a passage."
"All of us in the housing complex threw money outside the gate to hope that the mob would go away."

"When riding a motorbike, I wear a helmet, which is required, and bandana to hide my face."
"I started to ride a motorbike before the legal age to outrun the 'men squatting idly by the bus stop' I encounter on my way to school. They call me *amoi*." (*Amoi* is a derogatory term in Chinese for little girl).
"My grandmother keep our Chinese religious altar behind the wall so no one knew we were Chinese."
"I thought the world was coming to an end for the Chinese. But when I returned to school after the curfew, it was as if nothing had happened among my *pribumi* classmates and professors."
"We don't wear crosses or carry our bibles to avoid attack"
"We hide our Christmas tree away from view"

Finally, evidence of the persecution against the Chinese in Indonesia is reflected in their relationship with the government. With the State, they were the subject of dozens of laws that placed constraints on them compared to other groups. The stigmatization against the Chinese is experienced in everyday encounters with fellow Indonesians, the police, and government officials who define them as Chinese more than their own sense of "Chinese-ness" or their practice of "Chinese" cultures and customs. Indeed, the asylees even minimized contacts with the government including, for example, not applying for a marriage certificate "because it would involve having contact with the government, which means having to pay money." They avoided political activities because they felt they did not quite belong there. The victims of sexual violence and their witnesses vehemently refused to have contacts with the hospitals and the police. To do so is to incur more loss monetarily, to have their names dragged through the presses, not to mention that they would not be believed to begin with. Some have forfeited long years of training in professional degrees because of discrimination. When all else failed, they resorted to bribing in order to lubricate encounters with the state.

Textbox 3.4: ***Relationship with the Government and the* Pribumi**

"I did not report to the hospital after a rape. We have to pay a bribe."
"I did not report to the police. We have to bribe."
"We did not apply for a marriage certificate. We wanted to minimize contact with the government."
"I had to give up my medical degree training. They kept asking me for more and more money when I took the medical examination."
"The *pribumi* government servants would not cooperate with me in my work as a lawyer once I was not longer an apprentice under my *pribumi* mentor. I finally gave up my law practice because they threatened me with a big *parang* knife when I went to investigate a land dispute in the village."

These stories of the asylum seekers are consistent with the history of the Chinese in Indonesia and the periodic anti-Chinese spasms, with the most recent social upheaval in 1998, followed by a series of church bombings in 2000. The May 1998 riot took place the year after the Asian Financial Crisis. The anti-Chinese insanity of systematic rape, arson, and attack took place while the local police stood by. It led journalist McGurn (1998) to refer it to as the Indonesian *Kristallnacht*. Anti-Chinese violence is not new. Thus, compared to other anti-Chinese purges in Indonesia, the accounts that gave the figure of 150 rapes and more than a thousand deaths during the three days of carnage in May 1998 are not high. However, the viciousness of the violence led to an unprecedented mass exodus of ethnic Chinese who were convinced that they would never be accepted as equal citizens and would never be physically safe in the country that has been their home for generations (Purdey 2005).

These stories are also consistent with the data compiled by Mizhan Khan and Deepa Khosla (1999) for the Minorities at Risk (MAR) Project. The MAR Project was launched in 1986 and has been based at the University of Maryland's Center for International Development and Conflict Management since 1988. MAR monitors and analyzes the status and conflicts of politically active groups in all countries with a population of at least five hundred thousand. MAR's extensive database tracks groups on political, economic and cultural dimensions and provides standardized information to researchers, educators and the general public, contributing to the understanding of conflicts involving relevant groups.

Persecution against the Chinese in Indonesia goes back to the times of the Dutch colonial rule. Under the Dutch, Chinese Indonesians were treated as "Foreign Orientals." In addition to being excluded from the moral community of the nation, Chinese in Indonesia under Sukarno, the first president, were suspected of being communists, which led to a pogrom of more than sixty thousand in the 1960s. Under Suharto, the second president, they were subjected to a policy of forced assimilation, having been targeted for exclusion among the hundreds of ethnic and cultural groups in Indonesia. They were stripped of their name, language, and culture, as mentioned earlier. Besides being labeled as of "foreign descent," (*keturangan asing*) they were also "not of the soil" non-*pribumi*. Because the Chinese are defined as non-*pribumi*, they could never be of the soil, and therefore they are forever foreigners in the Indonesian imagination. In addition, *Cina*, a derogatory term similar to the English "Chink," was officially used to refer to the Chinese, despite the Chinese's preference to refer to themselves with an alternative term, *Thionghoa* (Jesudason 2001, 65), a term which means Chinese but derived from the Hokkien (Fujian) dialect spoken by most Chinese in Indonesia. That is, the Chinese in Indonesia became what Benedict Anderson refers to as a "pariah mercantile" population (Anderson 1991)—an unwanted and excluded minority used as scapegoats in times of civil unrest, with animosity towards them implicitly supported by state policies.

All Indonesian Chinese, regardless of their assimilation, were subjected to the same racialization. Objectively, their physical features—"race"—were important to the mass attackers in their search for blame in times of national crises. They were not judged by their subjective sense of loyalty and their contribution to Indonesia, but by their appearance alone. The Indonesian Chinese became a symbol of the country's trouble. They were attacked because of the country's belief that they did not belong there. They were racialized as foreigners and therefore subjected to censorship. This objective sense of who they are by other Indonesians became the dynamic that structured their outlook in life, and their everyday decisions. Therefore, it is not about their subjective identity but instead about an identity imposed on them from the outside. In the parlance of the conventional "race" language in the United States, Dewi was a different "race." The Indonesians' racialization of them for targeting and exclusion is the same as the use of the word "race" in committing racism. Their physical body defined their identity. They were attacked because of their Chinese looks. Women were raped because of their Chinese body. The Chinatowns were torched and churches burnt because they were inhabited by Chinese. The Chinese Indonesians were made acutely aware of their own particularity: their own history, culture, and the material being of their imputed "Chinese race."

Based on all of this documented evidence, I was able to conclude objectively that, in Indonesia, it was the observable attributes of the Chinese Indonesian (equivalent to "race") that were the basis of the attack and persecution against the asylum seekers. The word "race" may not have been used, but it was the local understanding that the Chinese possess particularities that can be identified, differentiated from the locals, and therefore can serve as grounds for attack and persecution.

Preparing the case for Dewi was a long process of working through the dilemma presented by the different perspectives on the idea of "race" with careful ethnographic research and by applying the idea of racialization. The authentication of the "Chinese" Indonesian has included an externally-defined identity which is based on their relationship to the State and to other groups in Indonesia, most of it structured by conflict and persecution, which affects how they live their lives. Based on these ideas, I was able to prepare a coherent narrative for Dewi—without using the idea of "race" as employed in the American tradition—to argue that she was persecuted through her physical attributes that came to define a local Chinese collectivity.

In a 2005 update on the May 1998 riots, the United States Department of State reported that the Indonesian government failed to make progress in establishing accountability because of the failure of civilian witnesses and government, military, and police officials to comply with the investigation (U.S. Department of State 2005). The Indonesian government's failure to establish "accountability" continues to obscure the identity of the perpetrators of Indonesia's violence. However, elicited through the asylum seekers in the United States, the violence perpetrated against them was not random, but was committed by members known to the State, and the State was unwilling or unable to stop the violence.

To the attackers, Chinese Indonesians were homogenized into a monolithic entity and attributed with simplistic characterization that led to the belief or conclusion that they must be rich and do not quite belong in Indonesia—as sanctioned by the State's many policies—and therefore, are fair game for attack and harassment. This categorization of the diverse "Chinese" population misses the mark in the nation's attempt to integrate its diverse populations. The racializing of the Chinese as the "Other" (as well as the anti-Christian activities which are not discussed here) took place in the context of Indonesia's struggle for self-identity.

The experience of the Chinese in Indonesia can best be understood as Suharto's attempt to control and manage its diverse population. In the construction of the Indonesian nation, the Chinese were racialized and ethnicized as a problem, their cultural rights denied, and they were considered as not quite belonging there. The effect on the Chinese is most acutely captured by the character in Edwin's (2008) movie, *Blind Pig Who Wants to Fly*. A young character in the film was asked what he wanted to be when he grew up. He answered, "Anything but a Chinese." Through Edwin's choice of the metaphor, who compares the Chinese Indonesians to a blind pig, tethered to a rope, walking with its head down, but wanting to fly. The filmmaker reflects his intentions and the Chinese moral relations to the Indonesian world: the Chinese as the most hated group in Indonesia. As previously discussed, the pig is *haram* in Islam. Haram, in Arabic, meaning sinful and referring to anything that is forbidden. By portraying the Chinese as a pig, it symbolizes their sinful and forbidden state in relation to Indonesia's larger moral and Islamic community. To Chinese Indonesians attempting to survive the policies of cultural erasure promulgated by the government that affected all aspects of their lives, they have withdrawn from civic engagement with the larger society. Indeed, they feel that simply being Chinese is an affront to others, or *haram*, like the pig, in the religiously conservative sector of Indonesia. Through self-censorship, parents have forbidden their children from playing outside to avoid trouble with the locals; or to speak their own language in public to prevent being hurt. They are to deny and forget that they are Chinese at all.

To make Indonesia a better place for all, the Chinese Indonesians must be included in this national and community-building effort, so that those who have left in terror may return home again. Even though a number among the original one hundred thousand have returned home, many remain as "illegals" in the United States, lacking the funds and resources to apply for asylum.

Dewi's companion, Meiji Sopoto, whom I met the first day, asked me if I was available to testify in court as an anthropological expert witness during Dewi's asylum Merit Hearing. I declined, as I had to be at a conference in Shanghai that summer. During that summer, while checking my email in a smoke-filled room of young Chinese playing video games, Meiji Sopoto informed me that Judge Gembacz had granted Dewi asylum. Dewi was one lucky asylum seeker.

In my analysis, I was able to objectively verify their "culture" with ethnographic interviews and verify persecution against them on account of their "race" through an examination of the racialized attacks against them. I have taken cautious considerations against essentializing their "culture" and reifying their "race," a precaution against the challenges the government might make during the court hearing. By establishing this "ethnographic authority" through anthropological research, I was able to contribute to the "authority" that speaks to the meaning of Chinese-ness among the Chinese Indonesians (Wang and Wang 2003). Based on this analysis, I was able to conclude that the exodus of the Chinese Indonesian asylum seekers was due to Suharto's failed policy of forced assimilation, which impacted their self-identity and their relationship with other Indonesians at all levels of society. If the Chinese Indonesian migrants in the United States, many of them illegal, decide to go home again, a rebuilding of Indonesian society must include the involvement of the Chinese Indonesian in civic engagement, rather than demonizing them as *persona non grata*.

In my limited exposure to cases of persecution on account of "race," I was left to wonder how other immigration officers and judges made decisions based on "race" without using the idea of racialization to show persecution based on "race."

Chapter 4

A Student Protester from a Myanmar Prison

In 2003, Mr. Goodsell asked me to meet Mr. Khun Yaw. My biggest challenge was figuring out what Bohmer and Shuman (2008) referred to as the question of "how to prove he is who he says he is?" in the identity of an asylum seeker.[1] Khun Yaw was a thirty-seven-year-old male claiming to be a Chinese from Myanmar. He claimed to have been imprisoned and tortured for four and a half years in the Insein Prison, in Yangon, near the old capital of Myanmar, for his involvement in the student protests. He carried a Malaysian passport and possessed a photocopy of a Burmese passport. When questioned, he explained that during the excitement of arriving in Long Beach, California, he forgot to reclaim the original passport. Speaking a mixture of Mandarin Chinese and English, Khun Yaw said he was a *huaqiao,* a Chinese who resides abroad, or "Overseas Chinese."

Mr. Goodsell told me he had a hunch that Khun Yaw was telling the truth, but he needed reasonable explanation to support his credibility. Based on a quick first impression, Khun Yaw could be a Chinese from almost anywhere. If he claimed to be from Burma, I would need to eliminate the possibility that he was not a Chinese from China, Hong Kong, Taiwan, Malaysia, Singapore, Thailand, or any country where there is an "Overseas Chinese" population.

Mr. Goodsell's old office in South Pasadena was quiet and spacious. Khun Yaw and I sat down comfortably in the waiting room and began our interview. Khun Yaw had a fair complexion and was of medium height, but he was quite stocky for a Chinese man. He could have been a fellow customer at a Chinese restaurant in San Gabriel Valley, just a few miles from Mr. Goodsell's office. I asked Khun Yaw if he knew Burmese. He said yes. I told him to say something to me in Burmese, not that I knew any Burmese, but he wouldn't do it. He said the Burmese had tortured him so hard in prison, he had sworn not to speak in that language ever again. I could not force him, so I asked him what had happened. He showed me scars on his chin and wrist. He pulled up the long sleeve of his white shirt to show me other scars on his body. Again, I asked him to tell me what had happened. He began to stutter and scratched his head, trying to remember. He said they beat him so hard that he had "forgotten many things."

Troubled by Khun Yaw's inability to recall details, I wondered how I could write about his identity in a way that Mr. Goodsell could use to build an argument in his case. I did not want to traumatize him with questions regarding his prison experience. I changed the subject and asked him questions related to his family and his background, letting him guide me on subjects he felt comfortable talking about. Khun Yaw said he was born in Yangon (formerly known as Rangoon), Myanmar (formerly known as Burma). His father migrated from Shanghai to Burma in his twenties and never returned to his native land again. His mother was born in Myanmar to grandparents who migrated from China. His family spoke a mixture of Mandarin and Burmese, the national language of Myanmar. Khun Yaw learned spoken Mandarin Chinese from his parents and a little writing from school. He answered questions related to his relatives on both sides of his parents' family, but said his parents had little contact with their parents, especially after he was sent to jail. I asked Khun Yaw about his wife, whom he married just before he went to college. He started to stutter again when he said, "my wife is a *Mian Dian ren*," which means "a person from Burma" in Chinese. I asked him how he met her. He said "She was walking on the street near my house. I thought she was pretty so I started to talk to her. I asked her if she was free and I took her out for dinner and a movie." Khun Yaw continued stuttering as he talked about his wife. I left the subject gently.

In interviewing Khun Yaw, I was reminded of the first rule in doing ethnography: establish rapport. Anthropologists normally spend a year or more in the field to make sense of a people's culture and here I was, hoping for revelation after only a couple of hours. I slowed down and continued to listen deeply. Khun Yaw and I chatted about schools, the traditions he observed, the festivals his family celebrated, and the food he ate. By focusing on the practices of his everyday life, I was also paving a way to ascertain his identity as a Chinese.

EDUCATION

Between the first meeting and subsequent interviews, I learned that Khun Yaw attended a government-run elementary school where he had one subject in Chinese, two in English, and one in Burmese. It was in school that he learned to write some rudimentary Chinese. Because of Khun Yaw's fluency in Mandarin, his schoolmates viewed him as a *huaqiao* ("Overseas Chinese"), rather than as a Burmese. After high school, Khun Yaw attended university, where he studied history and science. The instruction was in English and Burmese. This is commonly referred to as a "Form" system in Burmese education, and is a legacy of colonial rule common among former British colonies. This information helped me to place him as coming from one of the former British colonies in Southeast Asia: Burma, Malaysia, Singapore, and Hong Kong.

RELIGION

Khun Yaw shared that his father *pai-shen*, or literally, "worships" *shen*, or deities. Scholars refer to Chinese religion as Shenism to reflect the syncretic nature of Chinese beliefs (Thompson 1995). "We worship three gods. One is *Kuan Yin* [The Goddess of Mercy], one is Buddha, and one is a 'Four-Face Buddha.' My mother and I also worship with my father. During *da ze zi* [festive days], when we make offering to the deities, we use whatever fruits available at hand because *Kuan Yin* does not eat meat. We make some vegetable buns and use these as offering to her."

FOOD

In Khun Yaw's home, the food they eat "is like Thai food. It is slightly peppery." Besides regular rice, they also eat glutinous rice and vegetables, including some Burmese dishes. A common Burmese dish is half-ripened papaya cut into long, thin strips, with pepper, oil, and vinegar. Another Burmese dish—*pa o tor*—is chicken encased in mud and roasted. Other dishes include long beans stir-fried with dried tiny shrimp, stir-fried *chai sin* vegetable and "water spinach," fried eggs and chicken *tom yam*. In fact, most dishes are similar to Thai food, containing sweet and sour flavoring.

FESTIVALS CELEBRATED

Khun Yaw said the Chinese in Myanmar celebrate Chinese New Year but also Burmese New Year: "two New Years." The Burmese New Year depends on the Burmese calendar, so it is not the same date on the Western calendar. Other holidays in the country include Burmese Independence Day, Labor Day, and Christmas. For Chinese New Year, he said, "my family buys special foods for the occasion: *kropok* [a Malay word referring to deep-fried shrimp chips], coconut cookies, and egg sponge cake, as well as an orange drink which we would add sugar and water." Other special holidays include visiting the graves of the grandparents (*ching ming*) and the Mid-Autumn Festival.

NEIGHBORHOOD

Khun Yaw talked about his home in San Chaung in the outskirts of Yangon. He said it had a mix of *huaqiao* and Burmese. To the left of his family's "shop-house," which sold fruit, there was a clothing store owned by a "Yangon man and a woman, and their servant." A "shop-house" is a type of building commonly seen in Asia. They are mostly two or three stories high, with a shop on the ground floor and a residence above. People call the woman "auntie." The store selling sweets and toys to the right was owned by a *huaqiao*—addressed as "Uncle Tin" by others. Behind his house, there was a grocery store owned by a man addressed as "Uncle Tong." In the commercial area, made up of about two major streets, people spoke a mix of Burmese, Mandarin, and the Chinese dialects of Cantonese and Hakka. The choice of language depended on the linguistic background of the person. The common terms for addressing other Chinese included *Ah Pah* and *Ah Sou* ("uncle" and "aunt" in Cantonese).

COMMUNAL RELATIONS

In the neighborhood where Khun Yaw grew up, there was a mix of Chinese and Burmese. In terms of their relationship with each other, Khun Yaw said, "the Chinese and the Burmese were like two factions. The Chinese *huaqiao* were nicer to other Chinese *huaqiao*; the Burmese were a little better to other Burmese." At the time he was in elementary school, there were anti-Chinese activities. He goes on to say, "but the problems were resolved when the two groups stopped fighting—one group went here, the other went there. Eventually the Burmese started talking to us again. As a whole, the Chinese were discriminated against. The government favors the Burmese in housing, loans, and issuing of licenses."

AFTER THE FIRST MEETING

By the time I had finished asking him detailed questions about his religious practices at home, the foods he ate, and the customs and festivals he celebrated, I was certain of Khun Yaw's Chinese identity. Several hours had gone by, yet many things were still a mystery to me. Was he using forgetfulness to avoid answering some questions? If he said he was a Chinese, could he be a Chinese from Malaysia or Singapore, or a Chinese from the People's Republic of China, Taiwan or Hong Kong? I wanted to trust him, but I was thinking ahead to what the government and the judge would ask him. I needed concrete proof in order to write and speak about his identity with confidence. If I could not uncover information on who he was, he would have no chance in court when questioned about his identity. When I changed the subject back to the torture he had suffered in prison, he would begin scratching his head. I waited, because I needed to know his experience in prison as well as the journey that had finally brought him to the Port of Long Beach. How did he get here and how did he get help going to the city to apply for asylum? The journey seems impossible to a person who has not gone through the same experience.

Between his stuttering and his "forget[ting] many things," Khun Yaw did not make sense right away. His answers came out in disconnected bits and pieces. I repeated my questions, approaching the same subject from many angles. I assigned the bits of information into different categories for later use, like building a huge jigsaw puzzle. I told Khun Yaw that I would telephone him for further details and meet again after I had drafted a report. After having "established rapport" with him, the details came more easily during our many phone conversations, allowing me to finally piece his story together. Between the first and second meeting with Khun Yaw, I worked furiously to learn about Burma. It had crossed my mind that perhaps I should consult with another anthropologist. But who would I call? There are famous historians and journalists who report on Burma, but where would I find a colleague who knew about contemporary issues in Burma and was available to interview Khun Yaw at such short notice? What I needed was someone who could interview him, and figure out his identity with proof, right away.

It was fortuitous that I was teaching a course on Peoples of Asia at the time. To supplement my own learning, I used the occasion to assign class readings on Burma, starting with basic information from Lynn Pan's (1999) *The Encyclopedia on Overseas Chinese* and ending with *Political Systems of Highland Burma* by Edmond R. Leach (1967) that proved unhelpful to me in learning about Khun Yaw's identity. I purchased a VHS copy of *Beyond Rangoon*, released in 1995, and watched it in class with my students. The film is about an American tourist caught up in the Burmese student protest movement in 1988. It shows the brutality of military rule and the killing of civilians. In discussing the connections between military rule, the student movement, and my writing of a report on Khun Yaw's prison experience, one of my students revealed that the name of the instrument used to torture Khun Yaw was a "brass knuckle."

With readings and research on the Chinese in Myanmar, I was able to place Khun Yaw as an ethnic minority in Myanmar. Things he had said about his neighborhood and his relationship with his community began to make sense to me. With this information on the relationship among ethnic groups in his community, I was eager to learn if there was any anti-*huaqiao* sentiment for the attorney to use to build an argument of persecution based on "race" or culture or nationality.

MEETING KHUN YAW TWO MONTHS LATER

At the second meeting two months later in Mr. Goodsell's office, and after about twenty hours of phone conversations with Khun Yaw, I was thinking of his Malaysian passport. I greeted him with *Selamat Pagi*. Khun Yaw did not respond to my "Good Morning" in Bahasa Malaysia. Greetings like *Selamat Pagi* and *Selamat Petang* are common courtesies that people in Malaysia greet each other with. It is used across all ethnic groups and socioeconomic classes throughout Malaysia. So, if Khun Yaw did not respond to my greeting, he may not know the common greetings from Malaysia and therefore may not have come from there, despite carrying a Malaysian passport. (In talking with him, he had never claimed he was from Malaysia). Later in the interview, I switched my conversation with him from Mandarin to Cantonese; which did not elicit any response from him either. This helped me rule out the possibility of him coming from Hong Kong, Malaysia, or Singapore, where most people knew Cantonese.

While we were talking in Mandarin Chinese, I asked Khun Yaw to write some Chinese characters, from one to ten. Khun Yaw missed three of the ten, which suggested that he lacked extensive formal systematic learning in Chinese. This helped me rule out the possibility of him coming from China and Taiwan. When I mentioned Khun Yaw's case to a medical doctor a couple of years later, he suggested Khun Yaw may have sustained brain injury from the trauma in jail, and that he could be suffering from post-traumatic stress disorder (PTSD). Those possibilities never occurred to me because I was focused intensely on an anthropological perspective. Given the range of conditions asylum seekers present when seeking help, this suggests the importance of medical and psychological diagnosis from the outset. But these resources are rarely available given the lack of an infrastructure to help asylum seekers.

The impact of trauma has an effect on how an asylum seeker is able to recall or disclose certain events. Head trauma, depression, PTSD, dissociation, and the fact that they have chosen not to recall these events until their actual interview, which can bring about a host of emotions they have not yet dealt with. These things need to be addressed, as their difficulty recalling events tend to be viewed as "inconsistencies" or "lying," resulting in a decrease in perceived credibility, affecting the overall outcome of their case (Einhorn and Berhold 2015, 34–40).

After countless hours of interviews, I was finally able to sketch out the student protest that led to his imprisonment, the beatings in jail, and later, the escape from Myanmar.

EVENTS LEADING TO PRISON

In 1988, while Khun Yaw was teaching at a high school, he joined colleagues from a Teacher's Union to attend a protest against the government for their unfair treatment against the students and the teachers. In 1993, curious about the student activities at the Yangon Institute of Technology, Khun Yaw attended one. In November 1996, while Khun Yaw was studying English at Yangon University, his professor and teaching assistant told the students in the class to join them in a demonstration against the government. Khun Yaw said,

> He was our professor so we listened to him and went to protest. We were given banners, but before we had a good look at the banners, the police came. Our demonstration was against the government for 'not respecting us.' Our teachers asked us so we followed. It was my second demonstration.

Khun Yaw explained:

> During the demonstration, there were lots of people protesting. About an hour into the demonstration, the soldiers came, and the protesters scattered. There were about 500 people remaining. The police fired their guns into the air and they used water cannons to shoot at us. They kicked and hit those they caught with sticks. They were beaten on the head, including some girl students. Many people were bleeding from their heads and their mouths. The girl students returned the beating by scratching at the police. People everywhere were shouting against the government. When they were arresting people, I ran and managed to escape. The students ran but they were all arrested.

However, very early the next morning, on November 27, 1996, the soldiers went to his house to arrest him. There were about six or seven soldiers and police. They asked him to sit down and then searched his house. Khun Yaw said his parents and his wife were at home. His parents were terrified and his wife was crying. When they found papers that were anti-government, they took him to Insein Jail, sometimes simply known as Yangon Jail. What had happened to Khun Yaw was a rather common experience among dissidents and asylum seekers to the United States. Similarly, Bridget Haas (2017), writing about an asylum seeker who had fled her native Cameroon, was detained and tortured by the military police in response to her activism in her homeland.

TORTURE IN PRISON

Khun Yaw recalled his first day in jail:

> They started to beat me with big sticks. Later, they put a bag over my head, and they carried some kind of instrument in the hand, protruding from between their fingers of a closed fist, like where the ring is [a 'brass knuckle']. They hit me on my face, my body and then they kicked me.

When Khun Yaw spoke about the beating in prison, he showed me the scars on his body. He said:

> They locked me up for four and a half years. Every week they would take me to beat me up. They beat me up until I was injured and then when I was well, they would take me out to beat me again. They covered up my face and beat me. They hit me on my face and on my arms. They also kicked me and when they see that I didn't have 'any energy left,' they would take me back to the cell. When they see that I was a little better, they call me out and beat me again. Later they didn't beat me with the metal instrument, they only wrapped their hands with cloth and they pounded me with their fists. The beatings stopped after a month and a half. But I was in jail for four and half years.

Khun Yaw continued:

> While I was in jail I saw the students who were arrested too. All the students arrested were beaten by the guards, but because I don't look Burmese, the prison guards beat me with the metal instrument in their hands. They didn't beat the Burmese with the same weapon. When they beat me they called out in Burmese "bpee! bpee! bpee!" meaning "Hit! Hit! Hit!" I would cry from the pain. I was bleeding here and here [as he pointed to his old wounds]. I thought I was going to die in prison and would never get out. There is a doctor in the prison. During first month I saw the doctor four times. He applied something to my wounds. The guards were beating other people too. Some were beaten until they collapsed and not moving and then they would be pulled away. It was so terrible; their faces were broken and their mouths were broken and the floor was covered with blood. Two of the people who were badly beaten were taken away. I don't know what happened to them. Two other people replaced them in their cells.

I asked Khun Yaw what else happened in prison, besides the horrible beatings. Khun Yaw said:

> During the time in jail they made us make shoes with straw and leather. When we were done with the shoes, we had lunch, and then we would clean the toilets or mop the floor or do laundry. In jail we ate rice, vegetables, and some meat. The food was bad and there wasn't enough. They gave me less food and made me work harder than the Burmese. For example, there were two sets of bowls; the larger ones were for the Burmese and the small ones for the Chinese. The Chinese were given vegetable with one to two bits of pork but the Burmese had about six to seven bits. I was always hungry and I would drink water from the tap to fill up my stomach. Sometime, the Burmese prisoners would give me one or two bits of meat from their ration.

MY "EUREKA" MOMENT ON KHUN YAW'S IDENTITY

When Khun Yaw was telling me about the food he had in prison, I knew it was my "Eureka" moment. When he said he had pork in prison, I immediately ruled out his Malaysian origin. Malaysia, as a country with a large Muslim population and Islam as its official religion, never serves pork in any state-operated institution. Khun Yaw was not aware he had just revealed the real "gold" of his identity. I was so excited that I telephoned Mr. Goodsell almost immediately to report that his hunch about Khun Yaw was correct: I had "proof" Khun Yaw was from Myanmar.

By now, through a process of elimination, I had placed his identity squarely as a Burmese *huaqiao* Chinese. Despite not possessing a legal document showing his identity, he could not be a Chinese from any of the neighboring countries with Chinese populations. For the moment, however, I had to continue learning about Khun Yaw's experience in prison.

> During the four and half years in jail I didn't make a phone call or write a letter. While I was in jail, my wife and my parents didn't come to see me because they were afraid to see the painful condition I was in; "it was too terrible to see." During my more than four years there, I only saw about three visitors who came to the prison. I hated my teachers for getting me into trouble but there was nothing I can do about it. After four and a half years in prison, I was released, probably because of good behavior; I was very obedient and didn't make any trouble for them. After my release, they told me I must report at the police station every week. And if there was an emergency in the country, I had to go back to jail. They told me if I didn't report they would put me in jail again. I reported to the police every week. There was a book with my picture in it I had to go and sign every week. The nicer police would hand the book to me. The bad ones would throw the book at me.

> After my release, I couldn't adjust to life outside the prison. I couldn't eat and I couldn't sleep. I would dream and in my dream I saw the blood on the ground from the beating. I went to the doctor. He gave me sleeping pills and told me to take as needed. I didn't have the same feeling for my wife anymore. We lost all our friends and relatives. No one would come to our house because they were afraid of trouble. I couldn't get a job. No one would hire a person who had been to jail. My father told me I must escape from the country. There was no future, no work and I was like a totally handicapped person—I might as well be dead.

THE ESCAPE FROM MYANMAR

Khun Yaw described his escape from Myanmar:

> A few months after I was released from prison, my father's friend told us he knew someone who could smuggle people out of Myanmar and take them to America. My father asked about the cost because we didn't have money. The broker is a Burmese. Using my father's land as collateral, the broker provided cash for us. We paid the smuggler $5,000 first and I was to pay another $5,000 when I get to the USA. I asked him what about my passport. He said he would give me a copy first. He told me to keep the copy in a safe place and the captain would give me the original when I get to the US. Getting the passport was included in the $10,000.

He added:

> The broker told me to quickly escape. The year I left was 2001, in the month of December. There was very little time to prepare for the escape. I grabbed a few items of clothing, some underwear, and some personal toiletries. I took along two things that happened to be around: a 'prison release paper' and a photo of myself when I was young.

Again, Khun Yaw's experience was very characteristics of other asylum seekers fleeing persecution, whose personal belongings and documents were hastily arranged, with family members pooling resources to procure a means of escape (Haas 2017, 81).

THE JOURNEY BY CARGO SHIP FROM YANGON TO TAIWAN TO SOUTHERN CALIFORNIA

Khun Yaw described his journey to the United States:

> There were five other men on the ship, two Chinese and three Burmese. We sat in the middle of the ship, with just enough room to lie down. We used our

jackets as cover when we were cold. There were all these boxes around us. We could only see a tiny slit of light from between the boxes. The captain, who was Burmese, gave us bottled water and dried food like cracker and fruits. To urinate, we would do it in one corner. To defecate, we did it into a paper bag. When we had enough soiled bags, we would ask the broker to take it out to throw into the ocean.

It took about a month to go from Yangon to Taiwan. The cargo ship stopped at ports along the way but we didn't get out. In Taiwan, the cargo ship stopped for a month, but we didn't get out either. Between Taiwan and the United States, it probably took about two and half weeks, but I don't really know. We slept, ate, and slept again. The men and I talked but there wasn't much to talk about. It was all dark inside. If we saw some light it was day. If there was no light, it was night. Just before the ship arrived in Long Beach, the captain told us that we were docking in Long Beach. I was so afraid I would be arrested and returned to Yangon.

LONG BEACH, CALIFORNIA

I was also curious as to how Khun Yaw had made his way to a port city in Southern California and eventually found help as a stranger to America. Through more questioning, he shared, "After arriving in Long Beach, the captain collected the remaining $5,000 from me and told all six of us that as soon as we dock in Long Beach, he would open the door and we should run." In the rush to get out, Khun Yaw said the captain didn't give him his "original passport" that was promised him. But Khun Yaw said he remembered to tell the captain to tell his family that he had arrived safely in America. He was not sure whether or not the captain conveyed his message to his family. After running to a highway, Khun Yaw said he waited for several hours before he saw a taxi. He asked the driver, in English, to take him to the downtown area of Long Beach. He told the driver he didn't have much money—he had only about $100. For a drive of about 10 minutes he was charged about $30. After arriving in downtown Long Beach, he walked around for about three hours, looking for people who could be from Myanmar based on their looks so he could ask for help. He confessed he asked about nine people who appeared to be Burmese whether they were Burmese before he came across one who was actually Burmese. The other men were Indonesian, Cambodian, Sri Lankan, and Vietnamese. He asked the ninth man, in the Burmese language, "Are you Burmese?" The man replied "yes" and Khun Yaw asked him for help in English. The Burmese man called his friend on a public phone to take them to his house in Culver City, a city in west Los Angeles. The Burmese man's friend found Khun Yaw a job at a Chinese restaurant in Long Beach. Khun Yaw said he worked for six months and then found another job in the City of San Gabriel, a city to the east of Los Angeles, through a temporary job agency.

By the time Khun Yaw had provided me with great details of his journey from Myanmar to Long Beach, how he talked to nine people before he found a fellow countryman to help him, I felt his story became more plausible. Khun Yaw said asking for help after he arrived in Long Beach was the last time he spoke Burmese since arriving in the United States. After all the pain he had suffered in prison, Burmese was one language he wanted to forget. When he told me his feelings regarding the Burmese language for the second time, I wondered whether he had made an exception to write in Burmese for me. Or was there something more to his connection to Burma?

"PA-O"?

While conducting research on Khun Yaw, I was very intrigued by the entry of "Pa-O" under the box for ethnicity in Khun Yaw's asylum application. In 2003, "Pa-O" did not appear on any of the internet search engines. After many hours of research on obscure tribal populations in Burma, the second "Eureka" moment came when I discovered "Pa-O" was one of the Shan ethnic groups, among over one hundred ethnic groups in Burma. So, did Khun Yaw assume a Burmese ethnic identity when he applied for asylum?

I was curious to get to the heart of Khun Yaw's Burmese connection. In reviewing my notes, Khun Yaw had said his wife was a *Mian dian ren* (a Burmese, in Chinese). I recalled that he stuttered when speaking about his wife. From the details he had shared, his wife only had an elementary school education, and she had a brother who repaired bicycles for a living. When Khun Yaw and his wife were married, they lived with his parents, where his wife helped with their business selling fruit. They spoke a mixture of Burmese and Chinese, and his wife was a "Pa-O" ethnic minority.

If Khun Yaw's wife was a "Pa-O," he had assumed his wife's ethnic identity. From my interviews, I had determined Khun Yaw was very comfortable and secure in his identity as a *huaqiao* Chinese. My explanation for his claim of "Pa-O" identity when he applied for asylum was because he was afraid the outside world would not know where to place a person of Burmese Chinese origin. Therefore, he assumed his wife's "Pa-O" ethnic label. That is, in the event he should be arrested outside of Burma, he would be returned to Myanmar, rather than being sent to China.[2]

A few months later, after I had prepared Khun Yaw's report and was already quite certain of his identity, I asked Khun Yaw to write down the numbers "One, Two, and Three" in the Burmese script. Khun Yaw did. When I checked on the Burmese words later, the script was a perfect match to the

Burmese writing I had come to recognize. That is, even though Khun Yaw had told me he had sworn not to say anything in Burmese, he was able to write down some concrete evidence of his identity. Perhaps talking about details of the ordinary aspects of his life over the last few months had allowed us to build trust. Or, perhaps it had allowed him to view himself as a complete person with a history, a past, and a possible future, despite having suffered horribly in prison.

THE JUDGE'S DECISION

After Mr. Goodsell filed Khun Yaw's petition for asylum, we waited. When Khun Yaw appeared in court for his Merit Hearing with the Immigration Judge, Mr. Goodsell presented all my explanations to account for Khun Yaw's authenticity and credibility. The Judge appeared to be satisfied. However, before ending the hearing, she requested one more piece of evidence before she would grant him asylum: Khun Yaw would provide the immigration court his "High School Leaving Certificate" as evidence that he was from Myanmar. Mr. Goodsell commented, "The judge was willing to grant him asylum but she needed something to hang the case on."

After leaving Myanmar, Khun Yaw did not have any contact with his parents or wife for fear of jeopardizing their safety. His family also did not have a telephone. He had told the smuggler on the cargo ship to inform his parents of his safe arrival, but he was not sure if the message was ever delivered. He also worried how his parents were managing after having used their land as a collateral to pay the smuggler. Having escaped while he was under "conditional discharge," he would be arrested as soon as he returned to Myanmar. Given such circumstances, how was he supposed to produce a copy of his "High School Leaving Certificate?" Even if such records were ever kept, I could not imagine a school clerk in Yangon would process such a request, and then send it to Khun Yaw, in his/her own time, and pay for the postage. Given the years of military rule and control, the clerk would need to clear it with the principal first, if not higher authorities. I had no idea how the Judge's request would be possible to carry out. How could the Judge expect him to obtain a copy of his High School Leaving Certificate given the distance, separation, and hostile military regime?

I was stunned at the Judge's request. Mr. Goodsell said the Judge had a bad reputation in San Francisco and was sent to Los Angeles. We were unfortunate to have her on our case.

Khun Yaw, Mr. Goodsell, and I discussed how Khun Yaw could comply with the Judge's request. We suggested Khun Yaw ask a friend to go to Myanmar to visit the high school he had attended to obtain a copy of his "High School

Leaving Certificate." Months later, on the day Khun Yaw was to appear in court, he showed up at the attorney's office where we were to meet before going to court together. I had brought Khun Yaw a box of chocolates because it was close to Christmas. Mr. Goodsell said, "Look, Khun Yaw, the professor brought you a Christmas present." Khun Yaw took it from my hands without acknowledging it. Instead, he thanked us for helping with the case and then showed us a fake green card. He waved good-bye and left the office. Khun Yaw had obtained his green card fraudulently. He knew he would never be granted asylum had he tried to follow the judge's orders. Instead, he had taken the matter into his own hands and purchased a fake identity card. In a sense, Khun Yaw had committed asylum fraud because he failed to produce a document required by the asylum court. Without the required documentation to prove his credibility, he would be deported. Khun Yaw did not make himself available for deportation. Instead, he "disappeared" into the great metropolis of the City of the Angels.

Mr. Goodsell's response: "He will survive."

In 2015, when Aung San Suu Kyi won a landslide victory in the first democratic election, I thought of Khun Yaw's participation in a student protest against the government more than a decade ago. Even though Khun Yaw said it was only his second student protest, he had been to a number of student meetings in a number of universities. Even though he said he was merely an obedient student following his professor's call to demonstrate against the government, his presence in that student protest, along with many others in Myanmar, fueled the political turmoil, which continued up until the democratic election in November 2015. I wondered if these events would help Khun Yaw to go home again to his parents and his wife. Perhaps with the new openness of Myanmar, he will be able to locate his family and eventually have more than a "prison release paper" and a childhood photo of himself to remind him of his past. Perhaps he will be able to obtain a "High School Leaving Certificate" after all, so that he can make things right, legally.

Asylum seekers, by law, are not required to produce evidentiary proofs. When fleeing from persecution, most of them are unable to obtain documentation from their tormentors. However, we have an asylum system that forces the asylum seekers to do the impossible. Due to the demands of one ignorant judge, people are forced to "disappear" in the United States.

NOTES

1. After Dewi Wisante won her asylum, Mr. Kenneth Goodsell, who regularly worked with Dr. Nauman's immigration agency, contacted me to help him with his Indonesian cases. That was the beginning of a decade-long fruitful partnership of

collaboration between law and anthropology, which is the theme of this book. When Mr. Goodsell asked me to worked on Khun Yaw's case, we had already established a great working relationship, and he essentially let me figure out the identity of the asylum seeker by myself.

2. This was similar to my experience with the Vietnamese Boat People in Pulau Bidong in the mid-1980s. I had learned to speak rudimentary Vietnamese before arriving in Pulau Bidong for my research, hoping to use Vietnamese to communicate with the Vietnamese Boat People. But to my surprise, I discovered that most of the Vietnamese Boat People were Chinese Vietnamese. They spoke fluent Cantonese (and I am sure they also speak fluent Vietnamese). As a result, I used Cantonese to conduct my interviews in the refugee camps. When processing for settlement to a third country, the Chinese Vietnamese refugees told the United Nations High Commissioner for Refugees (UNHCR) staff that they were Vietnamese. (Indeed, they were also Vietnamese based on culture. But that is a subject for another discussion.) In the Chinese Vietnamese encounter with the international organizations, they were afraid they would be mistaken as Chinese from China and be returned to China, when in fact Vietnam had been their home for generations. So, like the Chinese Vietnamese Boat People, Khun Yaw had preemptively taken into account the outsiders' ignorance of the Chinese Burmese and assumed a Burmese "Pa-O" identity, which is also his wife's identity.

Part II

PERSECUTION ON ACCOUNT OF RELIGION

Chapter 5

A Buddhist Monk, a Catholic Woman, a Christian Pastor

How do asylum adjudicators learn about the religions of the petitioners and figure out if the asylum seekers were persecuted on account of their religion? Asylum adjudicators, from lawyers, government attorneys, and judges, to those in the legal consultation services such as the *lüshilou* in the Mandarin-speaking community in Los Angeles, are not trained in matters of theology, religion, culture, and community, nor on the country-specific conditions on these matters that prompted the asylee to flee his or her country in the first place.

In this chapter, I tell the stories of three Chinese Indonesian asylum seekers—a Buddhist monk, a Catholic woman, and a Christian pastor—to account for the dynamics of religion that affected their asylum applications. Even though I was not specifically asked to verify their religion, as I attempted to ascertain their Indonesian Chinese identity, religion played a part in the persecution against them and in shaping their identity. As a result, the cases are as much about religion as "race"—or to be precise, a racialized perception by others and an understanding of themselves as a racialized people.

LOCATING THE "RELIGION" OF A CHINESE BUDDHIST

Anthropological research on asylum cases is conducted by extended interviews, and is often done without the opportunity to make real-time observations of the petitioners' practices in motion, whether based on religion or other habits. My descriptions of the asylum seekers are, for the most part, based on what they have said and what they have shown me, and are triangulated with published research on the subject, rather than based on actual observations of the persecution against them in their homeland.

Mr. Budi had applied for asylum protection, but there were questions swirling around his case about why he had four names. Was he a fraud? Did he create these multiple names and identities to cheat the asylum system? When I was asked by Dr. Nauman's immigration services agency to help on the case, I was not specifically asked to ascertain the persecution on account of Mr. Budi's Chinese Indonesian "race" identity, or his religion, but on the confusion over his names. Mr. Goodsell, to whom the case was referred, was not particularly enthusiastic about the case but Dr. Nauman seemed to believe in Budi. Upon closer questioning, including the mapping of his name over the history of Indonesia and on his experience as a Chinese Indonesian in the United States, it was easy to understand the reason he possessed multiple names without assuming he had them for nefarious intention.

Born a third generation Chinese Indonesian, Budi had a Chinese name—three characters representing his family name, his generation name and his given name—which his mother had written for him, and which Budi had kept as an image in his cellular phone. On Budi's birth certificate, the Chinese name was written with Dutch Indonesian orthography. Under Suharto's policy of forced assimilation, Budi then changed his name to a "non-Chinese sounding" one. He adopted "Budi" as a part of his name. After he arrived in California, his Chinese friends from the People's Republic of China helped him render the spellings of the two versions of his Chinese name into Pinyin, a phonetic system used in China. And finally, Budi took a Buddhist name when he was initiated into Buddhist monkhood upon completing a program at the International Buddhist Progressive Society in Hacienda Heights in East San Gabriel Valley, east of downtown Los Angeles. Using the most common Chinese family name 張 as an example, it is possible to illustrate why Budi has four names. First, 張, rendered as "Tjio" in Dutch orthography would be written as "Zhang" in Pinyin, thus giving him two names from the same Chinese character. Second, the "non-Chinese sounding" Indonesian name "Budi" and the Buddhist name add a third and a fourth name.

To document persecution on account of religion, how does one know what constitutes the religion of an asylum seeker? The documentary, *Well-Founded Fear*, mentioned earlier, featured a young man claiming persecution on account of his Jewish faith. To authenticate his Jewishness, the judge asked him to recite passages of a Jewish prayer. In preparing Mr. Budi for his court appearance, would the judge ask for specifics of his religious practices? Would the judge know if Budi was reciting a Buddhist chant properly? And what would I do to show he was persecuted because of his "Chinese religious practices?"

Indonesia's constitution recognizes religious freedom. Under Sukarno, the first president, six major religions were permitted—Islam, Protestantism, Catholicism, Buddhism, Hinduism and Confucianism. Suharto, the second president, along with his attempt to erase everything that was culturally Chinese, also "derecognized Confucianism" (Suryadinata 2004). When the Chinese Indonesians were faced with persecution because of their Chinese religion, many converted to Christianity. Among the seventeen Chinese Indonesian asylum seekers I have interviewed, about half of them are Catholics and Christians, with the other half being Buddhist, practitioners of Confucianism, and other traditional Chinese religions. Some of the families have converted from Confucianism to Christianity. Further, members in a single family may consist of several different religions, with the result that in any household one may see a syncretic practice of different customs dictated by different religions.

Drawing on extensive anthropological accounts on the practices of Chinese folk religion, I sketched out the everyday practices of the Chinese Indonesian related to religious beliefs in order to support Budi's claim of his identity. Practice of Chinese "religion" is not associated with a formal structure such as a church or temple membership, or regular attendance. The Chinese traditional belief system involves ancestors and a pantheon of gods, deities, and ghosts, which are represented by statuettes, images, and writings on tablets. It is about the relationship the family has with its dead ancestors through the practices of making offerings on particular days on family altars. It is also about their relationship to the different gods, deities, and spirits whose shrines are located in different parts of the home and its surrounding. The forms of offerings appropriate for the various classes of supernatural beings and the locations of placement for these beings are very specific. Buddha, often represented by a statue of *Kuan Yin*, or the Goddess of Mercy, is always placed on an altar in the main living room. The God of Heaven, or *Tian Gong*, is represented by a tablet, and placed on a small altar mounted by the front door, facing skyward, and above the level of the head of an adult. The Kitchen God, made famous by Amy Tan's novel, *The Kitchen God's Wife*, is usually represented by a red strip of paper with the words "Kitchen God" placed over the stove. Statues of deities "adopted" by the family and pictures of ancestors are placed in the main family sitting room, facing the front door and above the level of an adult's head. The only god placed below eye level is the Earth Deity (*Tu Ti Gong*), found below the family altar, and facing the front of the house, whose job is to protect the family. The "Ghosts," such as the "Hungry Ghosts," representing those who had died an untimely death, are placated with offerings directly on the ground, outside the backdoor, at the appropriate festival. In folk terms, the Chinese refer to their practice as *bai shen*, literally, "worshipping the god." Historian Thompson (1995) uses the term "Shenism" to convey this complex belief system. Sometimes, the term Confucianism is also used to refer to the Chinese religious belief system. Given such a belief system, the basis for identifying the practice of Chinese "religion" is to observe the images representing these gods, deities, ancestors, and ghosts located both inside and outside the house, and the practices associated with each one throughout the year.

I was particularly interested in understanding Mr. Budi's claim of "religion" while he was in Indonesia. Since I was not able to observe his actual practices in Indonesia, he showed me a stack of 3x5 photographs of his family and his home. One picture shows the main sitting room with an ancestral altar including wooden tablets with the names of his ancestors either carved or written on framed pieces of paper. Other pictures show portraits of his ancestors hanging on a wall over a side table. Some show ancestral tombstones engraved with their Chinese names from the era when written Chinese was permitted in Indonesia. Each god, deity, ghost, and ancestor is also associated with different types of food the family offers during specific days of the month. Some of these practices require visits to the temple or to the grave sites. Due to anti-Chinese attacks, Mr. Budi and his family would close the door whenever they worshipped. This custom of hiding their religious practices is very similar to other Chinese Indonesian asylum seekers I have interviewed. One family, for instance, did not place *Tian Gong,* or the God of Heaven, by the front door facing skyward, and at a height above an average adult. Instead, this mightiest god of their pantheon is placed on a low table, hidden inside the family courtyard, invisible to passersby. Without the specific anthropological knowledge of the proper placement of *Tian Gong*, one might assume that the presence of the Mightiest God altar on a table in an interior side yard was normal and would not have suspected its presence as an altered practice to avoid anti-Chinese attacks. Without those visible signs of religion from the outside, the asylum seekers were not targeted. To practice their religion freely was to invite attack, thereby risking their lives merely to "light a few joss-sticks" as one asylee puts it, referring her custom of placing a lighted incense at the tablet of each of the deities and ancestors in the morning. To understand persecution on account of religion, therefore, requires careful interviews to uncover the layers of information that requires anthropological knowledge of both the community and their religious practices under conditions of persecution on account of their "Chinese religion."

A CATHOLIC WOMAN'S RELIGIOUS INVISIBILITY AND PERSECUTION

When Dr. Nauman's Immigration Services asked me to help Ms. Beatrice Wilan on her asylum application, there were no instructions as to what argument to focus on based on the grounds outlined by the Refugee Convention. Neither was there any instruction from Ms. Wilan's attorney whose office was in Northern California. My job was simply to figure out why this forty-year-old, pale-complexioned, Chinese Indonesian woman with a deep sorrowful look applied for asylum. I made arrangements to meet her and proceeded with the interview.

Ms. Beatrice Wilan was married to Mr. Liem who owned a motorcycle repair shop in a small town outside Jakarta. The couple and their two teenage boys lived upstairs above the repair shop. After a tumultuous student demonstration in 1994, Mr. Liem moved his family to a "safe" community in Central Java, two hours' drive away from Jakarta. Ms. Wilan was born into a Catholic family and baptized as Beatrice. She played the organ in her community church, where she also volunteered. She quit her job as a hairdresser and devoted herself to raising her children. Focusing on home and church, she primarily socialized with her group of fellow churchgoers.

During one fateful day of the Indonesian riot in May 1998, Ms. Wilan was home with her children while her husband was at work at the repair shop. When Ms. Wilan could not reach her husband by phone, she thought he might have gone to the rural areas to deliver bicycle spare parts, something he did frequently. As the riots in Jakarta continued, Ms. Milan was alarmed when her husband had not contacted her for a second day. She took a train to the city where she had planned to stop at her friend Ah Ling's furniture shop. From there, she could catch a minibus to her husband's shop after her visit. While visiting her friend, about a dozen *pribumi* attackers stormed into the shop. They looted, smashed the contents, and set it on fire, while shouting "*Cina! Cina! Bunuh Cina! Ambil! Cepat ambil!*" (Chinese! Chinese! Kill the Chinese! Take! Quickly take!). Ms. Wilan, Ah Ling, and Ah Ling's husband hid in the kitchen at the back of the shop. Ms. Wilan thought she was going to die until a man pulled her and her friends out through the back door and brought them to a church where about a hundred other people were seeking refuge. Ms. Wilan was terrified. She had heard enough stories about anti-Chinese atrocities, but to experience it firsthand was terrifying. It was a close call.

In the night, she wondered who would care for her children if she had died in the mob attack, and why had her husband not called? Where could he be? But she dared not think of anything negative about him; she was only hoping for the best. The next morning, the church offered the shelter seekers bread, but Ms. Wilan was too distraught to eat. Later, a person from the church brought her to the train station where she took a train home instead of visiting her husband's shop, as she had originally planned. On the way home, a group of young men taunted her by recounting their exploitation of the Chinese. One of them said, "Oh, on that day, there was a fair skin Chinese girl, I opened her clothes and I touched her here and there." Ms. Wilan knew that was meant to frighten her.

Upon returning home, Ms. Wilan told neither her sons nor her friends at church what had happened, because "people at the church are used to things like that" and even if she had told them, they would only say "pray, pray, pray." She tried to call Ah Ling but could not reach her. A few days later, when she finally reached Ah Ling, she learned that everything in the furniture store and living quarter upstairs was taken. What the mob could not take—the walls, the floors and the ceilings—were destroyed. Ah Ling also said that the mob had tried to set fire to the shop, as evidenced by some half-burnt newspapers, "but it was saved by a fallen statuette of Mary, as it must have put out the flame," reasoned Ah Ling.

Four days later, Ms. Wilan's husband's brother and his wife came to tell her that Ah Liem's store had been burnt and they were taking her to have a look. When she arrived, she found that "everything at the spare parts store was broken and someone had set fire to the building." She did not go upstairs to the charred living quarters that had once been her home; she dared not imagine what had happened to her husband, maintaining hope that he was still alive and possibly out making a delivery to one of the villages.

Her brother-in-law owned a similar spare parts store in Jakarta. He told Mrs. Wilan that his store and his home were spared because he had bribed the police for protection. Her brother-in-law consoled her, saying he would call the police and look for her husband. He advised her to return to Central Java to take care of the children. Upon her return to Central Java, the priest at church told the congregation about the brutal death of his younger brother the week before and warned them to be watchful and avoid going out unless they had to. The priest's younger brother was giving a friend a ride but his car was stopped by a mob in Jakarta. The mob pulled the brother out, shot him, and beat up the friend, who survived the attack to tell what had befallen the priest's brother.

While the Chinese and the Catholic community were being besieged by violence, Ms. Wilan herself told the children that their father would come home someday. She remained hopeful because there was still no news from her brother-in-law. Secretly, she feared the worst, but she said she dared not imagine what could have happened to her husband. She couldn't cry; she said she couldn't go around with "red eyes" when "I've to be out with the priest or the women at church to visit the sick at the hospital or their home almost every day." But Ms. Wilan said her heart began to ache and at times she couldn't breathe. She had also developed a painful growth in her throat/neck that lasted for nine months until one day she went to a church well known for a "charismatic healer" where she "cried and cried and coughed and coughed" until "a deep cough dislodged the growth in [her] throat." Secretly, Ms. Wilan said she felt depressed, anxious, fearful, and inadequate because she had not learned to take care of herself or become more informed about the world to understand why things happened. Over the course of our interviews she shared fresh memories of the bouts of anti-Chinese violence when she was a child in Sumatra. She remembered the beaten Chinese men and women were taken to her kindergarten across from her home, which was later burnt down. She was so sick she did not attend school for three years.

Later that year after her close encounter with the mob at Ah Ling's shop, Ms. Wilan's fifteen year-old son was kidnapped and beaten by three *pribumi* boys. He was released after the victim of the accident that prompted the assault revealed it was a case of mistaken identity. Ms. Wilan said the trauma over her son nearly killed her.

In October 2000, during the Feast Day of Maria, her church received a threatening message that it would be the next bombing target. The priest advised the congregation to minimize their stay at the church. During the Feast Day of Maria, it was customary for the ten Catholic families in her area to take turns praying in one family's home each night. That year, for fear of being a target of the agitated Muslims, the priest also advised the families to forgo the practice of communal prayer. Ms. Wilan said she was acutely aware that during violent anti-Chinese and anti-Christian times, her Chinese ethnic background and her Catholic religion made her an easy target. Ms. Wilan described her encounters with the radical Muslims who hate the *kifirs*—the infidels. "Whenever a radical Muslim sees a Christian, he would move away as far as possible because we Christians are the infidels. We are '*haram*'—dirty." To survive, she said she avoided advertising the fact that she was a Catholic. She had stopped carrying a bible when she went visiting other families or the Catholics at the hospital. She also stopped wearing a necklace with a cross, which her mother had given her. During Christmas, she would also hide the Christmas tree and other decorations from the views of passers-by to avoid incurring the wrath of the "fanatical" Muslims. Between waiting for news of her missing husband, the kidnapping of her son, the attack and arson while she was at her friend's shop, the death of the priest's brother, and the news of the atrocities against the Chinese and Christians circulating among her friends and relatives, Ms. Wilan was severely traumatized. Later in the year, when a friend told her about the possibility of going to America, she used the money her brother-in-law had given her from the sale of her husband's shop lot to apply for a visa. She "fled Indonesia" after her parents came to look after her children. A month after she arrived in California, she heard about the wave of church bombings throughout Indonesia in December 2000 where many were killed.

Religion is a matter of faith, and is not visible from one's appearance. Yet, as mentioned earlier, there were practices associated with being a Catholic that Ms. Wilan had already avoided to minimize her exposure to danger. Because of her preemptive actions to limit danger as a Catholic, she was never personally "targeted" or persecuted on account of her religion, even though the Catholic churches, with their distinctive architectural structures, are visible, and have been targets of vandalism and church bombings. The targeting of Chinese Indonesians was overwhelming in Ms. Wilan's case and the immigration court hearing on her case was focused on her "Chinese race" identity, rather than her background as a Catholic woman, which did not come up.

In January 2005, Judge Rener used my arguments to grant Ms. Wilan "Withholding from Removal." With the ruling, she could not immediately relocate her family to the United States, but she could work legally, get a social security card, and apply for a driver's license without fear of being "removed" or deported back to Indonesia.

A PIOUS PASTOR'S FORGIVENESS AND HIS WIFE'S ASYLUM APPLICATION

Mr. Yohanan was a pastor at a church serving a small Indonesian community in the American Midwest. There he met his wife, Ms. Cora Sonata, whose parents had sent her to Chicago in 2002 to escape the Indonesian riots, during which Cora and her family had survived a mob attack and her father had lost his business. During the difficult days after the May 1998 riot, Cora's family survived by living in a garage in a Javanese area, while keeping a low profile. Cora said her father bribed the Javanese to keep the family alive. In my interview with Cora, I also learned that she had been sexually assaulted by a group of *pribumi* men. After arriving in the United States, Cora applied for asylum protection when she learned of the opportunity. Her husband's application was "attached" to her application. I interviewed him after I had completed my interview with Cora Sonata.

Mr. Yohanan was a third generation Chinese, born in Jakarta. His grandfather was an elder in the Protestant Church of Indonesia. Mr. Yohanan attended a "new denomination church" which he explained as being different from the long-established Catholic churches in Indonesia. The new denomination churches were viewed as too Western and therefore seen as a "threat" in a mostly Muslim nation. Therefore, many of these newer churches did not have church buildings of their own, but held their services in hotel banquet rooms or in office conference rooms to avoid the church burning and attacks suffered by many older, well-established, and physically identifiable Catholic churches. Despite the precaution, Mr. Yohanan told me of an incident that took place in 1994 where a mob of fifteen to twenty men blocked the bank building where his church was holding its Sunday service in downtown Jakarta. After much negotiation by church officials, the mob demanded a "toll" in exchange for removing the blockade. From that point, churchgoers were charged a "toll" to attend services at the bank, which they paid every Sunday, and suffered in silence. The churchgoers' acquiescence to the mob's demands protected members from physical harm for several years, but in the 1998 riot, the bank where services were held was vandalized, alongside other businesses in the area.

Mr. Yohanan attended university in the United States in 1994. Upon his graduation, he devoted his time to the Indonesian Full Gospel Fellowship, which intensified his faith. He eventually joined a summer mission to Asia, with a week in Indonesia in June of 1998, a month after the May 1998 riots. During the trip to Indonesia, Mr. Yohanan noticed rubble from the burnt out Chinese shops and the "curse" words that had been scrawled on the walls, targeting the Chinese minorities. Friends warned him to remain "humble, not to provoke, and do what they ask."

Mr. Yohanan said he was safe in the summer mission to Asia because they held services in "neutral" places that were marked as areas "open-for-evangelism" by his church. There was an American in the team, which meant that the *pribumi* would have to think twice before attacking the Chinese because the American's presence made the group a little safer. The mission also worked closely with another church, the World Harvest, which provided relief work. Upon his return to the United States, he was asked to establish branches of the Indonesian church in a number of different states, over the next several years.

During the few days in Jakarta in June 1998, Mr. Yohanan visited his mother who had lost both her home and car to arson prior to his arrival. His mother had sent him a letter documenting her suffering as a part of his asylum application. Mr. Yohanan's parents fled to Singapore after the riot. In my interview with Mr. Yohanan about how he felt about the attackers, he refused to tell me. To my surprise, unlike many other Chinese Indonesian asylum seekers I had interviewed who were eager to tell their stories, Mr. Yohanan was unwilling to express any feelings of fear, anger, or empathetic accounts of the trauma his mother or wife had suffered. In his voice, there was no animosity, no hatred, no digging into his memories for more stories of persecution that could bolster his asylum application, even though the major international media were carrying news of the church burnings, church bombings, and anti-Christian vandalism in many parts of Indonesia. In the end, out of frustration, I told Mr. Yohanan that if I needed a good Christian pastor I would go to him for help, but if he wanted to apply for asylum, he must let me know how he felt about what had happened to him, his church, his wife, and his mother, as a part of the narrative I was preparing for his asylum application. He kept quiet despite repeated questioning. Unable to elicit details on his feelings, I submitted a report to their attorney, Mr. Mattern. In my report, I drew primarily from Ms.

Cora Sonata's accounts of sexual assault, and details of her family's escape from an angry mob. I described Mr. Yohanan's observation of Jakarta in June 1998 and his mother's personal experience during the riot a month before his visit without giving Mr. Yohanan's personal opinion to those experiences. Mr. Mattern incorporated my narratives into a petition to the government. Just weeks before they went into their Merit Hearing, Ms. Cora Sonata told me they were both returning to Indonesia. Mr. Yohanan had forgiven his wife's sexual attackers and his mother's arsonist. He said there was much work to do as an evangelical Christian pastor in the untapped Indonesian missionary field. Mr. Yohanan gave up his asylum application to do God's work. Mr. Mattern called me to inform me his clients had withdrawn their petition, even though he thought they had a good chance of gaining asylum.

As an anthropologist, I wanted to explore Coras' feelings about her husband's wish to return to Indonesia. However, from the standpoint of an expert witness whose service was requested by her attorney, when the asylum seekers withdrew their petition, my duties ended and there was no professional reason for me to gather that information. Therefore, my personal curiosity was kept at bay. Nonetheless, I could not help myself in regarding Cora Sonata's situation as an "attrition," a term Koss (2006, 209) uses to refer to the lack of access and the multiple layers of impediments in the justice system in cases involving sexually abused women whose stories never come to light (Koss 2006). I also thought of Mr. Yohanan's unwillingness to mention those who had hurt his mother, his wife, and the Chinese Indonesian, due to his deep religious piety and devotion to the practice of forgiveness. The Refugee Convention is designed to protect victims of persecution such as Ms. Cora Sonata, Ms. Yohanan's mother, and the Chinese-Christian victims of the Indonesian riot. Working from the standpoint of a human rights violation, I wondered—at what point does religious piety end and human rights begin?

The explication of these three asylum seekers whose persecution was related to matters of religion shows that religion intersects with asylum applications, not only in terms of theology, but with the lived experiences in their local culture and society. Asylum seekers who have been persecuted on account of their beliefs may not know their right to such claims. Attorneys helping asylum seekers may also hesitate to use religion as the basis for advocating asylum, unless there is strong and clear evidence of persecution on account of religion. In the cases of Ms. Wilan and Mr. Budi, they both hid their religious practices. By hiding their religious affiliation and practices, radicals who hate their religion are not given the opportunity to attack. When asylum seekers preemptively prevent being attacked, they eliminate any evidence for persecution on account of religion. Without clear evidence of attack, does it mean they are not persecuted? The stories of these asylum seekers highlight the role of religion in asylum cases: as evidence of persecution, the theology of Buddhism, Catholicism and Christianity by themselves are not as important as the asylum seekers' practices of hiding their religion. Deciphering the rather typical syncretic religious practices of the Chinese Indonesians requires knowing the specific rituals and symbols, and the offerings to a class of supernatural beings involving gods, ghosts, and ancestors. This knowledge is important in so far as it is used for verifying the "religious" identity of the asylum seeker, and not so much the authenticity of the religion or the person's religiosity. That is, the research in proving religious persecution against the asylum seekers rests on the sociocultural reconstruction of their beliefs, their practices, and their fears, rather than on the asylum seeker's theological and religious knowledge.

In Indonesia, for both Christians and practitioners of Chinese religion, even though their right of religious freedom is technically protected by law, they must withhold their expressions of religiosity from public view to prevent being targeted by the radical elements in society. In these three Chinese Indonesian cases, religion was not mentioned as a ground for persecution; it was their "Chinese race" that was highlighted as the basis of persecution. To Ms. Wilan, it was the anti-Chinese violence that led to the death of the priest's brother, the church bombing, and the presumed death of her husband. To Mr. Budi, it was the suspicion regarding his four aliases, rather than his attempt to hide his Chinese religious practices that was at question. And in the case of Mr. Yohanna, it was his desire to evangelize in Indonesia that competed with his wife's torment from sexual violence that drove her to seek asylum. As can be seen from the stories of a devout Catholic woman, a Buddhist monk, and an Evangelical pastor, their motivations for asylum petition are complex, and the role of religion plays out in different ways. Asylum adjudication, done fairly, must unearth the deeper layers of the lived experiences of the asylum seeker's religion. Without this knowledge about the asylum petitioner's practice of religion, the adjudicators depend on their racialized identity in Indonesia.

Chapter 6

Did Jesus Walk Through a Field of Wheat or a Field of Grass?

Coauthored with Joann Yeh

Given that religion's influence is so thoroughly embedded in the behavior and decisions of its followers, how do asylum adjudicators respond to the hidden religious ideas in the lives of asylum seekers? In this chapter, Attorney Joann Yeh and I present three case studies to highlight the difficulties of proving persecution based on religion through encounters with three asylum seekers from China.

Joann Yeh "inherited" the cases from another attorney who was unavailable for the hearing, and therefore did not have the chance to prepare the petitioners from the beginning. Joann Yeh and I documented and recounted the unfolding of the courtroom drama during the Merit Hearing when Government Counsels grappled with religious persecution in China. The first case was on the persecution against Mr. Wu for his practice of Christianity as a member of a Chinese Christian house church. The second was the persecution against Ms. Yang's practice of *I-Kuan Tao*, a modern syncretic religious practice originating in Taiwan. The third case was on Ms. Liu and was about another Chinese Christian house church. This third case was overturned by the Ninth Circuit Court of Appeals and returned to the Immigration Court. The Government Attorney and the Immigration Judge then tried to circumvent the Ninth Circuit Court's decision solely due to the fact that it was a "Chinese Christian" case.

CASE #1: MR. WU'S UNDERGROUND HOUSE CHURCH

Mr. Wu was a Chinese national seeking asylum on religious grounds. He was an active Christian, having been imprisoned and beaten by the Chinese police for participating in house church activities, which are officially banned by the Chinese government. In court, Mr. Wu was not an ideal witness, as he mumbled often and had clearly not spent adequate time preparing for the case, something that asylees are strongly encouraged to do by their attorneys prior to coming to court. Nevertheless, the questions posed by the Government Attorney (GA), who acts much like a prosecutor in immigration court, were aggressive and badgering. Joann recounted the Merit Hearing wherein the GA questioned Mr. Wu's credibility as a Christian.

THE NUMBERS OF BIBLES IN THE HOUSE AND THE DAY OF CHRISTMAS

When asked to recount the details of the police raid in the house church that resulted in Mr. Wu's arrest, the GA demanded to know how many bibles were visible when the police entered the residence. When Mr. Wu said he thought there were maybe "a couple," the GA demanded an exact number. Finally, he said, "Maybe five or so." The GA then gleefully directed the Immigration Judge's attention to the written statement Mr. Wu had submitted with his original asylum application, in which he said there were "eight bibles."

The GA then proceeded to ask Mr. Wu if he knew the date that Christmas is celebrated. He said yes, of course, it's December 25. Again, the GA smugly told the judge that in Mr. Wu's statement, he had said he was baptized on November 24, 2006, which he also said was "Christmas Day." When Joann Yeh looked at the original statement that Mr. Wu had handwritten in Chinese and the accompanying English translation to verify the GA's conclusion, Joann Yeh saw that the original statement did not have anything written after "November 24, 2006," which had been listed as Mr. Wu's date of baptism. In the English translation, however, the translator had added an additional sentence: "This is Christmas Day." Joann Yeh immediately objected on grounds that the translation that the GA was basing her argument on was incorrect. The Judge overruled Joann Yeh and told her she was interrupting testimony and that she could have her turn "later."

Joann Yeh noted that the Judge was going against all established practice in a legitimate court of law by not allowing objections by counsel during cross-examination. In all courts of law, attorneys are allowed to object to prevent a miscarriage of justice and to preserve a record that there was something the attorney found objectionable in a court proceeding. In fact, the Federal Rules of Civil Procedure not only specifically allow for objections, they explicitly state that objections have to be made in a timely manner or the objection is lost (Fed. Rules of Civ. Proc. 51c). In other words, if an objection is not made at the time of the objectionable question, it is assumed that the opposing attorney has no problem with anything that was put on the record. However, as immigration courts are not constitutionally authorized courts of law, but rather an administrative review board; they are not bound by the Federal Rules of Civil Procedure or any other rules or standards of laws or ethics.

Another serious problem highlighted in Mr. Wu's case is the role of the court interpreter. Interpreters are hired by the immigration court through a third party contractor, and complaints made about incompetent or ineffective interpreters are largely ignored. In Mr. Wu's case, the interpreter repeatedly mistranslated questions that the GA and the Immigration Judge asked, causing Mr. Wu confusion. Furthermore, this led the GA and Immigration Judge to accuse him of being "nonresponsive" and "vague." Since the most important aspect of the hearing is establishing the asylee's credibility, any impression that the asylee is not being forthcoming with answers or is stalling gives the immigration judge an opening to find that he/she is not credible. Since Joann Yeh is fluent in Mandarin Chinese and could tell that questions and answers were being incorrectly translated, she again objected repeatedly. Again, the Immigration Judge was angered that an attempt to object was even made. When Joann Yeh was allowed to speak, she reiterated that the written statement had been mistranslated and the courtroom interpreters had mistranslated several of the questions and the respondent's answers. None of her objections were mentioned at all in the Immigration Judge's final decision.

WAS MR. WU A TRUCK DRIVER OR AN ARTIST?

Before the GA was ready to rest her cross-examination, she started asking Mr. Wu what he did for a living back in China. It had already been established in previous testimony that he was a commercial driver. The GA was clearly intent, however, on forcing him to confirm it on the record no less than three times. When she got her third confirmation, she then asked repeatedly if he had ever been an artist. Joann Yeh objected to the question's relevance and was admonished again for "interrupting." Finally, the GA proceeded to show that she had proof that Mr. Wu had entered the United States on a B2 visitor visa meant for business travel. His visa application had apparently stated that he was an artist and needed a visa to come to the United States to attend a conference. The GA was clearly using this and the line of questioning to prove that he was a liar and therefore not credible. Even though Joann Yeh again objected, the Immigration Judge overruled her, allowing the interrogation to continue.

"Were you lying then or are you lying now?" This is an oft-used question popular in legal television dramas and movies but was clearly irrelevant and inappropriate here. Under established law, the government is not allowed to use the fact that an asylee entered the United States illegally, used falsified documents, or lied to gain a valid visa for entry into the United States. The reasoning is that if a person is fleeing persecution, he will use any means necessary to get somewhere safe, which would then seem to substantiate a case of persecution rather than undermine it. Again, when Joann Yeh made her objection, the Immigration Judge was hostile and appeared offended.

After both sides had rested, the Immigration Judge left to make her decision.

For cases filed in federal district court or even state court, the judge will adjourn the proceedings and draft a written opinion over several weeks unless the proceedings are expedited. This allows the judge to consolidate all the testimony and facts, apply precedent (previously decided binding case law), and render a decision. In immigration court, however, the immigration judge leaves for an hour or two in most cases, then orally reads his/her decision into the record. In Mr. Wu's case, what the Immigration Judge used as grounds for her findings was shocking.

First, she said that the fact that Mr. Wu could not remember if there were five or eight bibles laying in the open when the police raided the Christian house church he was attending was a sign that he was not being truthful.

Second, she found it hard to believe that a true Christian would think that November 24 was Christmas Day—even though it had been made very clear on the record that he had never said nor believed it and whoever had done the translation had incomprehensibly added that statement. Furthermore, she had not even bothered to ask the interpreter to verify whether Mr. Wu's written statement in Chinese matched with the English translation.

Third, she said that during the cross-examination by the GA, Mr. Wu was asked what the sermon was when the police raided the house church. He had responded that it was about Jesus and his disciples walking through a field. When the Immigration Judge pushed him to clarify what kind of field it was, he had said he thought it was a field of grass. In her opinion, the Immigration Judge said that "a real Christian would know that this particular scripture is referring to a field of wheat and not a field of grass." So, not only did the Immigration Judge act as an arbiter of facts and law, she somehow was now also allowed to use her own personal "expertise" as a practicing Christian to influence her decision. This is a tremendous overstep of the authority of the immigration judge, which, given the amorphous legal stature that it occupies, is difficult to ascertain. In no legitimate court of law is anyone's opinion allowed to be presented, much less used in deciding the outcome of the case, unless that person has been qualified and verified as an expert in the field and sworn in as an expert witness.

The only apparent consequence for an immigration judge who substitutes her own experience with the Christian religion in the place of law and facts is that the decision can be overturned on appeal. Even if an immigration judge's decision is repeatedly overturned on appeal, he or she has no incentive to change his or her behavior because neither his or her compensation nor reputation is substantially affected, unlike a federal district court judge, whose record of being overturned is publicly available and will be used by counsel in court to question a judge's competence.

In addition, this particular Immigration Judge has a reputation for being biased against cases where the asylum applicant is Chinese and particularly if the asylee is claiming persecution on grounds of being a Christian. As one attorney who frequently practices in the Los Angeles Immigration Court said to Joann Yeh on her first appearance before this Judge, "Judge [] hates Chinese Christian cases. She thinks they are all fake."

CASE #2: IS MS. YANG'S *I-KUAN TAO* A CULT OR A RELIGION?

In Ms. Yang's case, she was a practitioner of *I-Kuan Tao*, a religion started in China and popularized in Taiwan in the 1970s, incorporating aspects of Buddhism, Daoism, Confucianism, Christianity, and Islam. She had been arrested and jailed for a week for participating in *I-Kuan Tao* activities in China, where it is banned as a cult. In the United States, she had settled in Southern California and was attending services at a Kuang Ming Saint Dao Temple in in the city of El Monte. She had applied for asylum within the required one year of her arrival, but the case had been dragging on for more than three years.

Upon arrival to the courtroom on the morning of Ms. Yang's Merit Hearing, Lily Hsu, the GA handling the case, approached Joann Yeh and said that she had to recuse herself from the case. She appeared reluctant to explain why. So, they waited until the case was called by the Immigration Judge. After questioning by the Immigration Judge, GA Lily Hsu stated that she was recusing herself because she is a member of a Kuang Ming Saint Tao Temple, and was, in fact, quite active. In addition, she knew of and recognized a woman Ms. Yang had brought with her to testify about Ms. Yang's involvement and commitment to the Temple. The Immigration Judge agreed it was a situation warranting the GA's recusal even if it meant postponing the hearing for at least six months due to no other GA being available that day. Joann Yeh questioned why Ms. Hsu's religious practice would create a conflict of interest, but was largely ignored. This seemed incongruous—where was the potential conflict? If the GA had been a part-time pastor in a Chinese Christian Church, would she have to recuse herself from all cases where the asylee feared persecution based on being Christian? How does the attorney's personal religion have any bearing on whether the asylee is credible or whether she is able to prove her case?

Upon further research and discussion with other attorneys who regularly appeared in immigration court, and based on her own past experiences with these types of cases involving lesser known religions that sometimes get categorized as cults, Joann Yeh came to a disturbing conclusion as to why the GA so badly wanted to recuse herself. In these cases, the government presents its case by trying to delegitimize the religion in question and carefully (to avoid any First Amendment freedom of religion issues) attempt to imply that it is a cult or that there is a high likelihood that the respondent found a "convenient" religion that no one can verify the status of. In those cases, sometimes the only information the respondent can give the Immigration Judge to educate him on the religion is a printout of a Wikipedia page, which the GA will discreetly use to his advantage. This is the standard method of attack in these cases of non-mainstream religions. In Ms. Yang's case, this strategy became unavailable because the GA could not or would not be able to paint *I-Kuan* Tao as a fringe cult that doesn't really have an accepted mode of worship, such as attending Mass for Catholics or observing the Sabbath for Jews. This would be especially difficult if she were recognized by Ms. Yang's character witness, who would undoubtedly indicate Ms. Hsu was an active member of the temple were she called to testify.

So, rather than attempt to litigate the case based on Ms. Yang's credibility and testimony, the government chose to preserve their tactics of delegitimizing a non-mainstream religion. To the Immigration Judge's credit, she ruled that if at the next scheduled hearing, Ms. Hsu was again the only attorney available and she again felt that she had to recuse herself, the Judge would allow the case to proceed without a GA at all.

CASE #3: THE INFILTRATION OF UNINTENTIONAL BIAS

Ms. Liu was an asylum seeker from China, fearing persecution because she was a practicing Christian. She had already been denied asylum by an immigration judge, but that decision had been reversed when it was appealed to the Ninth Circuit Court of Appeals. Specifically, the original Immigration Judge had found her not to be credible solely on the basis that she had cried during her testimony when she was talking about her son but not when she was talking about her religion. The Ninth Circuit found that this was an unacceptable basis for a credibility finding and reversed the decision, essentially granting Ms. Liu asylum. It did, however, allow another immigration judge to make "additional findings of fact," meaning a new denial of asylum could only be based on new facts that had not been previously presented to the court.

What should have been a relatively routine procedure quickly turned absurd when the Government Attorney attempted a series of tactics to circumvent the Ninth Circuit reversal. First, before the case was even called by the Judge, the GA made a motion to reinstate the previous decision. This was in blatant defiance of the Ninth Circuit ruling, but the GA wanted a quick win and was clearly hoping the Immigration Judge would see it as a tidy resolution and simply go along with it. Upon immediate objection by Joann Yeh, the Judge said it would be dealt with when the case was called, which he would move up on the docket. When the case was called, the GA again tried to have the Judge simply reinstate the previous denial of asylum. Again, Joann Yeh objected that doing so was clearly in violation of the Ninth Circuit's ruling, to which the GA simply replied, "Well, the applicant can just appeal again if she wants." The presiding judge, Judge O'Connor, is one of the more reasonable and fair ones on the Los Angeles Immigration Court, and immediately indicated that he would not do that and had to respect the Ninth Circuit Court of Appeals' decision. He did, however, say that they could discuss what further findings could be made. He asked Joann Yeh what evidence and what witnesses she would be presenting. After she answered that she would be calling several members of Ms. Liu's church, Judge O'Connor made an odd comment: "So, we're going to get the usual parade and song and dance of how great a Christian she is, right?" When Joann Yeh expressed a little shock that he would trivialize sworn testimony in this way, he responded, "Yeah, but we know what they're going to say, right?" It is important to note that Judge O'Connor's tone was not mean or mocking and he appeared to simply want to streamline the proceedings. Nevertheless, his comments clearly indicated a disturbing jadedness about cases on the basis of religion—the assumption that part of the routine strategy is that the asylum seeker will "parade" a line of character witnesses, whose testimony the court already thinks it knows. The problem is that the evidence is not given the value it deserves and is not objectively judged each time it is presented.

The GA continued to attempt to find a way to reinstate the denial of Ms. Liu's asylum, knowing full well she had no new facts or evidence to unearth that would prove Ms. Liu's case was either fraudulent or that she was not credible. After stalling for half an hour while she fruitlessly flipped through Ms. Liu's file, hoping for some magical fraudulent fact to appear, Joann Yeh objected that the GA was abusing her authority and purposely delaying resolution of the case. The GA responded that she "did not appreciate opposing counsel's attitude" and then said to the Judge, "Well, I disagree with the Ninth Circuit's decision." The fact that she believed her mere dislike of the higher court's binding decision should influence the Judge's actions and decisions was disturbing, and demonstrates the problematic aspect that immigration courts are not real court of law. Judge O'Connor responded that while he did not like the Ninth Circuit's decision either, at least it had not been his decision that was overturned and the GA was not the original GA on the case so it "was no skin off our backs." Again, while Judge O'Connor was merely trying to convince the GA to give up her attempt to reinstate the previous decision, his comments indicated a concerning view of how immigration courts proceed. If it had been his decision originally that had been overturned, would he have made more of an effort to deny Ms. Liu's asylum case a second time?

After once again noting the GA's dislike of the Ninth Circuit's decision and ruling, Judge O'Connor finally addressed the GA by name, and indicated that she needed to give up: "Sometimes you have to know when to quit." Despite showing some reluctance to grant the asylum, Judge O'Connor finally did, but not without one more question: "So, Ms. Yeh, *since we know what your witnesses are going to say*, and Counsel, since you have nothing new to present, I think we can just go ahead and grant the case. Okay with everyone?" (emphasis added).

While it was a relief that the Immigration Judge did not delay or complicate the proceedings as a form of retaliation for an overturned decision, which he could have easily done, especially with the Government Attorney egging him on at every opportunity, Ms. Liu's case highlights both the potentially disastrous situation of an unchecked government attorney trying to get a quick fix for a case they thought they had already won and the inherent bias that immigration judges—even the good ones—have about certain cases. These are not merely "legal" battles that have to be dealt with, but problems unique to the asylum system and the US government's peculiar set of rules for the immigration courts, an issue we discussed in chapter 14, "Article I Court in a World of Uncertainties."

Our documentation of these three cases provides a rare opportunity to look at asylum Merit Hearings on persecution on account of religion. A startling realization for us is: "Who is qualified to interpret matters of religion?"

The inescapable conclusion to which these three case studies leads is that even with the strongest cases involving religion, the decision rests on officers and judges who are often not able, and many times not willing, to examine the case neutrally on the facts, testimony and relevant laws. Instead, these adjudicators appear to rely on gut feelings, personal notions, and beliefs about what constitutes a religion, and more incredibly, what being a committed practitioner of any such religion looks like. To pretend that the results of these proceedings were the outcome of any "judicial" process and should therefore be given that respect is wholly absurd.

In a written report or the UNHCR and the Church World Services, T. Jeremy Gunn (2002), regarding the claims of persecution on the basis of religion, argued that they are likely to be among "the most complex, arcane, and incomprehensible but will need to be decided by an adjudicator." Furthermore, he stated, "however impossible it might be to provide an accurate and complete definition of 'religion,' or however incompetent judges and lawyers may be to offer such definition, the legal system nevertheless requires them to do exactly that . . . judges are required to interpret 'religion' whether or not they are competent to do so" (6).

To deconstruct these bizarre court battles, one could blame Article I court which lacks funding for legal clerks to provide government attorneys and immigration judges with relevant research or the hiring of expert witnesses. Yet, until the law changes, this is what an asylee has to navigate. To minimize the questioning by the government attorneys and the immigration judge, Attorney Joann Yeh's experience has been to ensure that inconsistencies are accounted for before the court hearing.

If an anthropologist or a historian trained in religion were allowed to collaborate on these three cases, they could discuss the variations of the same religion as a result of borrowing and syncretism. All religions are interpreted and expressed locally, thereby accounting for local variations. This can tactically prevent the kinds of canonical arguments in court for the Wu and Yang cases. However, as noted above, these cases were from the case files of Attorney Joann Yeh without the benefit of social science input. Our documentation is to present a rare account of the actual proceeding of religion cases from the Federal Court in Los Angeles.

We conclude by suggesting asylum attorneys take into account the potential contribution of collaboration between lawyers and scholars of religious practices who could clarify on matters of culture, religion, and community.

Chapter 7

An Apostate from Indonesia:

A Convert from Islam to Catholicism

When Attorney Goodsell asked me to work on a case involving a young non-Chinese Indonesian asylum applicant, I was very excited. All of my cases up to that point had been with minority Chinese Indonesians suffering persecution in the hands of attackers variously described as Indonesians, natives, Muslims, *pribumi* or the indigenous people. The chance to work with a native *pribumi* was a welcomed change and an opportunity to gain another point of view. When Mr. Goodsell added that the asylum seeker was a convert from Islam, I knew the challenge would be profound.

When I mentioned the case to colleagues who knew about law or Islam, the obvious comment was that if Mr. Situ Tanjung was a Muslim from Indonesia, his conversion would make him an apostate. An apostate from Islam means death. At the time in 2006, circulating in the global media was a story about the fate of a man named Abdul Rahman, a Muslim from Afghanistan who converted to Christianity while working in neighboring Pakistan. The Afghanistan Karzai government sentenced him to death for apostasy. The Vatican intervened, and the Italian government granted him asylum to save his life. This idea of death of a Muslim convert weighed heavily on me. Who could I ask? I thought about several colleagues at my university who are either Muslim or have worked on religion. I did not specifically ask them for help; I had only mentioned the case and the issues I had encountered. I had learned a long time ago that although a person may be of a particular ethnicity or religion, this does not guarantee that he or she will know about the ethnic culture, the religion, language, or politics, associated with that particular ethnic group or religion. To do so is to assume a perfect alignment between ethnicity, language, culture, religion, nationality, and citizenship. Therefore, I simply waited for their response. A colleague who teaches a course on the History of the Middle East summed up the complexity of issues related to religion by telling me that he declares to his students that "if any of you think of me through any of the characteristics associated with a Muslim, I will show you are all wrong!"

When I made the appointment with Situ Tanjung, I proceeded with uncertainty on the case. Situ Tanjung was a college-aged young man. By his appearance, demeanor, and nonaccented English, he could be any other "cool dude" from Southern California. Situated at the crossroads of the world where all ethnicities, faiths, cultures, colors, and creeds percolate through the City of Los Angeles, any hope of determining the ethnic or religious origin by superficial markers was a task I would never attempt. Situ Tanjung told me he was born in Indonesia, but came to United States at a young age with his parents who had a business in Los Angeles. His parents, both Muslim, are prominent opposition figures in Indonesian politics from the island of Sumatra and have returned to Indonesia upon their retirement. Situ Tanjung did not want to return with them. He said he did not follow his parents' religion because he had converted to Catholicism. Except for brief trips to Indonesia, the United States was home to him.

Situ Tanjung's petition for asylum was a particularly difficult one. Unlike other asylum seekers from abroad who were escaping persecution of one kind or other, Situ Tanjung grew up in the United States and had not suffered any past persecution. Growing up as a Muslim in the United States, he also did not mention encountering any problems as a Muslim minority, a group particularly stereotyped after September 11, 2001. Therefore, I was not able to write him up as having been persecuted in the United States due to his religion by using terms such as racism and hate crimes. Even though I was aware that according to asylum laws, the fear of the possibility of future persecution is itself a sufficient ground for an asylum petition, if Situ Tanjung had changed out of his faith, no one, not even his parents, knew of his conversion. His conversion from Islam to Catholicism had yet to be borne out for a convincing case of apostasy. Furthermore, unlike "race," which is identifiable physically, and is immutable, religion is a matter of belief and faith, often adopted by choice, unless one is born into it. Therefore, it would be difficult to ascertain his identity by appearance and by cultural or religious markers alone. If Situ Tanjung was a former Muslim, would the judge overseeing his case quiz him on his Islamic knowledge, and what aspects of Islam would the judge ask? Would the judge even know about Islam? If Situ Tanjung is a convert to Catholicism, how does one prove his religious identity, and who qualifies to assess his canonical authenticity? In addition, how does one predict the possibility of future persecution based on his religious conversion? My concern in handling a delicate issue of apostasy was: would I be willing to state that death is imminent for an apostate stepping off the plane in Jakarta?

As I reflected on these questions, I needed to learn more about Situ Tanjong's religious identity. Without his parents' testimony, I would have to depend exclusively on Situ Tanjung's words regarding his former faith. It was not sufficient to merely ask someone his religion when law stresses evidentiary proofs, as we have seen with the judge quizzing the Jewish asylum petitioner in the documentary *Well-Founded Fear*. Therefore, in helping Attorney Goodsell prepare the case, I had to determine Situ Tanjung's identity with certainty. My approach was to learn about Situ Tanjung's California upbringing and his Muslim background leading to his conversion to Catholicism. That is, if he was a Muslim by birth, how does one know a Muslim (or a Christian, or a Chinese) is a Muslim (is a Christian, is a Chinese)? And how Muslim must a Muslim be? Core beliefs of a religion can vary from place to place. Dru Gladney (1998), an anthropological expert on Islam in China, discovered that the variety of Islamic practices vary tremendously even among the Hui Chinese Muslims. Take eating pork as an example. To the Chinese Muslims in Xinjiang Province in China's Northwest, eating pork is a taboo. But, to the Chinese Muslims in Fujian Province in China's Southeast Coast, pork is a part of their diet, yet, they claim a Muslim identity (Gladney 1998). In fact, even among those who follow strict dietary practices, there are still variations within their practices. The more observant will only consume *halal* meat, meat that has been blessed by the *imam* and eat food prepared by utensils untouched by pork.

Having grown up in a country with a Muslim majority in Malaysia, and having hosted Muslim houseguests in my home in Los Angeles over the years, including a Hui Muslim from the Xinjiang Muslim Autonomous Region in China, I am mindful of the diversity of practices in a Muslim person's daily rituals. That is, a practice may be a taboo to an observant, conservative Muslim, but is permissible to another with more relaxed orthodoxy. Therefore, my focus on learning about Situ Tanjung's religious identity would have to be based on the more mundane everyday practices such as eating, living, and falling in love while growing up in California rather than by judging his behavior against the precepts of Islam.

SITU TANJUNG'S MUSLIM BACKGROUND AND HIS CALIFORNIA UPBRINGING

In Los Angeles, Situ Tanjung grew up living with his parents and two sisters. He attended high school in California and completed a bachelor's degree at a local university. His two sisters have both married out of their faith. Situ Tanjung said his parents observed the five pillars of Islam—The Profession of Faith, Daily Prayers, Almsgiving, Fasting during Ramadan, and Pilgrimage to Mecca—but they were not strict about raising their children as Muslim. His major religious influence came from watching his parents pray five times a day and fast during Ramadan. When he was young, his parents told him to pray but he said they never taught him how to pray properly. During Ramadan, the family fasted during the day but ate before sunrise and after sunset for a whole month like other Muslims. He said his parents did not ask him to fast because they wanted him to focus on school and sports, especially since Situ Tanjung was working as a coach for a school sports team. When his parents celebrated *idul fitri*, to break the fast, Situ Tanjung said he knew it only as Indonesian New Year and a cultural holiday, and had never learned the meaning behind the fasting. Situ Tanjung said he did not know of any other holidays celebrated by Muslims or Indonesians.

While growing up in Los Angeles, Situ Tanjung was also never sent to an Islamic school to learn Arabic. He said his parents had never read the Koran to the children. In fact, Situ Tanjung said, "I have never read the Koran myself." When Situ Tanjung was a child attending California public schools, he said he ate school cafeteria food. "My parents never told me what to avoid. As a child I didn't know one kind of meat from another. I just saw food as food. I did not question what I was eating. At home as a Muslim family, we did not have pork, but we were not particular about observing halal dietary rules. My family ate at Coco's, Denny's, IHOP, and ordered everything except menu items with pork."

Due to Situ Tanjung's participation in various sports, his friends were of the multiple ethnicities of Southern California, with a predominance of Asian Americans—Filipinos, Vietnamese, and Chinese—along with Mexicans and Anglos. Even though Situ Tanjung knew about an Indonesian student group at his university, he said he did not know anyone from the group, and there was nothing that he had in common with them. Situ Tanjung volunteered the information that he drank beer, wine and other alcoholic drinks with his college friends. "But I am not an alcoholic," he added. I think he had provided me with that bit of information because he knew alcohol is forbidden in Islam and he wanted to clarify his practice as a Muslim. Through his many friends, especially a former Catholic Vietnamese girlfriend, Situ Tanjung attended youth activities such as Midnight Mass, Easter Sunday services, and other observances at Our Lady of Loretto in Los Angeles and at other churches in the San Gabriel Valley. Over the years, Situ Tanjung said, "When it came to a matter of spiritual issues, I tend to draw on the Church for inspiration."

CONVERSION TO CATHOLICISM

With his Filipino friend as a sponsor, Situ Tanjung was baptized at a multi-ethnic church in the city of Alhambra, California. Situ Tanjung said he chose the name "Michael" to indicate the shift in his identity of becoming a Catholic. In the Hebrew tradition, Michael is one of the seven archangels and the only one identified as an archangel in the Bible. The name, "Michael," means "a gift from God, who is like God." Michael Situ Tanjung said he is not a rebel fighting against his family or his religion. Instead, he explained, "I converted for myself. It was a religion I could relate to. . . . I needed a faith I could understand. My girlfriends were all Catholic and my current girlfriend is a Filipina and a Catholic. I feel connected to the religion." Michael Situ Tanjung's sisters knew of his conversion. He said, "They supported me because it is my life." At the time of his asylum application, Michael Situ Tanjung said he had yet to tell his parents of his conversion. If his parents' reaction to his conversion remained an unknown, I was curious about their reaction when his sisters married out of their faith. Michael said his parents did not object to his sisters marrying non-Muslims.

Allowing one's children to marry across religions would be considered a normal practice in California, but according to Islamic culture, when a daughter marries, a father is supposed to "give his daughter" to another Muslim man only. When a man marries a woman from another faith, she is supposed to convert to Islam before she can marry him. When Michael Situ Tanjung's older sister decided to marry a Chinese American of the Christian faith, he said his father did not insist that she marry only a Muslim man. His father hosted a wedding reception at their home but did not invite any of his Indonesian colleagues. "My parents kept the weddings a secret from all their friends and relatives in Indonesia to protect themselves from people who might blame them for not bringing up good Muslim children." Michael Situ Tanjung thought, "My parents must have received a lot of gossip because my sister married a non-Muslim, and a Chinese no less. If my father's family in Indonesia knew about it they would probably have said 'You don't do it!' But I think my parents adopted a policy of 'you don't tell them, they don't know, and no one will talk about it.'" He continued, "My parents' actions were radical and courageous among Indonesians. As Muslims, their actions were radical because they did not push Islam on us, or insist that we must marry only a Muslim. I think my parents protected us and allowed my sisters to marry the men of their choice. We did not talk about it, but they probably had to put up a front among their Indonesian colleagues, friends, and relatives." Michael said that he has his mother's blessing should he decide to marry his current Catholic girlfriend. If Michael Situ Tanjung has kept his conversion from his parents, and his parents have kept his sisters marrying out of their faith from their family, colleagues, and friends in Indonesia, what would happen if or when they learned of Michael Situ Tanjung's conversion? Before I could think about that question, I wanted to learn about Michael Situ Tanjung's visit to Indonesia, which he had mentioned in passing.

MICHAEL SITU TANJUNG'S VISITS TO INDONESIA

Michael Situ Tanjung had returned to Indonesia with his parents on a number of occasions over their twenty-plus years of living in the United States, with his last visit at the age of fifteen. During their one-month visit, he said his mother constantly tried to make him behave according to local *adat* (custom), as well as monitoring his "ill-bred" American behavior to prevent him from getting the family into trouble. In eliciting details from Michael Situ Tanjung, he said his mother's sanctions against his Californian American behaviors included, a) speaking in English, b) making eye contact with strangers, c) staring at things around him, d) wearing American shoes, and e) "looking foreign." To "fit in" even among his relatives, Michael Situ Tanjung would have to try to "pass" as a "local" which he said he was not sure how to do.

Michael Situ Tanjung vividly remembered how his Californian American persona almost caused them trouble. He said he was with his mother at the market where they were followed by two men. His mother held him close and whispered to him "not to speak in English," "not to make eye contact," and "look straight." They managed to lose the men by quickly walking through the market. Michael Situ Tanjung concluded that his mother's analysis was that he was pegged as a foreigner, and targeted for either a robbery or kidnapping. Or, perhaps, there were things his mother was not telling him.

Reflecting on Michael Situ Tanjung's experience in the land of his birth, I realized that Michael Situ Tanjung was not socialized as a native Indonesian during his twenty-plus years in Los Angeles. Instead, he has become an "Angeleno." He does not speak, read, or write the Indonesian language like a native, but neither is he a foreigner in Indonesia. The foreigners typically stay at the local Marriott hotel, shop at the Sogo Department store in Jakarta, and hang out at the local discotheques. For a "foreign local" like Michael Situ Tanjung, with ancestral roots in Indonesia, he is expected to behave like a local, or he must take his chances at being arrested or creating trouble for his family when his is among his relatives. While Michael Situ Tanjung was able to depend completely on his mother to hold him close when he was younger, now, as an adult, he was expected to have the social and linguistic skills expected of a native in Indonesia.

After several in-depth interviews, I was able to prepare a report on Michael Situ Tanjung's fear of return to Indonesia based on his conversion to Catholicism and his cultural background as a Californian. In the report, I wrote sections on his California upbringing, his visits to Indonesia, his religious beliefs, and his conversion to Catholicism. I included a brief analysis on the consequences of his conversion on his parents and Situ Tanjung himself if he should return to Indonesia. I also wrote a short analysis on conversion out of Islam, citing the case of Abdul Rahman in Afghanistan as well as the rise of radical Islam and anti-Americanism in Indonesia.

Attorney Goodsell liked my report, but added, "How about another report on 'What happens to an apostate in Islam?'" The task was daunting. I am not a historian of Islam. It was also taking me away from the comfort zone of an ethnographer, doing in-depth interviews juxtaposed with observations and local fieldwork to make sense of a person's identity. Conducting a search on library databases around 2006 and 2007 produced only a few articles on the legal consequences of apostasy in the late Ottoman Empire and in Egypt, but nothing on Indonesia. I had, in fact, asked Situ Tanjung to research the local Indonesian newspapers on what would happen to an apostate from Islam. He gave me copies of some newspaper clippings in Bahasa Indonesia, but the bits of news reporting of punishments for one offense or the other did not make sense without additional research on the local contexts. In this extensive search, I was looking for a *definitive case,* as in the examples of Mr. Abdul Rahman or the case of Ms. Lina Joy, an apostate in neighboring Malaysia, to show the Government Counsel and the Judge that Michael Situ Tanjung could suffer a similar fate should he return as an apostate in Indonesia.

Working on the apostasy case five years after September 11, 2001, Islam was a subject of intense public interest. Islam is a religion of peace, as proclaimed by many Muslims, but this contradicted the stark reality of the recent American experience with terrorism when airplanes brought down the Twin Towers in New York City. A discussion on the contradictions within a religion, on religion and violence, and on the motives of the attackers, while interesting and on the public's mind, were not the goals of an asylum report. I reminded myself that my job was to prepare a report for the judge, the government counsel, and other adjudicators who may not be familiar with apostasy and what would happen to an apostate from Islam. The report was to help an asylum petitioner who is afraid to return home, and who may not even be able to articulate what it means to be an apostate himself. Clearly, Michael Situ Tanjung was not rebelling against his parents or his former religion. He merely fell in love with a few Asian girls and their Catholic religion: his heart was swayed by both the women and their faith. The question for me was: what will happen to such a man upon his return to Indonesia? Except for the definitive cases in Indonesia similar to Abdul Rahman in Afghanistan (and

Lina Joy in Malaysia), I had to support my argument by drawing on reports published by the international media, human rights organizations, and mainstream journals well known to the American-educated public, such as judges and attorneys. With these resources, I prepared a report entitled "Supporting Document on Situ (Michael) Tanjung's Application for Asylum in the United States on his Fear of Return to Indonesia on Grounds of Apostasy."

In this report, I tried to answer the following questions: a) Why did Situ Tanjung convert to Catholicism? b) What are some recent examples of apostasy from Iran, Afghanistan, and Malaysia? c) What happens to an apostate from Islam? d) Why is the treatment of an apostate so harsh? And e) What will happen to Situ Tanjung when he returns to Indonesia?

Apostasy, according to the Koran, is death. Apostasy is not in the penal code of many Islamic countries, but many Islamic jurists follow their own interpretation of the Koran. Michael Situ Tanjung's return to Indonesia as a convert from Islam to Catholicism is the most serious offense against Islam. Given the current religious and social climate in Indonesia, as reported by the *International Religious Freedom Report* in 2007, and released by the US Department of State, Bureau of Democracy, Human Rights, and Labor, his fate is uncertain, with death being a possibility.

MICHAEL SITU TANJUNG'S CONVERSION TO CATHOLICISM

Michael Situ Tanjung's conversion to Catholicism is a natural outcome of his formative years of a very Californian childhood. In the United States, religious freedom is a taken-for-granted practice for Americans. Faith is a personal matter. Within the same family, husband and wife, and children and parents, need not share the same religion. In the multicultural and multireligious Southern California, the promotion of interfaith dialogues has included joint celebrations of different faiths and denominations. After September 11, Muslim groups have invited non-Muslims to "Open Mosque Days" and celebrations marking the end of Ramadan. Among immigrant groups, religion serves an important social function. It provides an instant social network of support for the various needs of an immigrant. Along the way, a few change their religion. For example, Cambodian refugees in Long Beach have converted to Christianity to please their American sponsors (Hott and Levin 1991). Among contemporary Mexican Catholics, converting to Evangelical Protestantism is a way to avoid cumbersome and expensive rituals (Dow 2005). In the relaxed secular atmosphere of Southern California, Situ Tanjung's parents did not bring him up as a "proper" Muslim or a "proper" Indonesian, if there is such a thing.

In Southern California, there is no known Indonesian language school or mosque. The major gathering place for Indonesians consists of a weekly food court at a hotel parking lot in the city of Duarte, a suburban city in San Gabriel Valley, to the east of Los Angeles. Half of those gathered there, enjoying their weekly *meegoreng* fried noodles while sipping *kopi* drinks, were Dutch Indonesian senior citizens and other Indonesians yearning for Indonesian food. Without an Indonesian enclave such as a "Little Indonesia" or "Little Jakarta" to serve as a cultural and religious wellspring of Indonesian tradition, Situ Tanjung grew up like most Californian teenagers and young adults: he was not exposed to Islam in school, had never learned Arabic, or read the Koran. With their parents' blessings, his two siblings both married outside their faith, their ethnicity, and their nationality. Michael Situ Tanjung shares more in terms of class and culture with other middle-class Americans of Asian and Latino origin in Los Angeles than with the Dutch Indonesians and Indonesian-speaking Indonesians in Duarte, California, or the group of Indonesian students at his university. In short, Michael Situ Tanjung is a Californian and an Angeleno.

SOME RECENT EXAMPLES OF APOSTASY FROM IRAN, AFGHANISTAN, AND MALAYSIA

In Iran, according to Amnesty International (2007), more than two hundred Iranian of Baha'i faith have been executed, mostly during the 1980s, apparently in connection with their religious beliefs or activities. In the same report, Amnesty International also documented the persecution of religious minorities and the harassment faced by converts. It specifically acknowledges that for some ten years there has been no known use of the death penalty for "apostasy" and such a risk is likely to be low. However, what is disturbing is the increasing use of the death penalty on other fabricated charges. For example, drug smuggling charges have been filed against converts who also faced pretrial detention where they are at risk of torture.

In Afghanistan, Abdul Rahman, a Muslim who converted to Christianity, was threatened with the death sentence. When Afghanistan's leading clerics endorsed his death, they were on solid grounds of Islamic scripture and tradition. World leaders, including the Pope appealed on his behalf. Mr. Rahman received a "dispensation" by the Karzai government for his mental condition. Unfortunately, Mr. Rahman remains guilty of apostasy on religious grounds.

In Malaysia, a predominantly Muslim country in neighboring Indonesia, with large Chinese and Indian populations of various faiths, the case of Lina Joy was documented extensively in the local media and the international organizations. Lina Joy was born Azlina binti Jailani, a Malay and a Muslim.

She had converted to Christianity in 1998 and endured extraordinary hurdles in her desire to marry the man in her life. She had received death threats, including calls to hunt her down. Her fiancé, a Christian of ethnic Indian background, had also received death threats. Her lawyer, Mr. Malik, a Muslim and a human rights lawyer, who presented a brief in support of Lina Joy to the appeals court, also received a death threat in a widely circulated email with the heading "Wanted Dead," with a photograph of Mr. Malik that was captioned: "This is the face of the traitorous lawyer to Islam who supports the Lina Joy apostasy case. Distribute to our friends so they can recognize this traitor. If you find him dead by the side of the road, do not help" (Perlez 2006). Mr. Benjamin Dawson, another lawyer who represented Ms. Lina Joy, said that with the threats against Lina Joy "so insistent, and the passions over her conversion so inflamed," he had concluded that there was no room for her and her fiancé in Malaysia. The most practical solution, he said, was for her to emigrate.

In Lina Joy's case, the question was whether or not her case belonged to the civil courts. Lina Joy thought she was no longer a Muslim, so she applied to the civil court for marriage.

In Malaysia, every person carries an Identity Card. The Constitution defines Malays as Muslims. All matters such as marriage, property, and divorce of the Muslims are handled by the Islamic Shariah courts. Lina Joy had applied to the civil courts to change from Muslim to Christian on her Malaysian Identity Card. The courts ruled that Lina Joy's request to change from Muslim to Christian had to be decided by the Shariah courts. At the Shariah court, she would be considered an apostate, and if she did not repent she would be sentenced to several years in an Islamic center for rehabilitation. The religious rehabilitation camp is like a prison protected by rings of barbed wire where the converts spend much of their time studying Islam.

According to Human Rights Watch, Muslims in Malaysia wishing to renounce Islam to profess other faiths or beliefs (apostasy), and Muslims who hold beliefs that deviate from Sunni Islam, are subject to criminal sanctions (Human Rights Watch 2006). Sharia law, which applies to ethnic Malays, "imposes criminal sanctions on those found to hold heretical beliefs that 'deviate' from Sunni Islam" (Amnesty International 2005).

WHAT HAPPENS TO AN APOSTATE FROM ISLAM?

My writing on apostasy for inclusion in Situ Tantung's report to the court was drawn primarily from the writings of Andrew G. Bostom, M.D., an associate professor of medicine at the Brown Medical School, author of *The Legacy of Jihad* (2005), *The Legacy of Islamic Anti-Semitism* (2008), and the article "Under the Scimitar of Damocles" which appeared in *American Thinker* on March 26, 2006. Another book, available during the time of my preparation of the case, was *Freedom of Religion, Apostasy, and Islam* by Abdullah Saeed and Hassan Saeed (2004). Abdullah Saeed is professor of Arab and Islamic Studies at the University of Melbourne in Australia, and Hassan Saeed is the Attorney General of the Maldives. Saeed and Saeed argue that the law of apostasy and its punishment by death in Islamic law are untenable in the modern world. Their book presented evidence that the law of apostasy conflicts with a variety of other Islamic texts and the current debate on the freedom of religion as a human right. Saeed and Saeed's writing on the contradictory evidence on apostasy in the Islamic texts are invaluable on a difficult and sensitive subject. It provides Koranic-based texts that show an alternative interpretation and the possibility of a hopeful future on the freedom of religion. It is the sort of reading professors love to assign to demonstrate another perspective so that the arguments are balanced.

In preparing the report on Michael Situ Tanjung, I constantly reminded myself that the aim of an asylum report as an expert witness is to argue the potential persecution an apostate asylee would face upon his return home if his asylum petition was rejected. Saeed and Saeed's immense scholarship, while convincing about a hopeful future, would fail to reassure an apostate under the stark reality of a narrative controlled by fundamentalist orthodoxy. Indeed, it might even be detrimental to the petitioner in an asylum court. From a scholarly perspective, my exclusion of certain arguments on apostasy may also appear selective and incomplete. From the perspective of helping an asylum petitioner, the diversity of opinions on apostasy might in fact provide a government counsel intent on denying the asylum petition with the argument that if there is flexibility in apostasy, there is nothing for Michael Situ Tanjung to fear upon his return to Indonesia.

Unlike the more "objective" and balanced positions one must take in presenting information on a subject to our anthropology students, the audience for advocating for the freedom of religion and discarding the punishment of apostasy is the Indonesian government and Muslim communities that regard even deviancy from orthodoxy as intolerable. With the focus on convincing the asylum adjudicators of the dire consequences of an apostate's fate should his asylum be rejected, I included unequivocal arguments intended to support the asylum petitioner. The following are excerpts from the report submitted to the court:

> According to the Koran 2:256, "There is no compulsion in religion." Yet, the death sentence or harsh punishment is firmly rooted in the holy texts and imposed on apostasy, or conversion from Islam, if a person refuses to reconvert to Islam.

"Muhammad said, 'Whoever changes his religion, kill him!'" (Al Bukhari, Vol. 9.57). This statement has been the standard throughout Islamic history for any who turn from Islam to another faith (usually Christianity).

Apostasy is a matter of treason and ideological treachery . . . the destiny of a person who has an inborn handicap is different from the destiny of one whose hand should be cut off due to the development of a dangerous and infectious disease. The apostasy of a Muslim individual whose parents have also been Muslim is a very infectious, dangerous and incurable disease that appears in the body of the *ummah* (people) and threatens people's lives, and that it is why this rotten limb should be severed.

One of the most authoritative Koranic commentators, Baydawi (d.1315/16) states "Whosoever turns back from belief (*irtada*), openly or secretly, take him and kill him whosoever find him, like any other infidel. Separate yourself from him altogether. Do not accept intercession in his regard" (as cited in Bostom 2006, 33–34).

WHY IS THE TREATMENT OF AN APOSTATE SO HARSH?

In asking why Islam punishes an apostate harshly, again, I cited the writings of Bostom (2006) in the report:

> The commonest argument in support of the death penalty for the apostate is based on the principle that Islam is not only a religion, but also a social and political order. A person who disagrees with the basis of organized society has only two alternatives open to him: he may either go out of the boundaries of the society's operation or submit to deprivation of all rights as a citizen. As the latter state would be worse than death, it is better to kill him (16).
>
> Generally, the danger the apostate constitutes for Islamic society is emphasized. By abandoning Islam, one rebels against the Islamic state and society. Therefore, it is highly probable that the apostate will attempt to destroy the structure of Islamic society and to change the contents of the Islamic religion. Moreover, having lost his loyalty to Islam, he is prone to support foreign nations against the Islamic state. (16–17). So the apostate must be put to death for the protection of Islamic society. (17) Now that the state no longer punishes the apostate anymore, there are some Moslems who hold the view that the killing of an apostate has become a duty of individual Moslems. (18) A large majority of the Moslem still regard the apostate as traitors, who should be killed, or, in the best case, be treated as social outcasts. . . . These views, expressed by fundamentalist authors, are still very strong. This may explain why the fate of the apostate, which some authors expressly consider a form of punishment, has been maintained in most countries (25).

That is, while "there is no compulsion in Islam," there is plenty of human coercion in the name of Islam, as we have seen in the case of Abdul Rahman and Lina Joy.

WHAT WILL HAPPEN TO MR. MICHAEL SITU TANJUNG WHEN HE RETURNS TO INDONESIA?

In helping the asylum adjudicators anticipate what will happen to Situ Tanjung when he returns to Indonesia I speculated on Indonesia' reception of an apostate, assessed his re-integration into Indonesian society should he be returned, examined anti-American sentiment in Indonesia, and what will happen to his family if his apostasy became known to the community.

A country's reception of an apostate depends on the country's interpretation of the Koran, which depends on its religious climate. Traditional textbooks used to describe Indonesia as a tolerant country. Indonesia has a national motto allowing freedom of religion as long as people believe in one of the six recognized religions. However, in 2005, the Indonesian *Ulema* Council (MUI) issued a *fatwa* (religious edict) banning pluralism, liberalism and secularism (Junaidi 2007).

Today, Christians are having problems acquiring government permits to build churches. Many Christians have turned their private homes into places of worship by the Christian community. In June 2007, around one hundred and fifty members of the Mosque Movement Front (FPM) and the Anti-Apostasy Front took to the streets of Bandung to demand the closure of private homes being used for church activities (Suwarni 2007).

According to Human Rights Watch's *World Report 2007*, in the chapter, "Indonesia: Events of 2006," under the section, "Freedom of Religion":

> Instances of religious intolerance appeared to be on the rise in 2006 with attacks on Ahmadiyah places of worship and Christian churches. A Joint Decree No. 1/2006 on the establishment of places of worship, issued by the Religious Affairs Ministry and the Home Ministry in March 2006, requires a 90-member minimum congregation prior to the issuance of permits for a place of worship. The decree provoked a string of protests from minority religious groups, and prompted the forcible and sometimes violent closure of several Christian churches across Indonesia by vigilante groups."

Another example cited by Human Rights Watch was the conviction of Lia Aminuddin, the leader of a minority religious sect, the Kingdom of Eden, for blasphemy against Islam, and sentenced her to two years' imprisonment by the Central Jakarta District Court in June 2006 (Human Rights Watch 2007).

The Judge ruled that Lia Aminuddin "had blasphemed Islam by practicing prayers in two languages, allowing the consumption of pork, and making her own interpretations of the Koran." (*Jakarta Post* 2006).

In assessing Michael Situ Tanjung's "reintegration" into Indonesian society, I noted that according to Islam, if one is born a Muslim, one must always be a Muslim. Leaving Islam is apostasy. Given the rise in fundamentalism, religious violence, and intolerance in Indonesia, the country will not be kind to an apostate. Upon Michael Situ Tanjung's return to Indonesia, he must apply for a change of religion on his National Identity Card (KTP). The Government of Indonesia requires all adult citizens to carry a KTP, which, among other things, identifies the cardholder's religion. The card is used for all transactions with the government. Transactions with the government include matters such as registering for marriage, applying for a birth certificate, securing employment, obtaining a license, or seeking medical treatment. Changing his religion on his card will immediately expose his apostasy. Given the discrimination against unrecognized or minority religions, the discovery that Michael Situ Tanjung has converted out of Islam can only bring about unthinkable treatment. Situ Tanjung could decide not to reveal his apostasy by not changing his identity card and not using his identity card. In Indonesia, those who chose not to use their identity card by not registering their marriages or children's births risk future difficulties: a child without a birth certificate cannot enroll in school and may not qualify for scholarships. Individuals without birth certificates do not qualify for government jobs.

Unfortunately for Michael Situ Tanjung, he will also encounter anti-American sentiment in Indonesia upon his return. The October 2002 Bali bombings, the 2003 bombing of the JW Marriott hotel in Jakarta, and the 2004 bombing outside the Australian embassy all point to the attacks on Western-held interests. Recent targets against "Western" ideas include attacks on the publication *Playboy* magazine and raids at discothèques. An increase in radicalism of Islam in Indonesia today is accompanied by the imposition of Sharia laws in many parts of Indonesia, even though Indonesia is *not* an Islamic state. Anti-Christian violence in Indonesia can be understood as attacks against local deviation from the Sharia law. According to The Pew Research Center survey on global attitudes, Indonesia had a 75 percent favorable opinion towards the United States in 2000; it was 30 percent in 2006 (Eastwood 2007).

Michael Situ Tanjung's apostasy also poses a complicated dilemma for his family. His father is an important member of a political group that has been persecuted everywhere in Indonesia for political and other reasons stemming from the Suharto era. His maternal grandfather is an important member of the Indonesian government. But under the Sharia law, there is no mercy for deviation. If Michael Situ Tanjung's apostasy is discovered, his parents will be blamed for not having brought him up as a proper Muslim and for having tolerated his religious conversion. Will they be forced to disown or kill their son, or will they be punished as well?

AT THE MERIT HEARING

Mr. Goodsell submitted my two reports—one on my library research on apostasy and one on the interview on Michael Situ Tanjung as a "cool Californian dude"—to accompany his asylum application.

On the day of Michael Situ Tanjung's merit hearing, Judge Daw was the presiding asylum judge. Judge Daw, after having cleared the other cases on her calendar, turned to concentrate on Michael Situ Tanjung's file, and said, "I know what apostasy is." She wasn't speaking to anyone in particular because she had yet to call the counsel to begin the case. When an asylee's fate hangs on the judge's decision, we read meaning into every utterance. Is that good or bad for the case? Has she heard another case on apostasy in her caseload? Is there a relationship between Daw and Dawson, the Malaysian human rights lawyer who represented Lina Joy's apostasy case? Will she grant Situ Tanjung asylum? I held my breath.

After the Counsel for the Government sat down on one side, with Attorney Goodsell and asylum petitioner Michael Situ Tanjung on the other, Mr. Goodsell stood up to introduce me. He directed Judge Daw's attention towards me and said, "Professor Ngin is available to testify." I stood up from where I was sitting in the gallery. Only Michael Situ Tanjung's sister and her husband were in the audience, but I wanted the judge to know who I was. Judge Daw acknowledged my presence and wanted me sequestered. I gathered up my belongings and joined other family members of asylum seekers in a windowless waiting room, sitting on repurposed old church pews.

Around noon, Mr. Goodsell and Michael Situ Tanjung looked for me in the waiting room. Mr. Goodsell looked pleased and whispered something. We walked quickly down the hallway, passed through the security check on the way out, and remained silent in the elevator among other asylum seekers, families, attorneys, counsels, and judges. As we walked out into to the hot Los Angeles sun, Mr. Goodsell said the judge granted Michael Situ Tanjung asylum based on the argument that his cultural upbringing in Southern California would make it difficult for him to integrate into Indonesian society. He said there was no mention whatsoever of apostasy. Mr. Goodsell and I speculated that it might have had to do with President Obama's attempt to reach out to the Islamic world.

Mr. Goodsell and I wondered, "What if Judge Daw had granted Michael Situ Tanjung asylum by arguing the potential dire fate of an apostate?" We believed that if Judge Daw had granted Michael Situ Tanjung asylum based on apostasy, and if the Counsel for the Government were to appeal, the Government Counsel would have to argue that Judge Daw was wrong in granting Michael Situ Tanjung asylum. Instead, the Government Counsel could argue Michael Situ Tanjung would be safe to return to Indonesia as an apostate from Islam. The Bureau of Immigration Appeals (BIA) would then have to debate whether death would befall an apostate from Islam upon his return to Indonesia. A BIA decision that grants Situ Tanjung asylum based on apostasy is also to imply that Indonesia is a country with extreme views towards apostates, and that Situ Tanjung's fate is unthinkable. A BIA decision that denies Situ Tanjung that appeal based on apostasy is to suggest Indonesia would look kindly upon an apostate, and Situ Tanjung could return home as a Catholic without harm. Mr. Goodsell and I thought that perhaps Judge Daw wanted to prevent an entanglement with such a sensitive legal question. Therefore, she ruled by avoiding the subject of an apostate altogether and focused instead on a "cool California dude."

I was pleased that my due diligence in conducting ethnographic fieldwork on Situ Tanjung's *culture in California* was the deciding factor in a positive asylum outcome.

Persecution on the grounds of religion, as discussed earlier, and as documented in chapter 6, is one of the most difficult tasks for an asylum adjudicator. As demonstrated by the ethnographic evidence covered in chapter 5, a major difficulty stems from religion's embeddedness in a people's culture. To understand persecution on account of religion requires a deeper and more holistic inclusion of the asylum petitioner's cultural context in which he expresses his faith.

Even though the case began with an apostate from Islam, in the end, it was not the asylum petitioner's fear of persecution due to his rejection of Islam, or his embrace of Catholicism, but the availability of some anthropological information that provided Judge Daw with an argument from which to make a decision on Situ Tanjung's asylum application without entanglement with a potentially political and explosive issue. I think Judge Daw knew what "apostasy" means and the implications of her asylum decision all along.

Part III

PERSECUTION ON ACCOUNT OF MEMBERSHIP IN A PARTICULAR SOCIAL GROUP

Chapter 8

Ethnographic Details as Evidence of Rape and Pregnancy

In early 2005, Ms. Jeni Chuck Smith contacted Meiji Sopoto in Dr. Nauman's Immigration Services Office for help with her asylum application. Her application had already been rejected by an immigration officer and was similarly rejected by an asylum judge at a Merit Hearing. Her request to the Bureau of Immigration Appeals (BIA) was her last chance to avoid deportation, unless she found a way to make the case go all the way to the federal circuit courts, specifically the Ninth Circuit Court in California.

"They said there was a lack of emotion from the applicant," Sopoto told me when she called my office. "The attorney who had helped her before did not pursue the reasons for the name change and the treatment of ethnic Chinese in Indonesia. The Immigration Officer and the Asylum Judge focused primarily on suspicion rather than on the gang rape. We need to give her another chance; we have a very experienced attorney handling her case this time."

I agreed to interview Jeni for the full story and began contacting the attorney handling her appeal. The attorney, however, similarly entertained suspicions that Jeni was a fraud, asking "for a person coming from Sumatra, how did she get a name like Jeni Chuck Smith?"

Intrigued by Jeni's name and the challenge of helping on a case appealing to the Bureau of Immigration Appeals for consideration, I called Jeni to make arrangements for us to meet. Asylum seekers who are new to the United States usually lack resources to navigate a new environment, particularly so when this navigation involves finding a professor's office in a huge urban university with a perennial parking problem. Frustrated students are known to have simply skipped class rather than drive in circles looking for a parking spot, so I prepared myself to be extremely flexible in meeting Jeni. I gave her information on directions, parking, and public transportation, as well as informing her that she could come to my house if it was more convenient.

Then, I realized she was not local; Jeni lived in a small town some forty miles east of San Francisco, in Northern California, and four hundred miles from my city in Southern California.

I explored different ways for her to meet me in Southern California: by Greyhound buses, by train, and by plane. My teaching schedule was busy, but I was prepared to meet her somewhere if necessary. However, given her lack of resources and the lack of public transportation on weekends, nothing seemed to work for her. I decided to undertake a one-person, humanitarian mission to visit her when my family was making the four-hundred-mile trip to Northern California.

When we arrived in Northern California, I drove to Jeni's house by myself. I found Jeni living in a cold and dimly lit house with glass windows covered by condensation instead of window curtains. Her husband was away working at a Chinese restaurant. She held an infant in her arms as a little boy stood clutching to her legs while she moved across and between rooms, trying to show me the documents.

Since Jeni's attorney had doubts regarding her Chinese identity, I took great pains to gather details about her cultural background in order to establish that she was a Chinese from Indonesia, despite her Western-sounding name. From Jeni's declaration, sent over by her attorney, I had learned that Jeni's family was attacked during the May 1998 Indonesian riot, and that Jeni had been gang-raped, resulting in pregnancy.

I conducted the interview while Jeni was rocking a baby with one arm and calming the older one cuddled in her lap. During those precious quiet moments in between caring for her two children, she told me how she acquired the name "Jeni Chuck Smith." At birth, like all Indonesians, she was given only one name: Jeni. Under Suharto in the 1960s, when the government forced the Chinese to change their name to anything but Chinese, her father, Mr. Chung Yong Kin, changed his Chinese name to "Chuck Smith" because, "the government only said we cannot have Chinese names." Bailey and Lie (2013) state, "The attempts by the Indonesian state under Suharto to regulate Chinese Indonesian names and Chinese Indonesian resistance to such discrimination through distinctive names—as well as their ongoing use of names to mark ethnic boundaries—illustrate the social and political force that names can carry" (22). The Indonesian government did not say the Chinese cannot have other kinds of names. Therefore, by choosing a Western-sounding name, Jeni's father complied with a government regulation but refused to be subjected to the forced assimilation by choosing a local Indonesian or Muslim name like many other Indonesian Chinese had done. Jeni took her father's full name when she was required to have a last name to apply for a passport. Hence, Jeni Chuck Smith. Jeni's paternal grandparents are Hokkiens from the Fujian province in Southern China. Her parents are both Indonesian-born. Jeni did not know her maternal grandparents well because her mother "married out" and moved in with her husband's family upon marriage, in accordance with the Chinese custom of patrilocality. They also lived too far away for regular visits. Jeni grew up in the extended family home of her paternal grandparents in Indrapura, near Medan. Her parents moved into their own home when she was a teenager. Medan is the capital of the North Sumatra province in Indonesia. It has a population of over two million and is the fourth largest city after Jakarta, Surabaya, and Bandung. North Sumatra is a conservative Muslim area ruled by strict Sharia laws.

In her childhood home, Jeni learned the Hokkien dialect as well as a little Mandarin and Kejia/Hakka from her grandparents. Hokkien is the language of the Fujian people. *Kejia* or *Hakka*, in its local pronunciation, means "guest people." The Hakka people do not have their own province and are scattered throughout southern China, with many migrating to Southeast Asia. Jeni wrote me her name in the Chinese characters, explaining that "it means some kind of bird." She also wrote down her father's Chinese name from before he was forced to become Mr. Chuck Smith.

Jeni's grandparents owned a sundry shop in a shop-house very common in the old Chinatowns throughout Southeast Asia. On the upper floor of the shop-house was the family's living quarters. Their shop-house was located within the Chinese sections of Indrapura. Their neighbors in other shop-houses were also ethnic Chinese, while their customers were mostly Muslims and Batak, an indigenous people from the area who are Christian.

Until Jeni's father opened his own sundry shop in a different part of Medan, Jeni helped her grandparents at their shop. When Jeni was thirteen, her parents moved into their own shop-house a few miles away. Her father, Mr. Chung/Mr. Smith, worked as a snake trader. He collected snakes from native Batak people and processed them for sale: the meat went to the Batak, snake parts to the Chinese medicine shops, and skin to the snake skin traders. Her mother stayed at home to look after Jeni and her younger siblings.

In the homes of Jeni's parents and grandparents, the family observed many Chinese customs, including the making of offerings to the God of Heaven (*Tian Gong*), God of the Earth (*Tiju Kong*), and the Goddess of Mercy (*Kuan Yin*, a Bodhisattva) on the first and the fifteenth of the lunar month, similar to other Chinese Indonesians I had interviewed. Jeni and her mother also went to a small *Lao Bu* (Old Mother) temple in Indrapura during Chinese New Year. They celebrated the Lunar New Year at home. The celebration of Chinese Lunar New Year was forbidden when Jeni was growing up. It became public only after former president Megawati was elected. Other important celebrations in Jeni's home were *Cheng Beng* (*Ching Ming*, in pinyin), in which dead ancestors are remembered both at home and at the graveside with food offerings, and the Mid-Autumn Festival which takes place during the full moon of the eighth month, according to the lunar calendar. On the night of the Mid-Autumn Festival, family members gather around to celebrate, emphasizing the importance of and harmony within the family, while enjoying the bright full moon at night. The foods they ate were a combination of spicy Indonesian food and Chinese food, but the eating of pork dishes distinguished them from the local Muslim populations.

Recalling her childhood, Jeni said she had attended a "Muslim" school, where there were only "two or three Chinese and one or two Batak." She had one subject in Arabic, one in Islam, and one hour of English per week, besides the usual subjects taught in Bahasa Indonesia.

When she reached puberty, she was sexually molested by her "Muslim teacher," who would pinch her body "below the armpit and just behind [her] breast. He would smile and then pinch." Another Chinese girl was also targeted, but "the teacher did not do it to the Muslim girls." It was an example very familiar to scholars who conduct research on sexual violence (Green 2004, 113).

Jeni said her father complained to the principal, but no action was taken. She said she could not change schools, because it was the only middle school available in her neighborhood.

She attended a high school outside her neighborhood. In school, Jeni said her friendships with the Muslims and the Batak were not close (*dak dekat*), except for a friendship with one Muslim girl in middle school and a Batak in college. Their relationships consisted mostly of "saying hi." She explained that this was "because when they get mad at you, they will tell you, '*minggir kau cina!*' [You go away, Chinese!]." Her high school and college friends were mostly Chinese from the area. She said the Chinese girls "tried to avoid coming into contact with the Muslims and the Batak." She gave an example of taking public buses in the city, where the men would grope Chinese girls. Her college friends depended on each other for rides in their own cars.

Jeni's husband, Manny Tio, was a fisherman she met through a mutual friend. They were married in a traditional Chinese ceremony after ten months of dating. Jeni told me about the wedding.

At that time, Jeni was residing in her mother's house. On the morning of the wedding, her future husband and his entourage went to Jeni's house to bring the bride to his house according to Chinese custom.

"We had a ceremony where we served tea to his grandmother, his mother [his father had passed away], and other relatives. We *yi qu gong, er qu gong* [bowed to them] in order of seniority according to the generations they are from. In return, we received from them gifts of gold jewelry and *ang pau* [gifts of money in red envelopes]. After that, we prayed to the tablets of the Tio family's lineage ancestors [his grandfather and father] as well as the God of Heaven and the God of Earth."

Jeni repeated the same tea ceremony with her parents and relatives, and bowed to her own family's Chung altar of ancestors and deities. In the evening, there was a banquet for the relatives and friends of both families, with a total of twenty-eight tables for 224 guests.

"It was a small wedding compared to my sister's. When my sister got married there were 53 tables," Jeni explained, "Unlike in America, we did not register with the government to get a marriage certificate, because we don't use the marriage certificate for anything in my area. When we *pai jo kong* [prayed to the ancestral lineage tablets of the husband's family] we became married. Also, if you try to get a marriage certificate, it will cost a lot of money because you must bribe many people in government."

After their wedding, following traditional Chinese custom, Jeni moved into her husband's parent's home along the Sumatran coast facing the Strait of Malacca, where Manny's mother and sister resided. On weekends, Jeni and her husband would visit her own parents in Indrapura, three hours away by car.

Our interview had gone for one hour without interruption when her infant daughter woke up. Jeni carried her in a sling while she fed her with a bottle. Then the four-year old woke up from his nap. Jeni talked to him in Hokkien. He sat up, leaning against his mother. I was thankful and pressed Jeni to continue with two other major points I wanted to learn from her. She told me the horrifying experience of her family in two anti-Chinese riots in May and July of 1998 in Indrapura in North Sumatra. Her stories echoed the stories of many other Chinese Indonesian asylum seekers I had interviewed over the years. Even though it was interesting to hear a firsthand account from a Chinese Indonesian from Medan, I did not have time to ask her about her reactions to the attacks against the Chinese. But her stories were important evidence on persecution based on "race," which I had hoped would give credibility to her request for asylum, and had therefore included them in the report for the courts.

Recognizing how precious the time was because Jeni did not need to attend to her sleeping children, I wanted her to tell me about the rape. I told her I had already learned about it from her declaration, but I wanted to hear from her personally. When she spoke about the rape, her voice became softer, and more words came out in Bahasa Indonesian.

THE GANG RAPE

Jeni's husband owned a medium-sized fishing boat and a truck. He worked with five fishermen and a truck driver. Whenever the fishermen returned from sea, he went out to meet the fishing boats, collected the catch from his own boat as well as the catch from other boats, sorted them into containers, and brought the fish to the wholesalers. This work took him away for about a week at a time.

On a Saturday in 1999, Jeni said, *banyak ikan masok*, a large catch of fish had come in. Her husband would normally drive Jeni to her parents' house, but he did not have time that afternoon because the workers wanted him to *pergi cepat nya*, or to hurry over. Manny's extended family members, who were normally home, were not there that day. Jeni did not want to be home alone, so she decided to visit her parents during her husband's absence. The drive between her house along the coast and her parents' house in Indrapura takes about two and a half hours through a landscape dotted with small *kampongs*, or villages, oil palm, and rubber plantations. About an hour into her drive, two men on a motorbike created an "accident" to force her to stop her car. She said, "I don't think I knocked them down. They fell by themselves (*dia jatoh sendiri*). She stopped the car and got out to check the conditions of the two men. "I thought they appeared unhurt," she said. Then, other men appeared from nowhere and forced her to drive to a remote area where they brutally gang-raped her. The passage from my report to her attorney recalled Jeni's words to me: "The three men sat in the back of the car. While I was driving, from the rear view mirrors I noticed that the men were smiling. One of the men pointed a knife at my neck and forced me to drive. I offered them money but they keep asking me to drive." When they came to a desolate location—"there was no house but only trees"—the men forced her out of the car.

> They ripped off my clothes. They shouted "*Cina ta tau di-untung. Diam, kau amoi!*" [You Chinese never appreciate what you have. You shut up!] I cried and I screamed but there was no one there; they said "*bangsat cina!*" [You Chinese bastard!], and hit my face and pulled my hair. I said I will give you whatever you want, but please don't do this, but they kept saying "*Diam kau amoi*" [You Chinese girl shut up!] They hit me so hard my mouth was *darah mulut* [bleeding]. They pulled my hair. They opened my body; I tried to push them away. It was almost dark. They take off their clothes; the three took turn *bergantian*—[after you, me]. I was so tired; I fainted. About 9 p.m., two Indonesian women on bicycles gave me my clothes. They asked me if I wanted to go to the hospital, I just said I want to go to my car. . . . The three men had gone. My money all lost; my mobile phone gone.

Jeni described the men as "all in their 30s, all wearing *baju biasa*"—ordinary clothes of jeans and singlet t-shirts. Her mother later said that the men were probably the military (*tentara*), but not in uniform, because the rubber plantation and oil palm orchard (*kebun*) employ a lot of military people as security guards (*jaga*). She said, "I was in shock. I was dirty. I didn't feel anything. I just drove and drove to my mother's house. My mind was blank. I cannot think. But I had pain all over my body."

When Jeni arrived home, she said she did not call the police. Her mom considered it useless, and said, "You will lose. You will lose because everybody will know. Your name will be in the papers the next day. You'll lose money because you must also bribe the police."

Jeni's mother prepared her bath by boiling water to warm up the cold water (in a tropical climate, water tapped into the house is not heated). The next day, she prepared another bath, a *mandi bunga*, an herbal/flower bath consisting of seven kinds of flowers (*tujuh macam bunga*) which she bought from the market to help her *buang siah* or to rid the evil spirit. The next day, her mother also took Jeni to a *senseh*, a practitioner of traditional Chinese medicine. "I told the *senseh* my body was sick (*badan sakit*), the body was 'dirty'; I didn't tell him I was raped." Jeni was given Chinese herbal medicine, which her mother prepared into a decoction for her to drink.

When Jeni's husband learned of the incident from her mother, he was angry and wanted to go beat up the men. But she told him, "You don't know them. It was *bodoh, dat guna* [stupid and useless]."

Later that year, Jeni discovered that she had missed her menstrual period. Tests from two pharmacy pregnancy test kits were positive. Since her marriage, they had wanted to have children. When her husband learned that she was pregnant, he was elated. But Jeni feared that it could have been from the rape. "So I had an abortion because it may not be our baby." Jeni said she did not go to a hospital for an abortion because "they will ask many questions, and there will be a lot of paperwork." Jeni and her mother found a *kampong bidan*, a village midwife who performs abortions. At the midwife's house, she prepared a clear liquid, chanted a prayer over it, and told Jeni to drink it. "Then she asked me to lay down on a long table. She 'massaged' (*urut*) very hard my stomach, both in front and below. The *urut* was very, very painful. The *bidan* told me to continue *urut* after I get home." That night, she started to bleed. "There was a lot of blood, like my period, but more than usual, with some stuff that came out."

I held my breath when Jeni told me what she did after she was raped and became pregnant. I could not believe I was actually listening to the kind of data I had gathered for a World Health Organization project on Indigenous Fertility Regulation Methods (IFRM) almost three decades earlier. I only needed to use abbreviations for my note taking; I had been furiously writing Jeni's story all along before that. I reassured Jeni that I understood what she was telling me. I wanted Jeni to pay attention to the ordeal of the gang rape.

After the gang rape, Jeni said she felt dirty and shameful. She said she was very sad for a long time. "I *Saya dudok di-rumah* [stayed at home]. My husband did the marketing." She said she felt shameful even until today. After the trauma of the rape, Jeni began to hate men, especially *pribumi* men. She stopped wearing dresses, skirts, and shorts after the rape. She only wore pants. She did not have intimate relations with her husband for months. Later that year, Jeni's grandparents were going for their medical checkup in Penang, an island off the northwest coast of the Malayan Peninsula, across from the Strait of Malacca from Medan. Jeni's mother urged her to accompany her grandparents on the trip, saying that it would help her forget her sadness. Her mother told her, "try not to remember anything, try to forget it." While in Penang, Jeni said she realized the difference between Medan and Penang: Penang did not have *pai hua*, or a blanket anti-Chinese hatred and expulsion, whereas Medan was full of hatred against the Chinese. Upon her return, she told her mother that she wanted to flee Indonesia, perhaps to Australia or America. Her husband had also read in the newspapers that they could apply for a visa to come to America. They quickly left Indonesia and arrived in Los Angeles on a B-2 visa.

ETHNOGRAPHIC DETAILS AS EVIDENCE

After my return to Los Angeles, I quickly turned the twenty-five pages of notes into a draft report. I talked to Jeni on the telephone many times for clarification on details. I conducted research on *pai hua*—the history of anti-Chinese incidences in Indonesia—and was able to find corroborated accounts of violence from the intense reporting on Indonesia by the major international media (McGurn 1998; Mydans 1998), Human Rights Watch, US Department of State, and scholarly writing (Ressa 2003; Siegel 1986; Purdey 2005). These publications were consistent with the data compiled by Mizhan Khan and Deepa Khosla (1999) for the Minorities at Risk (MAR) Project.

Wanting to ensure that I had captured Jeni's words and interpreted her stories correctly, I also faxed a copy of the draft report to a number at the restaurant where Jeni's husband worked. He made sure to wait at the other end so that only he received the fax. When Jeni concurred with my interpretation of her account, I sent a signed copy to Jeni's attorney for her work on Jeni's appeal to the Bureau of Immigration Appeals.

In the report, I had emphasized specific cultural data to support Jeni's case. This included the anti-Chinese policy in Indonesia that led to a third generation Chinese acquiring the name "Jeni Chuck Smith." I also described in detail the tea ceremony and other customs related to Jeni's traditional Chinese wedding. Some aspects of the customs, such as bowing in front of the ancestral tablets, have gone out of fashion in other parts of the Chinese diaspora or when the Chinese adhered to newly adopted Christianity where the "ancestor worship" is the first to be removed. The tea ceremony—related to the showing of respect to the parents and elders—and the incorporation of the newlywed to the respective families, through the giving of gifts such as money or heirloom jewelry, is considered secular and usually retained. I described, in detail, the horrendous anti-Chinese attacks and arson of the Chinatown in Medan that destroyed Jeni's grandparents' shop and a second incident where arson almost killed Jeni's family.

Throughout the interview and in preparing the report, I returned to Meiji Sopoto's comment that "Jeni is honest, but they said she did not show emotions." Then she added, "People in those situations are not used to showing emotions." Einhorn and Berthold (2015, 41) argue that cultural characteristics and context play a big role in shaping what information is shared and with whom, as well as the presentation of asylum seekers in court proceedings. The context refers to the meaning and consequences of the trauma in the socio-political-historical-cultural-spiritual setting of the survivor. Bohmer and Shuman's (2008) work corroborates this idea, stating that cultural factors have an impact on the construction (and communication) of asylum applicants' narratives (402).

I thought about the question of how to capture emotions of trauma across time, space and culture. I was not in Sumatra when Jeni and her family were attacked, and when she was raped. But her "honesty" must now come from the "truths" of her spoken words. This was her appeal to the Bureau of Immigration Appeals. This was her last chance to avoid the deportation of herself, her husband, and her two American-born children. Her attorney wanted anthropological input, perhaps because she felt that my contribution could provide additional information not previously included, hopefully turning the tide of fate for Jeni, her husband Manny Tio, and their children.

But how could my interview and report serve as witness to their tragedies? When I interviewed Jeni, she did not break down and cry, therefore I could not describe her emotion in such a manner. Jeni and I knew time was precious. She was busy caring for her children and trying to focus on my incessant questioning. However, in the accounts Jeni provided, she recalled details that captured her emotions of fear, trauma, and her experience of the anti-Chinese incidents, including the gang rape. In my written ethnographic account to her attorney, I included verbatim the conversations using phrases in the Indonesian/Malay language that Jeni had reverted to when she was in distress. Exact words uttered by the rapists "*Cina tatau di-untong. Diam, kau moi.*" (You Chinese never appreciate what you have. You shut up! You *moi*!). *Moi* is derived from the Chinese word for younger sister. But in the Indonesian context, it has taken on a derogatory meaning, equivalent to "Chink" in the Chinese-American experience in the United States, when shouted at Chinese women. Jeni also used the word *bergantian* (after you, me) to describe the gang rape by the three men who had tricked their way into her car by blaming her for an accident that they themselves had staged. They then forced her to drive, supposedly to the hospital, while looking for a secluded location to rape her.

I tried to ask her about details of the incidents, without psychologizing or imputing how she might have felt. This awareness came from having testified in court and encountering government counsels who questioned my expertise. Indeed, while I was testifying on the case of another asylum seeker, the counsel for the government had asked me, "Are you a psychologist?" The answer was an easy "No." But the government counsel then came back with a second question, "How do you know how the rape victim felt if you are not a psychologist?" I believed I had said something along the lines of, "I have interviewed many women Vietnamese Boat People refugees in the Pulau Bidong and Sungei Besi refugee camps who were raped by the Thai pirates in the South China Sea. I have also interviewed other Indonesian Chinese women victims of sexual violence escaping the 1998 anti-Chinese riot. And I found the emotion of the asylum seeker in question consistent with those I had interviewed."

In my interview with women victims of sexual violence, I have used words such as fearful, shameful, traumatized, sad, and dirty because I am expected to describe briefly a sense of the state of well-being of the asylum seekers. But there was no way to verify the degree of pain or the depth of shame. Without training in psychology, the psychological aspects of violence and trauma were secondary to checking the ethnographic details I gathered through oral history.

Although members of a given cultural group share certain cultural characteristics, there can be individual differences between members of that culture, including their cultural beliefs, practices, and the meaning and ways of relating their experiences of various events. In addition, there can be significant individual differences between cultures in the expression of distress. It can be risky to make assumptions or interpret the applicant's demeanor and behavior based on one's own life experience or cultural lens. Unless these factors are presented by an expert in a way that is understandable to adjudicators not trained about trauma, memory, or culture or in such disciplines as psychology, social work, or anthropology, the asylum adjudicator may come to an erroneous credibility determination that may lead to the applicant being ordered deported (Einhorn and Berthold 2015, 41–42).

Focusing on my own anthropological expertise with regards to Jeni's case, I documented, in particular detail, Jeni's practices relating to post-rape cleansing, pregnancy, and abortion—the use of seven sacred flowers for an herbal bath to rid the body of evil (*buang siah*), the consultation with a local practitioner of Chinese medicine (*senseh*) for illness, and the use of a village midwife (*kampong bidan*) to manipulate her abdomen (*pulut*) to induce a miscarriage or abortion, which were all consistent with the cultural practices of the Chinese in the Indonesian/Malay context.

This expertise came from my research across the Strait of Malacca from Medan on the west coast of the Malayan Peninsula on a World Health Organization's (WHO) Expanded Programme on Research, Development and Research Training in Human Reproduction, directed by Alexander Kessler through the Task Force on Psychosocial Research in Family Planning coordinated by Anthropologist John F. Marshall. The research protocol was developed in Geneva. My research was funded by the WHO Task Force, the Institute for Medical Research in Kuala Lumpur, Malaysia, and the University of California International Center for Medical Research (UC-ICMR) (Newman 1985). The WHO project in the 1970s was interested in how men and women regulate their fertility around the world. Lucile Newman, a professor of anthropology at the joint program in Medical Anthropology at the University of California, Berkeley and the University of California, San Francisco (UCB/UCSF), was managing a team of researchers in various countries around the world. As a graduate student of Lucile Newman in the first year of the Medical Anthropology program at UCB/UCSF, I conducted research among the rural and urban Chinese communities in Malaysia on the Malayan side of the Strait of Malacca. My research on the indigenous fertility methods used by the women was published in an edited volume by Lucile Newman on *Women's Medicine* (1985). With that, I felt I could speak with confidence about Jeni's post-rape cultural practices.

The consistency between ethnographic details on her experiences related to rape, pregnancy, abortion, and cultural practices common among the Chinese in rural Indonesia is irrefutable evidence of her experience of rape. It is rare when one is able to speak with such confidence as an expert witness on social science cultural data, which can be used as evidentiary proof in an asylum case. I thought to myself, if the Counsel for the Government should ever ask me if Jeni could be lying, I could tell them, she would have to be a good anthropologist to know about such details. But of course, there is no place for the testimony of an expert witness in a case going to the Bureau of Immigration Appeals. My duty to Jeni Chuck Smith was complete once I had submitted the report.

I did not hear from Jeni's attorney regarding the outcome of her case; she was not obliged to inform me of the result. The government also publishes cases selectively. However, I could not help but to be curious about what had happened to Jeni and her two children born in the United States during the five years she was going through the asylum application process. I felt that if the expertise and ethnographic evidence of an anthropologist such as myself had been asked in the beginning of Jeni's asylum case, she would have had a better chance. But the request to work on the case came *after* she had been rejected twice already in the asylum application process. In 2014, when I asked Meiji Sopoto what happened in the case, she said that Jeni had probably left the country.

Chapter 9

Without Evidence and Without Witness

When Attorney Goodsell contacted me in 2003 about Mrs. Harianto, we had already successfully completed "proving" the "Chinese race" identity in about a dozen Chinese Indonesian cases. With Mrs. Harianto, there was something else that needed to be addressed besides proving her Chinese Indonesian identity. "Something happened to Mrs. Harianto, but she wouldn't talk about it." Mr. Goodsell had informed me, and then he added, "She has also missed the one-year rule. Perhaps you could talk to her." Applying for asylum protection within one year is crucial. Those who missed the one-year rule have a difficult time obtaining asylum unless their justifications are extraordinary. In helping Mr. Goodsell on the case, my job was then to find that "extraordinary" circumstances that had delayed her asylum application.

Mrs. Harianto, a fifty-two-year-old mother, and her husband, Mr. Harianto, had arrived in the United States on a tourist visa and overstayed after an extension. With expired visas, Mrs. Harianto and her husband were now "out of status" and their presence in the United States was illegal. They lived in constant fear of being arrested and deported. To make matters worse, their failure to apply for asylum within a year after arrival made their chances of getting asylum very slim.

I first met the Hariantos in Mr. Goodsell's office. Their sadness and desperation still haunts me to this day. Something horrific must have happened. She said she had tried to apply for asylum before, but each time she would withdraw her application at the last minute. Despite the passage of time, the trauma remains vivid and painful. Her reluctance to speak about the incident turned into delays, and those delays resulted in missing the one-year rule.

Based on this, how was I going to help Mrs. Harianto with her asylum application? If I was going to address whatever horrible trauma she had experienced as a woman, I had to keep in mind that the Refugee Convention does not specifically mention gender as one of its criteria for asylum protection. Instead, women seeking asylum have applied under a category known as "Membership in a Particular Social Group" (MPSG). Legal scholars have mentioned women forced into marriage, forced to have an abortion, or forced to have "female genital mutilation" being granted asylum under MPSG. Persecution based on sexual orientation comes under the ground of MPSG as well. However, many scholars have also described MPSG as being confusing, unclear, and marginalizing women's representation in court. Women are unable to speak and their trauma remains hidden.

How do I help Mrs. Harianto so that she qualifies under the grounds of MPSG?

In helping asylum seekers prepare a stronger narrative for submission to court, the unspeakable must be spoken, the unarticulated must be articulated, the hidden must be uncovered, and the silence must be broken to make full sense to the adjudicators.

Unsure of how I would argue that whatever had happened to Mrs. Harianto could come under the Refugee Convention ground of MPSG, I decided to learn first what had kept Mrs. Harianto from talking and to coax out the hidden, the unarticulated, the unspeakable, and the silenced.

We decided to meet at her residence because it would be more convenient than a long drive to my office in Los Angeles. I had considered Mr. Goodsell's office—which was also a long drive for the Hariantos—but his office feels like a busy waiting room at a county hospital filled with patients waiting to see their doctor.

MRS. HARIANTO'S STORY

During our interview at their modestly furnished apartment in a suburb of Los Angeles, Mr. Harianto spoke with me in a mixture of Mandarin, English, and Bahasa Indonesian. He demanded to know: "Do you know what happened to the Chinese in Indonesia? And the fighting between the Muslims and the Catholics in Ambon, Maluku, and Sulawesi? And the recent incidents affecting the Chinese?"

He was venting his sense of loss and frustration, and perhaps also to quiz me on my knowledge of the latest troubles in many Chinese communities in the archipelago. Given my very short visit in 1997, I do not claim expertise on Indonesia. But my many interviews with Chinese Indonesian asylum seekers had given me an intimate sense of the May 1998 anti-Chinese riots that were not even reported in the major newspapers. I think Mr. Harianto was pleased when I mentioned the work of Frans Hendra Winarta, a lawyer in Jakarta and a member of the International Bar Association Human Rights Institute (IBAHRI) under the leadership of Nelson Mandela.

When it came time to focus on the specifics of Mrs. Harianto's personal story, I noticed from the corner of my eyes, Mr. Harianto slowly walking away and disappearing into a room down the corridor. When I asked Mrs. Harianto to tell me what she remembered, her voice was barely audible; perhaps she was thinking her husband was still within earshot. As she spoke, she held her abdomen as if in pain. Tears flowed down her cheeks. Details came out in bits and pieces. I tried to be supportive. I paused. I let her talk. She paused. Things did not make sense at first but I could not press her too hard. I had no idea how long the interview would take.

Recalling the events that had been long repressed is never tidy. Talking about oneself is also not easy. So I began by asking Mrs. Harianto about her customs and her habits: her life before she got married, her role as a mother and an outstanding Chinese Catholic woman in her community.

Mrs. Harianto is of the Chinese Hakka dialect group. She spoke Dutch, Indonesian, some self-taught Mandarin, some English, which she mostly acquired after arriving in the United States, and *Kek*, the language of the Hakka people. Mr. Harianto had a manufacturing business outside of Jakarta. Their two grown children attended university in Jakarta. One of Mrs. Harianto's daily activities in Jakarta includes visits with her social circle of relatives and church people. She is Catholic, but observes many Chinese customs, festivals, and dietary practices. On that fateful day in May 1998, having heard about a riot near her children's university, she decided to go pick up her daughter who was still at school. During the short, ten-minute drive, two policemen stopped her car, ostensibly to check her identity papers. Mrs. Harianto protested, but they forced her to drive to a remote area until "the road had no asphalt" and then gang-raped her. She said she felt they may have drugged her with a piece of cloth over her mouth because she could not scream or fight back. Afterwards, they pushed her out her car and drove off. Mrs. Harianto said she could not get up, so she crawled until "the dirt reached the gravel." It was getting dark. A Chinese couple in a passing car stopped to enquire. Mrs. Harianto begged them to take her home, but the man was reluctant. He was afraid she might die in his car and he would have to be a witness. The woman had mercy, and gave Mrs. Harianto her jacket to cover up her torso, but they were still unsure about taking her. Mrs. Harianto pleaded for them to take her home. The couple finally agreed to take her, immediately speeding away the moment they dropped her off.

Upon returning home late in the night—four hours after she had left home for a ten-minute drive, Mrs. Harianto did not tell her husband what had happened. She went straight to her room and found dried blood on her lips and bruises on her face. She said she did not go to the hospital or report it to the police because, "How could we have gone to the police or the hospital? They wouldn't have believed us because we are Chinese. They would want money before they would do anything. . . . No one at the police station would believe me." Proving sexual violence as a persecution for asylum must include proving that the violence was not random, that it was done by agents of the government, and that the government did not or would not protect the person. In listening to the stories of the asylum seekers, their stories are similar: "they were too embarrassed, feared they would not be believed" (Koss 2006, 2).

The next morning, Mrs. Harianto went to hide at her sister's house, which had been left vacant after her foreign employer had evacuated the family and its dependents to Singapore. Mrs. Harianto had isolated herself socially because she felt "too dirty and too shameful" (*kotok* and *malu* in Malay) to face her own husband, her friends, and relatives. She said, "In that neighborhood no one knew who I was." She wanted to kill herself. She would cry for no reason. She instructed her daughter to inform everyone that she had gone abroad. She lived alone in shame, as if the shame was visible all over her face. Until her interview with me, she had never told anyone details of what had happened during the four hours in May 1998.

Mrs. Harianto whispered to me, "My husband is very understanding. I felt so dirty, so low and so ashamed." She confessed she felt sorry for him because she had not had sex with her husband since the horrific incident many years ago. "He is very gentle, loving and patient," she said, but she added, "Whenever he tries to touch me, even on my shoulder, I'll jerk and pull away. I just tell him I am tired."

WITHOUT EVIDENCE AND WITHOUT WITNESS

Despite not having medical and police reports as proof that rape actually took place, and despite having missed the one-year rule by several years, the judge granted Mrs. Harianto "withholding from withdrawal." That is, she did not have to be "withdrawn" or removed from the United States. I was not privileged to know the rationale for the judge's decision. Perhaps, she had mercy on her. Did Mrs. Harianto's story of crawling "until the dirt reached the gravel" strike a chord with the asylum adjudicator; or was it her regret over her inability to respond to her husband's tender advances?

Perhaps it could also be the report that I had submitted, with the compelling story that identified her as having "Membership in a Particular Social Group," as required by the Refugee Convention.

When Attorney Goodsell first contacted me, I was put in a quandary as to how to prepare her case. It was not to uncover her identity as a Chinese

Indonesian, but as a woman who had been persecuted due to her gender, which is not a recognized criterion for asylum protection. Instead, to be recognized as refugees, women asylum seekers must demonstrate they fear persecution on account of their "Membership in a Particular Social Group" (MPSG). As a ground for asylum protection, legal scholar Foster (2012) has referred to it as the "Ground with the Least Clarity." Its difficulty is due to its "lack of self-evident 'ordinary meaning' and its concomitant ability to encompass a wide range of evolving contemporary claims" (2). Many legal scholars and community activists working with asylum seekers have attempted to understand the definition of this criteria based on case laws and explanations provided by the United Nations High Commissioner for Refugees and the National Immigrant Justice Center.

If the definition of MPSG is unclear, it has also given the opportunity for asylum seekers who have been persecuted for various reasons to qualify under this ground. (See discussion by Musalo et. al. 2007). To provide more clarity in applying this definition, I turned the definition of MPSG, provided by the UNHCR guidelines, into three questions to help me think through Mrs. Harianto's situations:

a. What similar backgrounds, habits or social statuses are shared by women in similar situations?
b. What similar characteristics do these women share that distinguish them from society at large?
c. What reactions do people have towards such a group of women?

When the definition of MPSG is dissected, it is about social statuses and what perceptions and reactions people have toward women and men who have been abused. Following such a definition, the topic of statuses, roles, and people's perception towards those roles are very familiar to sociocultural anthropologists. The field's study of kinship and marriage, economy and society, wealth and power, religion and witchcraft, all relate to an individual's position and role in society in one way or another. Reflecting on my own anthropological research in multiple locations over the years, I was reminded that these were not typical skills possessed by an attorney.

Gender roles are acquired and learned through the symbols, meanings, values, and practices unique to each culture. The way we view the world, the way we are expected to behave, what we consider as appropriate behavior, and our identities, are all influenced by the sociocultural and political institutions and discourses in our surroundings. These institutions and discourses are part of the "regulatory regimes of power that produce particular kinds of subjects and subjectivities, such as the contented homemaker or the sexual deviant" (Shaw 2009, 14).

Though their gender issues are rarely emphasized, gender refers to men as well. In America, boys and girls are socialized differently, beginning with different colors for decorating a newborn's room, the different toys given to boys versus girls, and the ways in which society's expectations of how boys and men behave vary from expected behavior from girls and women. The consequences for those who do not conform to the norms are played out daily on the schoolyard where children are bullied.

Gender roles may be further distinguished from the positions women and men occupy in society. For example, depending on the culture, the position of a wife entitles a woman to a certain claim in her husband's family as a daughter-in-law, as a mother to their children, and as a kin to his relatives. The position of a daughter entitles a woman to certain claims in her parents' home (such as food and shelter), and those claims may change when her position changes to a married woman, depending on the culture.

Every role is relational. There are specific expectations between dyadic relationships between mother and daughter, mother-in-law and daughter-in-law, man and woman, and woman and woman. Depending on these relationships, individuals in society modify their behavior accordingly. There are things a woman will tell another woman that she may not tell a man, believing men do not care, do not know, or simply because they do not share the roles and the same experience.

Thus, due to the accident of their birth—or the stars they are born under—only women can procreate, and their body is the site of pregnancy, gestation, and lactation. A woman's biology may determine her female sex, but it is the culture of her world that determines a woman's position and identifies her as a marriageable girl, a good wife, a mother, a daughter, a daughter-in-law, or any other position within the web of kin. When a woman fails to perform the roles expected of her, due to her position, she can be forced to comply. Those in power can impose punishment on her, resulting in abuses such as domestic abuse or rape. Therefore, to understand why women are persecuted in society necessitates an understanding of their positions and roles in that particular society.

SHAME AS EVIDENCE

Violence against women is both a physical attack on the woman as a biological being and an attack on her gendered positions and roles in society. By making a distinction between sex and gender, it is possible to shift the focus of the persecution against a woman by elaborating on her gendered roles. That is, physical evidence may be absent, but damage to her social position remains. By examining damage to the women's social position through ethnographic interviews, it shifts the focus from violence to the physical body to violence against their gendered positions and roles.

Depending on the culture, sexual violence against a woman can generate shame in a woman, destroy the marriageable possibilities of a young woman, or create embarrassment in some cultures. Sexual abuse, or persecution, works on the level of a women's gendered position and social role in society. If a rape comes to be known, a woman's reputation can be damaged; changing people's reaction toward such a woman. In some societies, losing one's virginity can lead to ostracism and even death. Shame damages the rape victim's sense of self-worth by having to explain to others why and how it happened, at the risk of not being believed. Thus, by laying out the asylum seekers' claims of persecution as embedded within their local cultural norms and practices as evidence, it is more difficult to refute their experiences and label them as a fraud.

In helping Mrs. Harianto prepare her case for submission to the immigration court, I took an ethnographic approach by highlighting how shame affected her relationship with her husband and her community. It was gender roles, rather than the physical aspect of the rape, that structured her everyday life. Sexual violence against women leaves no evidence and no witnesses over time. It is the persecution against her social and cultural position that support her claims to asylum.

Besides the violent physical attacks on Mrs. Harianto, rape also attacks her society's idea of what it means to be a good woman and wife. Sociologists have determined that, "gender ideologies define masculinity through aggression, violence, domination, and power. Violence is then a means to exhibit these traits to oneself and others. Combined, women's unequal status and opportunities in society, culture, and law encourage violence against them. Therefore, measures of gender inequality may be important predictors of rape" (Green 2004, 112–13). Mrs. Harianto has built her social standing by being a good wife, a good mother, and a woman of esteem in the social circle of Chinese Catholics in Jakarta. Mrs. Harianto had worked as a nurse before marriage, but quit her job after her children were born. She raised their children while her husband built his business, both playing their traditional roles within the context of the Chinese community in Indonesia. By her fifties, she had reached the paragon of a good woman with a successful husband and two children attending university. Mrs. Harianto's sexual victimhood was not a result of her sexual misadventure, dysfunctionality of character, or being one who "invites" unwanted attention. The tragedy is that it is ordinary women tending to their gender roles. Persecutions against these women are not against "the other;" these rape victims are individuals we can relate to as ourselves and our female kin. Therefore, as a good wife, she was too ashamed to face her husband. Being a married Catholic woman, the rape was a violation of that sanctity. Sex is a subject that women in traditional and polite Chinese Catholic society do not talk about. If she were to reveal the incident, it would be embarrassing for her and for the people who hear it.

In Mrs. Harianto's situation, the rape was not due to her lack of vigilance in personal safety or in committing conducts unbecoming of her society's norms. She was socialized to perform her dutiful role as a mother protecting her daughter by preventing her from harm even in times that seem tenuous for her own safety. Mrs. Harianto did not deserve the trauma of a gang rape by the police who were supposed to be protecting her and her community. She did not report it to the police. It would be futile, not to mention the cost and the publicity that could further harm her.

The intentional trauma of this rape was also meant for the larger Chinese community. The rapists were sending a message: I can control your women and your people as well. The rapists were aware that the *malu* (shame) suffered would reverberate throughout the Chinese community. It would spread fear, just as other rapes singling out Chinese women were taking place in the community during the May 1998 riots as reported by the major media outlets. In just three days, the Volunteers for Humanity compiled 143 cases of rape/torture/sexual harassment/murder occurred in Indonesia, targeting Chinese populations (Wandita 1998, 38). Like Mrs. Harianto, many victims did not go to the police or to the hospitals because they feared public persecution and defamation of character. Because of this, the numbers compiled may only reflect a fraction of the actual victims. But these issues were secondary to Mrs. Harianto's personal trauma.

"Rape as a weapon of war" has emerged as a forceful legal argument, although much more difficult has been recognizing it as a solid ground for refugee status. Therefore, nongovernmental organization (NGO) reports and testimonies are strategically collected to present a singular argument, a "rape script" (Buss 2009). This mass data, however, ends up silencing, rejecting, and ignoring the testimony of an individual woman in need of protection and justice from the men and boys in her village, or the one nearby who sometimes wear military uniforms and other times does not (Ruffer 2013). The images of the military or rebel rape mask that these "official rape scripts" wear are often men and boys who, on another day, might be the schoolteacher, the businessman, neighbor, unemployed bandit, or schoolboy in love with the girl in the field, who have raped these same women throughout the course of their lives (Ruffer 2014).

For Mrs. Harianto, rather than worrying who these rapists were, it was for the protection of her personal and social identity that prevented her from disclosing the incident of rape. To disclose the rape and have it spread like news would be to destroy her sense of self and social well-being. It was Mrs. Harianto's fear of societal judgement within the context of her culture that defined her decision. The rapists persecuted her through her "membership" as a wife, in her relationship to her husband; and as a Catholic Chinese woman, in her relationship with others in her Indonesian Catholic Chinese community.

By contextualizing Mrs. Harianto's story with accounts of anti-Chinese and anti-Christian persecution, I tried to present her complete story in great detail in a document accompanying her application submitted by Attorney Goodsell. With all the relevant details regarding Mrs. Harianto available to both the Counsel for the Government, and the Immigration Judge, it would be harder for them to focus narrowly on the sexual aspects. Mrs. Harianto had missed the deadline by several years. If she had wanted to play the system, she could have applied for asylum soon after arriving in the United States in order to meet the one-year rule.

My ethnographic focus described detailed observations of Mrs. Harianto's emotions, actions, and cultural reasons for her behavior, that is, her gender roles in society. The experience of rape distinguishes Mrs. Harianto from other women in society, as required by the language of MPSG. The experience of rape, if known by others in the community, would lead to negative reactions toward Mrs. Harianto. Her feeling of shame is a response in anticipation of the embarrassment she would feel if others came to know about it.

This ethnographic focus on Mrs. Harianto's experience is in sharp contrast to the treatment of women by the legal system. Nicola Henry (2010), in her examination of wartime rape survivors at the trial of the International Criminal Tribunal for Yugoslavia (ICTY), found problems in the "crisis of representation" and the "crisis of law." That is, even though the events women have experienced are often too painful and they are unable to remember and to speak about it, they must "continually struggle to not only be understood but also to have their experiences believed, recognized, and validated" (1113).

When women victims present their case in court, the blood, the bruises, and other evidence on a woman's body have long faded. The perpetrators of the violence are long gone, and those who have terrorized the women have dispersed; there are no witnesses. Who would believe these women? The only proof that a woman's stories of violence have even happened is silenced by the stigma and taboo to talk about them. In the case of wartime trauma victims, Agamben (1999) and Henry (2010) attribute their silence to the limitation of language in representing trauma and in conveying the inexplicability of their experience. To recount the story is to be re-traumatized by the unspeakable. Not to speak about the unspeakable is to foreclose the possibility of any asylum claims. This "unspeakability" of rape trauma makes proper representation impossible. To make themselves believable, rape victims are known to have sought doctor's letters to draw on the weight of medical authority to validate the accounts they have gone through (Fassin and d'Halluin 2005, 602).

RAPE VICTIMS IN COURT

While women victims struggle to speak of the unspeakable and make themselves believed, law demands a witness to "accurately testify to certain events in a chronological and rational fashion" (Henry 2010, 1105). The narrow focus of the trial on rape is on the physical aspect of the rape itself. The court wants to know: Was there penetration? How many times did he/they do it? Why was there no mention of the rape in the first investigation? The focus is on the inconsistencies in reporting the rape, rather than on the number of considerations that could prevent a woman from speaking about her experience.

These externally imposed obstacles forces "silence on many victims in the aftermath, followed by the inarticulation of the experience and the distortion and manipulation of this within the public context" (Henry 2010, 1114). As a result, women are found not to be believable because of the "discrepancies" in their accounts, without any consideration to the effects of trauma on one's ability to recall such events in "a chronological or rational fashion."

Furthermore, as reported by Spijkerboer's (2000) examination of 252 women asylum claimants, he found a "tendency in refugee law practice to consider politics as the main issue in the refugee definition" (12–13). An asylum application is constructed by a myriad of people. The context of the construction of an asylum application, and the making of an asylum decision, is dominated by the notion of a "political refugee." As a consequence, "the question of what is political is of primary importance. Some acts are seen as insufficiently serious to constitute persecution while others are seen as serious but nevertheless as part of the normal situation in the country of origin" (45). In the process, the persecution of women is counted only as personal harm and not as political persecution (Kelly 1997), despite the fact that scholars have long recognized rape as a "weapon of war."

Due to the shame suffered and their reluctance to talk about it, women often miss the one-year deadline, consequently affecting women more than men. The gap between a woman's arrival in a country to finding the courage to file a petition can span several years, demonstrating that the victims "suffered from severe trauma and/or depression that prevented them from talking [about] the harm they suffered" (Arbel, Dauvergne, and Millbank 2014, 66). A group of physicians from Physicians for Human Rights have petitioned the abolishment of the "One Year Bar" for the law to take into account the special circumstances affecting women (Hustings 2010).

By linking the rape against Mrs. Harianto to the rape of the Chinese women in the community during May 1998 in Indonesia, I am also suggesting the political nature of the acts of rape, rather than on the randomness of the incident.

Despite these concerns, however, under an ideal ethnographic condition of empathetic asking and listening, her story slowly came out. The story that she revealed was more than just about the incidents of gang rape: it was about what the rape did in terms of shame and her sense of regret towards her caring husband.

In telling the story of Mrs. Harianto, I have tried to delink sex from gender. While her physical body may have healed, the wounds of her gender roles are irreparable. Therefore, she must escape by total social isolation or to a new country where she knows no one. In asylum petitions on MPSG, I have emphasized careful attention to documenting the damage and persecution in the absence of physical evidentiary proofs by providing a description of the social roles she played and an explanation on how the knowledge of her rape within her Chinese Catholic community would damage her social identity.

Years later, I telephoned Mrs. Harianto to ask for permission to include her story in my book. She told me that she had been looking for me all these years. "Everything is ok now," she said. I knew immediately what she meant by that. Even if time had not healed what had happened to her, she was finally able to resume an intimate relationship with her husband. She was able to reciprocate his love with care for him.

Chapter 10

Dowry Dispute:

A Case for the Law Firm of Seyfarth Shaw

Attorney Amanda Sonneborn from Seyfarth Shaw, a major law firm in Chicago called me in 2009 to help her client, Rani, daughter of Jayanathan, an Indian woman from Malaysia, and a victim of domestic violence who had applied for asylum in the United States. I was curious how Attorney Sonneborn found my name. Sonneborn told me that her law firm had undertaken a pro bono case from the National Immigration and Justice Center in Chicago, but did not have an expert on Indian women from Malaysia. She contacted about a dozen academics in Chicago and on the East Coast but none could help until someone mentioned Dr. Aihwa Ong, an anthropologist at the University of California at Berkeley who knew of my work. I wanted to tell Sonneborn I was neither an expert on Indians in Malaysia nor on domestic abuse, but who else could I refer the case to? Who would Rani turn to? By 2009, I had the experience of helping attorneys on about two dozen cases; the success of many of these asylum cases reminds me that anthropology can tell a better and more complete human story. Therefore, I agreed to talk to Rani.

I interviewed Rani through a number of conference calls set up by Sonneborn, who was in Chicago, with Rani in Indiana, and myself in Los Angeles. Through these calls, and later by direct phone contact with Rani, I was able to reconstruct her experience of persecution and her fear of returning to Malaysia.

RANI'S PROBLEMS

Rani's problems began when she was promised in marriage to Raju, son of Rajakumar, a fellow Malaysian of Indian origin, who had studied engineering in the United States. By Malaysian standard, his American engineering degree was considered an exceptionally handsome family investment, so he was a great catch. At first, Rani was a good match too. Her two year college education and some work experience outside the home were considered more than adequate by most families because most women in Malaysia (about 60 percent) do not even attend college.

Rani and Raju's marriage was arranged through family friends who knew both families. They met at Rani's house. Raju's family asked Rani's parents as dowry to buy him a car or a house, or a sum of Malaysian Ringgit $30,000 (about US$10,000; close to a year's salary for a teacher or a nurse in Malaysia). Rani's family agreed to provide a dowry, jewelry for Rani, as well as kitchen and household furnishings for the newlyweds.

Rani and Raju's engagement took place the day before Raju was to leave for his job in the United States. Rani's parents did not have enough money at hand for the full dowry but they promised to pay in full before the wedding. Both families went ahead without the complete sum of the promised dowry, with Rani's family paying for the engagement party.

Rani's parents are both Malaysian-born Indian from Kerala, located on the Southwestern tip of India. Her father holds a respectable white-collar job in a rubber plantation company. She has an unmarried older brother who lives at home with her parents. As a good daughter, she gives her whole paycheck from working as a waitress to her parents, keeping $100 for bus fare. At home, besides English and Malay, they speak Tamil and a closely related Malayalam Indian language.

Raju's parents are both Tamil-speaking, but of Telugu and Ceylonese origin. Raju is the only son, and lives at home with his parents and his unmarried sister. Telugu speakers are mainly from the states of Andhra Pradesh, Telangana, Puducherry in Central and Eastern India and the neighboring Southern state of Tamil Nadu. Tamils are the people from Tamil Nadu, and Kerala in Southwestern India.

Perhaps angry because of the inadequate dowry, Rani's future in-laws began to treat her as a maid, demanding that she cook, do the laundry and ironing—including those of Raju's sister's laundry—and to clean the house during her weekend visits. They would beat her when the work was not done to their standard. Her future father-in-law demanded money from Rani every month. If she refused to visit his parents' home, Raju would get upset.

Rani told me that Raju's family said she was of a different caste, not worthy of their son. They had invested a lot of money in him, and he could have married someone better. Rani herself believed she would never be good enough to satisfy them. To avoid shame to the family, her parents would not let her withdraw from the engagement; they were afraid their relatives, friends, and neighbors would gossip so they did not want to change the wedding plans. Her husband's family did not want to stop it either. Rani said,

"It was a terribly unhappy situation. I was only 21, scared, and did not know what to do. The only thing I could do was to obey them."

While working in the United States, Raju gave his paycheck to his parents, as a good son should. Later, Raju returned to Malaysia to marry Rani. Rani's mother gave her some gold jewelry, paid for the wedding, and dinner for one hundred guests. Rani said she did not know the exact amount her parents gave Raju's family in dowry.

A month after the wedding, Rani accompanied Raju to the United States.

RAJU'S VIOLENCE AGAINST RANI

While the couple was in the United States, Rani gave birth to their daughter. After two years in the United States, the couple and their baby returned to Malaysia. As is the custom, Rani and her daughter moved in with Raju's parents. However, Rani's in-laws resumed their abuse. Rani claimed that her in-laws constantly complained to her husband about her, who then began mentally and physically abusing Rani, too. Rani said, "When his parents complained about me, he would throw at me whatever was within reach—keys, biscuit tins, dishes, furniture."

"When they said the toilet was not cleaned properly, he would watch over the cleaning and when I did not do it right, he would scoop up the toilet water and throw it on my face."

"When they complained I did not cook properly, Raju would get angry, shout, and throw things at me and physically hurt me." "He would pull my hair, kick me, and hit me the way 'a boxer boxes his opponent.'"

"In fact, he would beat me so that his parents did not have to do it as much." That is, as a devoted son, he did it for them. The humiliation and beating took place in front of her daughter, her parents, his parents, and her brother. Rani said her husband told her he did not want her and their daughter in his life. He wanted to give his daughter up for adoption or to his sister.

Besides Raju's violent abuse of Rani, I also recorded specific episodes in great detail, told below, as a part of her asylum petition on the persecution she had suffered at the hands of her husband and her in-laws. I included her reports to the police, in which she was told to go back to her husband.

While listening to Rani, I was reminded of the similarity between her situation and research findings in China where "the husband is accorded with the ultimate authority in family issues, including financial decisions. The wife, however, is assigned with the role of a daughter, a wife, and a mother who is obedient to the father before marriage, to the husband after marriage" (Zheng 2015, 155–56), and where this patriarchal framework has created a space where intimate partner violence is viewed as a "private family issue," leading wives to accept these violations despite their constant humiliation and pain.

ABANDONMENT AND ENDANGERMENT OF RANI AND HER DAUGHTER

When Raju purchased a new home and moved Rani and their baby into it, his abuse became more premeditated. In one instance, Rani recalled her husband taking her and their daughter out for a drive; Rani had been delighted for the opportunity, but her husband took them to a remote area far outside the city where he forced them both out of the car, then left them behind. Forced to carry her daughter under the tropical sun for miles, Rani walked home. When she arrived, she was forced to wait outside as she had no key and no money for transportation to her parents' home. Instead, she waited, feeding her baby and being ignored by neighbors whom she was also too embarrassed to ask for help. Rani dozed off during the night while holding her baby in her arms.

The next morning, she woke, fed her baby, and then walked to a nearby park where she waited. When her husband returned around noon the following day, she said he did not speak to her. Raju merely stared, and out of fear, Rani refrained from confronting him, choosing not to question why he abandoned her and their baby. Rani was too afraid to speak because she was frightened Raju would beat her. She felt no one would defend her, so she endured it.

SLAVE-LIKE EXPLOITATION OF RANI'S LABOR

For a year and a half in 2007, Rani said her husband had an agreement with her that she was to make money for him while his parents would care for their granddaughter. Raju rented a stall in the market and told Rani to sell soda and burgers. Rani would work the whole day, from 9:00 a.m. to 11:00 p.m. She did not have any help and was forced to give all the money to her husband. Rani said, "I worked like a slave," and was constantly tired. Rani believed that perhaps the forced labor she performed for her husband was a way for him to make up the dowry money her parents had owed him. Rani said Raju rationalized her misery by saying "you are fated to marry me, and therefore this is your fate." Rani said she refused to accept her fate and later found a job as a preschool teacher. But Raju would physically injure her to keep her from going to work.

MAKING RANI A "BAD" WOMAN

Raju's treatment towards Rani took a strange turn when he invited strangers, men Rani had never met before, to the house and asked Rani to cook for them. While Rani was preparing food for the men, her husband would leave the house. She said the strangers would eat, get drunk, and sleep in the house. Rani did not feel safe when she was alone with the strangers. Immediately after cooking, she would lock herself and her daughter in the bedroom to prevent anything from happening. Rani suspected her husband wanted to make money by "selling her" to the strangers, or by creating an opportunity for them to have sex with her, or to rape her. She said it would be very easy for him to accuse her of inviting men to their home while he was away. With such an excuse, he could easily justify killing her. Rani had good reason not to ask her husband about the men. She said he became more violent and tried to rape her whenever she asked him about anything. To Rani, being killed by her husband was a constant, daily reality.

Rani was exhausted and needed help looking after the baby "so she could sleep for a couple of days." She told her family about her suffering, but they refused to help. Rani's mother thought her problem was due to "bad karma," and told her brother not to help her. After being violently abused by her husband, Rani would return to her parents' house where her mother would allow her to stay for only a couple of days.

Rani said she was hurting emotionally and physically from the cruelty inflicted by her husband and his family and the rejection from her own parents. She said her brain was hurting, and was desperate for help. Her brother told her to report to the police.

RANI GOES TO THE POLICE

Rani recounted the story: "When I went to the police, the woman officer sent me to the chief, also another woman. But the chief did not even try to see the bruises on my body. She only said, 'You cannot do that to your husband. You need to stay together. Otherwise, your husband will start drinking.' They gave me all the cultural reasons. I told the police officers about the rape, and asked them to put it in the report. They said he was my husband and they cannot put rape in a report."

Rani went to the police three times but was told the same thing every time. The final time Rani made a police report, she was told to get a doctor's report. When she returned with the report, the chief told her that she had already been there three times and were not interested in helping her. The chief stated,

"If you are not working on your marriage, we can't help you." She added, "Men have power, you must let men be themselves. If a husband has another woman, you can't ask about it, because that is how it is in the Muslim culture. Women must obey and let the husband do whatever he wants. That is how a marriage is going to work." The Malay woman police inspector, who is a Muslim, even told her, "You are so lucky, your husband has only one wife. My husband can have up to four wives." Rani thought to herself: "I am not a Malay and a Muslim. I am an Indian and a Hindu. The police were applying Muslim standards on me as a Hindu woman." She speculated that the police might restrain her husband if she had given a bribe. But she had no money for a bribe.

Rani said, "There was no help anywhere. My body was 'shutting down' from the beating and the bleeding." She planned to escape to the United States where she knew some people in the Midwest.

RANI'S ESCAPE TO THE UNITED STATES

Before leaving, Rani gathered all her personal documents and her daughter's American passport. She and her daughter stayed with different girlfriends in the city; each time they were only a few steps ahead of her husband and his friends from finding them. She applied for a tourist visa and borrowed money for an airline ticket. She arrived at the Midwest home of a friend of her husband's, also of Malaysian Indian origin, married to an American woman. The couple had invited her to visit if she should return to the United States. Rani took up their offer.

Rani said it was a strange situation. The couple picked her up from the airport in Chicago and drove her and her baby to their home in a city about a hundred miles south of Chicago in the state of Indiana. They asked her how much she had brought with her and made her buy them a computer. She bought one at Walmart for $800 and gave an additional $300 to their friend from the $2,000 she had brought with her. They obtained a social security number for Rani's American born baby. They wanted to use it to get food-stamps but Rani did not know if that was the real reason. They also wanted Rani to work as a hostess at a local bar because her husband's friend knew the owner. Rani refused. In the arrangement, they let her stay in their basement in exchange for housekeeping and babysitting. They gave her a cell phone but the husband's friend would check her calls on the phone every day.

In October 2007, Rani's daughter had a toothache. Without getting any help from her host, she asked for a ride from the host's sister to see a dentist who offered a "payment plan" in his advertisement. Rani also decided to use the opportunity to meet up with another friend she knew from her previous visit, and told her ride she would return home by herself.

Rani confided in her other friend, Lisa, a policewoman, who invited her to stay at her house until they figured out what to do with Rani and her baby.

When Rani's host learned that Rani had left the house she was furious and called the police to report her for "stealing." Fortunately, Lisa, intervened and immediately took Rani and her baby into her home. She also checked with her boss at the police station on how to help Rani in her situation.

While staying at Lisa's home, Rani learned about asylum from a fellow immigrant at a children's playground. She applied online and when she finally met with an immigration officer, she was advised to seek help from an attorney. Rani said she went from one attorney's office to another asking for help. Altogether, she visited twelve attorneys but none could help her. "I collected a lot of nice shiny brochures from those visits," she recalled. Fortunately, one attorney called someone he knew in New York City. Rani said she had told this particular attorney that she had exhausted her search for an attorney. The attorney told her to wait while he went to the next room to make a phone call. When he returned, he told Rani to call the National Immigration and Justice Center (NIJC) in Chicago. The NIJC contacted Seyfarth Shaw to help Rani.

After countless hours detailing Rani's experience of violence and abuse by her husband, I prepared a report and submitted it to Sonneborn in 2010. The case was postponed until 2011, then again until May 2014. The postponement gave us a chance to improve the asylum petition.

COLLABORATION BETWEEN LAW AND ANTHROPOLOGY

In December 2013, as the date for the Merit Hearing grew closer, Attorney Chris Busey was assigned to work on the case with me. Another attorney, Abigail Cahak, joined us as well. Attorney Busey told me that asylum work was new to him, whereas I had experience with more than two dozen cases by then. Up to that point, in my preparation of Rani's case, I was concentrating on documenting the details of violence against Rani by her husband, his family, and his friends in the United States.

In discussing the case with the attorneys, Attorney Busey suggested including in the report Malaysia's dual legal system of civil and Sharia laws, and the position of Indians in multiethnic Malaysia. Attorney Cahak suggested inclusion of gender issues, and questions on labor relations. They recommended several articles, which I incorporated into a new report.

At that point in my research on Rani, these topics seemed quite unrelated to her case of violent domestic abuse. The details of abuse by her husband were so overwhelming. By meticulously providing detailed documentation of the abuse Rani had suffered, and her repeated request for help from the police, I felt confident that Rani had demonstrated that the "government was unwilling and unable to help her." By its refusal to help, not to mention the police women's use of cultural and religious grounds to deny Rani help, I wondered how much more evidence we would need in order to prove she was persecuted because of her "Membership in a Particular Social Group"? (see part II). I was frustrated that a woman who barely survived violent domestic abuse must justify persecution against her by discussing theories on gender relations, labor relations, India's minority positions in Malaysia, and the country's dual legal systems.

I felt that these issues were only peripherally related for an asylum seeker desperate for help. I wondered if the difficulty stemmed from her gender, since persecution based on gender is not an automatic ground for asylum protection. I also thought perhaps issues of Indian women were foreign to an educated American public of attorneys in general, and especially that of an Indian woman from Malaysia in particular. Rani had visited about a dozen attorneys in a Midwestern city without getting help, and Attorney Amanda Sonnoeborn had contacted more than a dozen academics in the United States, including Ivy League institutions, and could not find an academic able to undertake Seyfarth Shaw's pro bono case with the National Immigration and Justice Center. I wondered how far I would have to go for my investigation to verify the truth of what happened to Rani, an asylum seeker whose identity, based on gender, color, caste, culture, religion, and education, was all wrapped up into the anthropological figure?

Working on Rani's case reminded me of Ms. Chun's forced abortion case (part IV, chapter 11) where the judge demanded to know whether Ms. Chun remembered the nurse showing her the aborted fetus from the left- or the right-hand side of the hospital bed. If the much-desired child was already aborted, why did it matter from which side of the bed she saw it? This incredulous question drove me to think of the expectations needed for an asylum case. At what point should I stop probing the asylum seekers with ridiculous questions so as to satisfy the unanticipated demands of the asylum adjudicators? Perhaps it was not simply about how much information or evidence the asylum adjudicators need in order to verify the truth of a case. In my exasperation, I was beginning to feel that it was a deliberate attempt to turn away the asylum seekers.

Providing documentation on persecution based on MPSG grounds appears to be governed by a different set of rules. When the asylum seeker's life was at stake, I had to keep pursuing the topics of gender, color, caste, culture, religion, and education regardless of their relevance to her abuse.

GENDER RELATIONS OR CASTE RELATIONS IN DOWRY DISPUTE?

While gender relations are topics covered easily by academics in the West, gender relations research is underdeveloped in Malaysia. Given Malaysia's multiethnic populations, with Malay being the majority (60 percent), Indian being the third largest (12 percent), and the Chinese in between (25 percent), few social science research priorities are focused on Indians, much less on gender relations within the Indian communities.

With the goal of leaving no stone unturned in helping Rani, I conducted a second round of interviews with her. I sent her a link to an article in the *Wall Street Journal* (December 13, 2013) of a story very similar to hers where a policewoman in Delhi died in the hands of her husband's parents due to her inability to provide more dowry. I asked Rani if the experience of the women in India sounded similar to hers; I wanted to know if the inadequate dowry caused her husband's family to be mean to her and whether caste played a part as well.

"Yes, inadequate dowry and caste did play a role in my abuse. And also his higher education and I did not have degree like he has," came the email reply.

When anthropologists teach about the society and culture of India, we often mention castes as one of the cultural attributes of Indian society (Heinz 1999). And even though the caste system was constitutionally abolished in India in 1950, it is still implemented in rural areas. Caste is almost never mentioned in the literature on Indians in Malaysia. On the other hand, according to news from the *Times of India* (2013) and from statistics published by the Indian government, one woman in India dies every hour due to "dowry death."

According to the custom on dowry, parents give their daughter a dowry at her wedding, as an inheritance from the parents to their daughter (Heinz 1999). Recent social science research on dowry discovered its metamorphosis from a gift from parents to a daughter into a reason for murder and abuse of young wives in modern day India. According to Oldenburg's (2002) historical research in the Punjab area of India, laws under British colonial rule prevented women from holding property. Traditional dowries intended for a daughter were then given to the husband. In time, with a monetized economy and opportunities for modern economic development, the dowry brought in by the bride has turned into a "cash cow" to finance the purchase of motorcycles, household furniture, the payment of tuition fees for a husband's college education, or his pet investment projects. If the first young wife is "killed accidently," often by a "kitchen fire," as reported in many news accounts of "dowry deaths," the husband is then free to marry another woman, with a new dowry that his family could expect from the woman's family.

In trying to understand the ferocity of violence that Raju and his family had inflicted on Rani, I speculated that perhaps Raju's family viewed their investment in Raju's American education as benefiting Rani through his higher income and higher status. Raju was presumably a "better catch" as a husband to Rani than she was as a wife to Raju, especially since she did not pay up her promised dowry. Rani had mentioned that she had less education than Raju a number of times. In India, education is equated with status, and in the marriage arrangement between Raju and Rani, her lesser education was another strike against her unless she could translate her lower education and social standing into monetary benefits to Raju's family.

In interpreting Rani's story closely, the caste origin of both families was never mentioned. I did not ask, because I considered caste confined to anthropological textbooks on India. I wondered however, did the "color" of Rani and Raju play a part in their relationship?

Color was mentioned during my second round of interviews with Rani. She said her husband and his family are of Telugu and Ceylonese mix and consider themselves north Indian because her husband is "very light skin[ned]." Rani's parents are from Kerala, and of "darker skin color."

I could not tell Rani's "color" because I conducted interviews with her by phone, texting, and email. I had never met Raju, or nor have I even seen a picture of him. My assessment of the importance of color in Indian society was based on the commercials on whitening creams and powders one sees on Indian televisions at Indian restaurants, as well as advertisements on internet websites. The message is clear: lighter skin color is better than darker skin color. Watching the nonstop Bollywood dancers on Indian television, I have often thought, "They do not look like the Tamil Indian friends, classmates, and neighbors I grew up with in Brickfields, now 'India Town,' in Kuala Lumpur."

India is a huge country; a diversity of peoples is expected. A hierarchy based on color was not unexpected but rarely brought up in my discussions of Indians in Malaysia. In the history of the Indians in Malaysia, the focus has always been about their position vis-à-vis the Malays and the Chinese in a Malay-dominated country. In the deal struck during Malaysia's independence in 1957, Malays were given special privileges while the Chinese and the Indians gained citizenship in the agreement. Ethnicity and religion have long been the dominant forces affecting Malaysian Indian life expressed in terms of communal relations. Discussion of the Indians is often centered on the lower socioeconomic indices of the Indian rubber estate workers who were brought to British Malaya to work in the plantation economy. The majority of the rubber plantation workers are Tamils from South India. The other group of Indians, less acknowledged in the literature, are the Indians who were brought there to run the railways and the civil service in the British colonial administration in Malaya. For example, Mr. Geraldo Gomes's parents were brought from Goa, a former Portuguese colony in Western India to start the Malaya symphony. Mr. Gomes was my high school music and history teacher at Vivekananda, an Indian missionary school. He was also a part of the Goan Indian diaspora, according to anthropologist Professor Alberto Gomes, his nephew, at the University of Latrobe in Australia, at a talk given at California State University, Los Angeles, some years ago. Many Malaysian attorneys are of Northern Indian Punjabi origin, based on their names such as Singh, Kaur, and Gill. Similarly, the *jaga*, or security guards, guarding Malaysian banks and jewelry stores, distinguishable by their turban required of all Sikh men, are also mostly from the Punjab area. Others, based on the languages they speak in Malaysia: Malayalam, Sinhalese, Tamil, Ceylonese—and names, such as Subramanian, Kumar, Pillay, Nathan, Jyothi, Prasad, are indicative of their diversity. In this great diversity, while caste may have been forgotten (on purpose by those from the lower castes), color may have emerged in Raju's family, to show their higher status, compared to the darker skin color belonging to Rani's parents' of South Indian origin.

Articulating Rani's hidden story reveals how her dowry conflict goes further back and is embedded in both India's history and Malaysia's history—and their contemporary developments. To Raju's family, Rani's background as a Tamil, whose father's work is related to the former rubber plantation, combined with Rani's relative lack of education, has justified their abuse when the dowry was not inadequate. That is, gender relations are expressed through a combination of caste, color, and class.

SHARIA LAW IN THE DOMESTIC ABUSE OF A HINDU WOMAN?

Most individuals have the impression that Malaysia is a beautiful, peaceful country. In the imaginations of such individuals, it does not have headline-grabbing natural disasters or man-made calamities. Until the disappearance of Flight MH 370, the shooting down of a Malaysian airline over Ukraine, the reporting of Anwar's sodomy trials, or Najib's scandal on the major international media, there was no reason to know about Malaysia.

With the West's interest in the Muslim world, the focus is often on the Middle East. Yet Southeast Asia is home to the world's largest Muslim population, found principally in Indonesia and Malaysia. However, Malaysia is overshadowed by the sheer size of the Muslim population in

Indonesia: 205 million in Indonesia compared to 16.8 in Malaysia (Malaysian Digest 2015; Islamic Tourism Centre of Malaysia 2017).

Given Malaysia's multiethnic and multireligious nature, Sharia law is not imposed on the non-Muslim. However, Malay men and women, who are good Muslims, must be mindful of Islam's teachings in everyday practices. That is, Islam is a way of life. As a result, the boundaries between Sharia laws, the *adat*, or customary practices of the indigenous Malay world, and the professional training of the modern civil servants, are blurred.

Therefore, the women police inspectors who saw Rani may have been sympathetic to the abuse she had suffered in the hands of her husband, but to them, Rani only has to deal with a husband who has only one wife. For Muslim women, their husbands can have up to four wives, and the wife has no say whatsoever whether he marries one, two, or three more women. Our views of the world are colored by our own experiences. The police inspector told her, "You are lucky, your husband has only one wife. My husband can have four." The police inspector implied that it was easier for a woman to deal with a husband who has only a wife versus a husband who can have up to four wives. Perhaps the woman police inspector was expressing her own vulnerability as a Muslim wife. If a Muslim husband does not want his wife, all he has to do is to pronounce three times his intention to divorce her, even though as a good husband he is expected to provide adequately for all his wives. But in all aspects of life, there is always a gap between the ideal and the actual. To women whose economic security depends on their husband, and to all the wives whose vows of love and devotion have been for their husband over the years, is this where the road will lead?

Around the time of Rani's report to the police for protection, an issue circulating around Malaysian media was the story of a Muslim man who divorced his wife by SMS, or text messaging. The Sharia court took up the matter and ruled that divorce by texting was legitimate. Sisters in Islam, a Malaysian nonprofit organization, took issue and argued matters of divorce cannot be terminated in such a callous fashion, but to no avail. Sisters in Islam then examined the Koran and used their Koran-based evidence to argue against divorce by texting/SMS, but they failed again to stop the Sharia court's interpretation.

Perhaps the Malaysian women police inspectors were voicing their own powerlessness as Muslim women who faced the possibility of a husband who could end an intimate relationship of marriage with such insensitivity (*Ilhan*), simply by announcing divorce by text/SMS. Therefore, in comparison with Rani's experience of domestic abuse, they were both victims of unequal gender relations, whether a Hindu woman under a transformed dowry system or a Muslim woman under Sharia law.

The implication of the unexpected remark by the police inspector suggests the need for culturally sensitive intellectual tools the police (as well as social workers and other agencies of the state) could use in providing service to a diverse citizenry. However, I did not include the need of the Muslim women police to receive more professional training working in a country with great diversity in my report. First of all, I maintain that the policy aspect of police cultural sensitivity training is irrelevant to the horrific abuse Rani has already suffered. Second, in the hands of an unsympathetic adjudicator, I could be asked, perhaps, "Aren't there Police Inspectors who are either Chinese or Indian?" or "Couldn't Rani go to a different police station and find a sympathetic police who would listen to her?" If the answer is "yes" to either question, it would be easy for the asylum adjudicators to argue that Rani could be returned to Malaysia and find a representative of the government who was willing to protect her. Even though that is a theoretical possibility, Rani may not be able to wait to be properly situated so that the chance of finding such a kinder police inspector will intersect with her life. Until then, Sharia law works through Muslim civil servants doing their job with unintended impacts even on a Hindu woman.

RANI'S MERIT HEARING

In April of 2014, I flew to Chicago and met Rani, her daughter, and her three attorneys at Seyfarth Shaw for the very first time. After a quick lunch, we walked over to the courthouse. At the courthouse, I later met Attorney Diane Tafur from the National Immigration and Justice Center, who had referred Rani's case to Seyfarth Shaw.

The attorneys and I strategized our court appearance. We decided it was best not to let Rani's daughter be present during Rani's testimony. However, it was also important for the judge and trial attorney to see her. So we decided that I would walk into the courtroom with Rani's daughter, predicting that the Judge would sequester me for Rani's testimony. Our predictions were correct, and I left the courtroom, taking Rani's daughter along with me.

The hearing dragged on. Rani's daughter and I chatted, sitting on chairs in the hallway. She told me she liked Chinese food but did not know how to make it. She said she wanted to learn. So, in the Chicago courtroom, I gave her instructions on how to make an "egg flower soup" by dropping a beaten egg into a boiling soup stock she is already familiar with from the seasoning package of Ramen noodles, with a reminder to make it under her mother's supervision.

It was getting late for an eight-to-five court day. The judge said he did not want to begin my testimony at 4:30 p.m. so he postponed it until the following month. However, he did agree to let me testify by phone with a landline from my office under the condition that my office be locked during the testimony.

On the day of the testimony in May of 2014, I woke up to a text from my son-in-law in London informing me that my daughter had just given birth to my first grandchild. I had no time to ask about the details, but was relieved to learn that both mother and child were well.

That morning, I had to concentrate on another mother and her child. I took an early train to the office, just in case there was a delay on the Metrolink. Outside my office door, I posted a sign, “Do Not Disturb. Interview in Progress.” In the morning, Chris Busey and I went over the major points of my testimony. Later, he monitored the progress from the courtroom in Chicago to alert me when I would be called to testify.

I cleared my office desk, turned off the computer, and I was ready for battle. I stood up during the interview even though no one was watching me. During the hearing, the government tried to disqualify me as an expert witness and relentlessly questioned me for three solid hours. I was shell-shocked by the time I came out of my office.

I had an anthropology class in the afternoon. My students were eager to hear about what had happened “in court” earlier in the day. I was happy to recall the details of the exchange for them.

DISQUALIFYING THE ANTHROPOLOGICAL EXPERT WITNESS

“Ms. Ngin, you have done research in Malaysia. But you have also done research in China and Indonesia. By doing research in the other areas, doesn’t that make your research too general?” the Government Counsel fired the first shot to try to disqualify me as an expert witness.

“In anthropology, we operate with two major principles. First, we use a holistic perspective where we take everything into account. Second, there is the comparative perspective where we are required to conduct research in other places for the purpose of making comparison.”

“Have you published any research on the Indian dowry system?”

“No.”

“Ms. Ngin, going down your resume, have you published any research on domestic abuse?”

“No.”

“Have you published any research on divorce?”

“No, but I have done research in the Indian community. . . .” I was going to talk about the Focus Group Discussions among the Indians in the town in

Nillai in Malaysia on intergenerational relations for the RAND Corporation when she interrupted my testimony.

"Given that she has not done research in the area related to the petitioner, I object to qualifying her as an expert."

Fortunately, the Judge came to my defense. "If her research is on family relations and on social relations, divorce falls within family relations."

Reluctantly, the Government Counsel allowed me to be qualified as a "lay witness" and not an expert witness. We moved on with the questioning. Later, Attorney Chris Busey questioned me about the research I had recently conducted with my students in Orange County, California. Students in my class participated in a project sponsored by the Orange County Human Relations Commission with the collaboration of three black churches in the county to listen to the voices of the congregation in response to the racist attacks against an African American family in the City of Yorba Linda in Orange County.

"Dr. Ngin, in your resume, you have published something on a 'Listening Session' in the African American churches in Orange County, California. Could you please explain that?"

"What does that have to do with dowry dispute in Malaysia?" The Government Counsel snapped at Attorney Chris Busey before I could proceed with the answer. I was surprised, but delighted by the question and answered immediately.

"It has to do with my research on social exclusion, whether it is racism against the African Americans in Orange County in California or against the Indians under Malaysia's version of affirmative action policy, known as the '*bumiputra* policy.'" My knowledge on exclusionary practices in both the United States and Malaysia seemed to have stopped the Government Counsel.

I also thought Attorney Busey's question was brilliant and strategic. Perhaps it was a subtle reminder to the Government Counsel, who is an African American, on the racism she herself, or someone she has known, might have experienced in the United States. Does the racism in the United States not remind her of the similar exclusion of Indians under Malaysia's *bumiputra* policy? How can she not see the parallel between the two minority groups who are both subjects of exclusion in their respective country?

Raju's family was probably thinking that they would not have had to spend huge sums paying for Raju's American engineering degree if he had been a Malay and therefore qualified for loans and scholarship under the *bumiputra* policy. Rani's family was also probably thinking if Rani had been a Malay, she would have qualified for financial support and gone beyond a two-year college education. But as these topics are considered seditious, they are not discussed in public, despite being on the mind of every non-*bumiputra* in Malaysia.

What I had at first considered tangentially related, the subject of labor relations actually came up in the questions regarding whether or not Rani could be relocated and find livelihood in Malaysia, should they be returned there. The Government Counsel asked me, "Could Rani not learn Chinese so she can get a job in the Chinese community?" If the Government Counsel thought the expertise of a sociocultural anthropologist should be narrow and particular, then her question on the likelihood of a twenty-eight-year-old Malaysian Indian woman learning Mandarin Chinese in order to get work in the Chinese community hinges on one that requires knowledge that is both broad and diffused. To come up with an answer that meets adequate academic standards, I would need to know about theories on foreign language acquisition by adults, the cultural histories on the confluences of the Indian and the Chinese diaspora meeting in a former British colony with its own nation-building language policies, Rani's socioeconomic background and language inclination, and the opportunity of her learning Mandarin Chinese in the crossroads of East and West. The court for an asylum petitioner's Merit Hearing is neither the appropriate place nor time to elaborate these strands of ideas, so I decided to answer the question with a firm "No" without further elaboration. I did not volunteer the information that Malay was the lingua franca in multiethnic Malaysia. It is also a language learned in school by all pupils. There is no need for Rani to learn Mandarin Chinese. If she found work in the Chinese community, she could easily speak in Malay, or English, to communicate with the Chinese. If she has a knack for learning a new language, she could also pick up any of the Chinese dialects of Cantonese or Hokkien, if she wants to, depending on where she ends up, just as I picked up rudimentary Tamil while growing up in an Indian community in Kuala Lumpur. I did not expect an attorney to have much knowledge on a country or a culture. Since there was no logic to her questioning, I concluded that it was aimed at rattling me in order to disqualify me.

Changing the subject, the Government Counsel asked me a question about Rani's husband wanting to meet his daughter and what that would entail psychologically for the father and the daughter. In my interviews with Rani, she had never mentioned anything about her husband wanting to meet his daughter. Have I missed anything? It was a subject I had not thought about and I did not know the answer. Thinking about what would happen if Rani should be returned to her husband, I stood my ground. So boldly, I asked, "Are you asking me a hypothetical question?" The Government Counsel did not pursue that line of questioning. Perhaps she was grasping for straws when she asked me that question. Reflecting on her question much later on, I realized it was intended to trap me into answering as a psychologist. Once I did, she would discredit me for posing as a psychologist and therefore disqualify me again.

Later that evening on the train home, I received a call on my mobile phone from Rani. She said that Diana Tafur, the attorney from the National Immigration and Justice Center, told her to call me and say, "The Judge agreed with the professor. I will get my asylum if the government does not appeal." From the reflection on the train window, I could see tears streaming down my face. The long ordeal was over for Rani and her daughter. I thought of my own daughter giving birth to her new baby that morning. While visiting my daughter and seeing my first grandson for the first time four months later, I apologized for not being there during the birth of her baby. My daughter said lovingly, "Mom, I understand you were in court to help another mother and her baby."

REFLECTING ON THE HEARING WITH THE ATTORNEYS

The next day, I joined Diana Tafur and Chris Busey on a phone call to discuss their impressions of the hearing in Chicago. Since then, I had time to ponder the questions from the government attorney, the most important of which was her wish to send Rani and her daughter back to Malaysia. Attorney Diane Tafur complimented me for refusing to back down on that question.

I had argued that if she were to return home, she would visit her mother who may let her stay for a few days, but according to Indian custom of patrilocality, a married woman's place is with her husband's family (Mahmud 2017). Rani's mother, like before, would send her daughter away. In addition, once Rani was home, relatives and friends would hear about it, as well as her husband's family through the temple they go to.

There was no reason to believe her husband would look kindly upon her. She had already shamed him by escaping his grip while she was in Malaysia. She caused him additional shame through his friend in the United States whom Rani stayed with when she first arrived. In fact, it could be the chance for Mr. Raju to punish her for the embarrassment she caused. If Rani was returned, could she become one of those women who are murdered in "dowry deaths"? If she has no future in the Indian community, her future getting a job with the government to become self-sufficient is equally bleak. As a single mother without the social support of family or community, there aren't too many jobs she can take. Given Malaysia's *bumiputra* policy, the chances of Rani getting a secure government job is quite slim. I thought to myself, perhaps Rani could work in the service sector given Malaysia's labor shortage. But, again, Rani also needs familial support for her daughter while she works. And the chances of discovery and death by her husband are forever present. For now, Rani and her daughter are assured of safety from abuse thanks to a judge who listened to the opinion of "a professor."

COLLABORATION BETWEEN ANTHROPOLOGY AND LAW

Anthropological collaboration with law can be used strategically to help in the adjudication of asylum cases. In helping the attorney of the asylum seeker, anthropology helps by telling a better story of persecution contextualized within the country of origin, the sociocultural background of the asylum seeker, and political and other issues in the community where the asylum seeker sought help. This more complete story humanizes the asylum seekers and makes their application sound more credible. In helping the judges, we provide a more holistic context for an asylum seeker's story and explanations for the need for an application and a favorable decision. In fact, in the case of Rani, the attorneys' suggestions to include topics that are only tangentially related to Rani's violent abuse led to a report that provided a much larger picture of the country's condition, information that made Rani's story seem more reasonable.

With technology such as conference calls and Skype, the anthropologist and attorneys working on the case do not even have to be in the same city or even meet face to face until the time when the anthropologist is called in to testify.

This collaboration also demonstrated how much it takes for an asylum seeker to have a positive outcome. Diana Tafur, the staff attorney at the Asylum Project at the National Immigration and Justice Center and four attorneys at Seyfarth Shaw were involved on the case at different times, all pro bono. Given the absurdity of the questions heard at Rani's hearing, a collaboration between law and anthropological input during evidence preparation might be the recourse for asylum cases.

PERMISSION FROM RANI TO TELL HER STORY: WHY DOES IT MATTER?

After Rani had been granted asylum, we chatted about how she viewed the whole process. Rani said she suffered beating and abuse for three years. She thought it was her fate, her life. I told her she was very courageous to have endured so much to save her own life and her daughter's life. She said there are a lot of women in abusive relationships. "There are lots of Muslim women who couldn't leave their husband. I know of no other Indian woman who has done what I have done. There are so many women who are afraid to leave their husband, even the women in the US."

I told Rani that she should not be treated like that. She said, "I understood why my husband would do it. But my in-laws were bad. When you asked me questions about their treatment it made me recall all the bad things. I was very upset. But I knew that I must tell you to save my life."

Rani saw it as an accomplishment in my life for helping women and children. I used the opportunity to ask for permission to use her story in my book.

"You know I am writing a book about the asylum seekers. Would it be ok if I use your story? I will not use your name, I will change the dates and all the details that will identify you and your family."

"Why do that? Please tell my story. If you don't tell, who would know about it? Have you seen the movie called 'Not without My Daughter?' My story is similar to her story. The woman walked in the desert until she reached the US Embassy to ask for help to save her daughter. I did it for my daughter."

Part IV

PERSECUTION ON ACCOUNT OF POLITICAL OPINION

Chapter 11

A Filial Daughter's Devotion to Falun Gong Practice

In late 2010, Mr. Goodsell called me regarding an asylum seeker who was persecuted because she was a practitioner of Falun Gong (FLG). Her father was also arrested because the government found Falun Gong literature hidden in the family rice barrel. He then added that his client had missed the asylum petition deadline by about five years, meaning that her chances of obtaining asylum were extremely slim, given she was well past the one-year deadline. We did not know of anyone who had been granted asylum after missing the deadline by so many years. I approached the case with much trepidation. My little knowledge of Falun Gong came from the occasional newspaper accounts where the Chinese government referred to Falun Gong as an "evil cult." In contrast to these claims, I have also seen practitioners of FLG sitting serenely in a lotus position with hands outstretched, doing exercises of breathing in and out on a busy sidewalk outside the Chinese Consulate in Los Angeles. The case invoked in me the iconic image of a rice barrel, found in every Chinese peasant household, with its content a sign of fullness, or hunger, for the family. I had an image of an old man kneeling and pleading for his life by an overturned rice barrel, perhaps for not paying his taxes, emptied by a greedy landlord.

I speculated with Mr. Goodsell that if FLG is considered an "evil cult," would it still be a case of religious persecution? Mr. Goodsell referred me to Falun Gong's official website which describes it as a Chinese practice that combines meditation with qigong exercise, and moral philosophy centered on the tenets of truthfulness, compassion, and forbearance (Chinese: 真、善、忍). The practice emphasizes morality and the cultivation of virtue, and is identified as a type of qigong practice. The website raised many questions for me. If these are the tenets of FLG, then why is the practice considered a threat to the Chinese government? There was much to learn. I was not sure what Mr.

Goodsell thought I could do. I agreed to meet Ms. Li, but made no promise to working on the case given my lack of familiarity with FLG.

When Ms. Li met me in my office, I shared my concern in regards to how her five-year delay would affect her chance at gaining asylum. Ms. Li told me she was not thinking about applying for asylum when she first arrived in the United States; she admitted that she wasn't aware of asylum as a concept, let alone a possibility. She had escaped China with the hope that the Chinese government's policy on Falun Gong would change so she could return home again, but things had not worked out the way she wanted. By the time she realized she should apply for asylum, no lawyer would take her case until she found Mr. Goodsell, who was willing to listen to her. I realized that if Mr. Goodsell felt he must listen to Ms. Li's story, she must have something important to say. Ms. Li told me she worked as a waitress in Koreatown about twenty minutes from my office. She would come once a week on her day off.

MS. LI'S STORY

Ms. Li and her husband are both of Korean origin. Her husband is a fellow engineering technician at a provincial government enterprise. He is the youngest of five siblings, four of whom work in Russia. Her in-laws lived with their older son, his wife, and two school-aged children, a boy and a girl. Her parents cared for them while their parents worked. Ms. Li and her husband lived in a small house built by her brother-in-law who had made some money in Russia. After the birth of their daughter, Ms. Li's husband was very disappointed. He was envious of his older brother's good fortune for having a son; he hoped to save money so that he could bribe the government to allow him to have another child, in the hopes that it would be a boy. Aware of his unhappiness, his siblings arranged a trip for him to the United States where he could ease his mind, learn English, and perhaps a new skill.

At first, Ms. Li's husband would call frequently from California, but his calls became less frequent after a year. During her husband's two years in the United States, her in-laws would visit her whenever they were in the city and would bring some money from her husband which he had sent to his mother.

After their daughter was born, Ms. Li stopped working for a year to care for the baby. During that year, she took her daughter to visit her parents frequently. It was at her parents' house that they shared how they had regained their health with FLG practices in 1997. Ms. Li began the FLG practice and was pleased with improvement in her own health.

MS. LI'S ARREST, DETENTION, BEATING, AND SURVEILLANCE FOR HER PRACTICE OF FALUN GONG

Ms. Li said that after her health became better from FLG practices, she looked for more opportunities to learn Falun Gong, and began to practice with a group at a public park in her city taught by Ms. Jing. Grateful for her newfound health, she even helped Ms. Jing teach the newcomers at the park, and began to "proselytize" among her friends.

On July 22, 1999, the Chinese government announced that Falun Gong was an "evil cult" (*xie jiao*) and "its principles were lies," with goals "to topple the Chinese government, bring harm to society, and poison the heart of the Chinese people" (Permanent Mission of the People's Republic of China to the UN 2001). Ms. Li and her friends felt that it was contrary to their experience. To them, Falun Gong was only a form of physical exercise. They found it useful to their health, and Falun Gong exercise had become a routine they could not do without.

On July 31, 1999, which was a Saturday, Ms. Li remembered that she went to a public park in her city in the Dongbei area of China bordering North Korea and Russia, just like any other weekend morning. Suddenly, two public security vans and about ten policemen came to the park. They jumped from the police van and surrounded the group of twenty to thirty people. The group had already lost members from its original size of fifty after the government's announcement. The police rounded those in front with sticks and told the others to leave. One policeman grabbed Ms. Li who was in the front, and another beat her with a long stick and pushed her into the back of a police van. Ms. Jing, the Falun Gong teacher, and several others to the front of the group were put in the same van and taken to a detention center.

At the detention center, Ms. Li was taken to a small room for questioning regarding every detail about her involvement with Falun Gong activities. Sitting across from the interrogator, she was asked about the reasons for her participation in Falun Gong, the dates she started, where she had learned it, who she had studied with, whether she teaches Falun Gong, and what other activities she took part in besides Falun Gong exercise.

Ms. Li said she practiced Falun Gong for good health at a public park with music from a tape recorder; she knew about the government's order to forbid Falun Gong, but she felt she was not anti-government, and she felt everyone could see for themselves when she exercised openly at the park. She enthusiastically shared information on her improved health condition and that she had not been to a doctor ever since she started practicing Falun Gong. She had nothing to hide. The police retorted, "If Falun Gong was so great why are there hospital and patients?" They proceeded to blame her for possessing "twisted logic." They told her Li Hong Zhi, the charismatic founder of Falun Gong, was trying to topple the Chinese government and was fooling its believers. When she disagreed with them, they accused her of arguing with them, and slapped her face. Ms. Li noticed blood flowing from the corner of her mouth and questioned the police's right to beat an innocent woman. The police became angrier. One of them picked up a chair and smashed her with it. The chair hit Ms. Li's knees and she fell to the ground. "Get up!" the police ordered her. Ms. Li was in pain and was crouching on the floor. "Sit up! You are lying about being hurt," the police demanded. When Ms. Li could not get up the police beat her again and pulled her up by her hair. They made her sit in her chair and continued with the questioning. "You must have committed a crime or else you wouldn't have been arrested," the police told her. "We do not arrest people unless we know people have committed a crime." Ms. Li said she was incredulous that the police blamed her for getting herself arrested instead of the government for arresting her.

After the interrogation, the police sent Ms. Li to re-education classes at the detention center where ten men and women accused of various crimes, were housed in one room. Each room is controlled by the criminal detainees who have been there longer than the newcomers. When meals are delivered, these detainees would deliberately push and spill the newcomers' food and drinks. The police knew about it, but took no action. As a result Ms. Li did not get much food or water while in detention. She developed a fever the second day. She told the police she had a fever and wanted a doctor, but they ignored her request. After her release on Wednesday, August 4, 1999, Ms. Li went to the hospital for her fever and the bruises on her knees. She showed me a copy of the doctor's receipt from her hospital visit.

THE STREET COMMITTEE'S VISIT AFTER MS. LI'S RELEASE FROM DETENTION

Soon after Ms. Li returned home from the hospital, members from the street committee visited her. Ms. Li believed the public security must have informed them of her arrest. "In China, they know as soon as something has happened to you." Ms. Li said she told them she was in pain from the police beating. She said the street committee members were surprised at the beating and detention. She was stunned when they told her it was not possible, and thought it was probably because Ms. Li had injured herself. After the first visit, the same street committee members and neighbors would visit her two or three times a week, which lasted for three months. Later, it became once a week for about a year and a half. Ms. Li said that at first, the street committee members would come into the house and ask if she was still learning and practicing Falun Gong. Later, they would walk around and inspect her house, listen to the music on her tapes, ask what she was reading, open her cupboards, and ask about her new purchases. During these visits, they would tell her about the consequences of being a member of Falun Gong. They reminded her that she was lucky, implying that if she practiced Falun Gong again, she would be given longer sentences. At first, Ms. Li did not know that she was under the government's surveillance. She would let her neighbors and street committee members come into the house to visit her, thinking that they were only concerned (*quan xin*) about her welfare. When the visits continued, she felt she could not trust her neighbors anymore. She wanted to leave this constant surveillance. After her release, Ms. Li was also required to report to the police once a week for six months. The police would ask: Are you practicing Falun Gong? Are you in contact with the other practitioners? Do you make phone calls to other Falun Gong practitioners? Do you know of others who are practicing Falun Gong? Ms. Li said she felt terrified during this whole process because she was a "model citizen" before she was arrested.

The Monday after her release on August 9, 1999, Ms. Li returned to work and was told she was fired due to her involvement in Falun Gong. She had supposedly given the company a bad reputation because she had committed a crime for not obeying the government's policy. Ms. Li said she knew it was coming because on Monday, July 26, 1999, before she was arrested at the public park, all the employees at her work unit had to fill out a form regarding the employees' experience with Falun Gong. Ms. Li did not answer the question and was warned by her work unit that unless she stopped practicing Falun Gong, she would be fired. They wanted her to learn about the government's policy to help remove the bad influence of Falun Gong.

MS. LI'S FATHER'S ARREST, JAIL, BEATING AND "RE-EDUCATION" BY THE GOVERNMENT FOR HIS PRACTICE OF FALUN GONG

On August 12, 1999, the street committee in Ms. Li's father's neighborhood visited her father's home, supposedly to "help them improve their understanding and to remove the evils of Falun Gong." Ms. Li said that her parents knew they would receive a visit from the street committee so they had already burnt their Falun Gong material. When a group consisting of one woman and two men came to visit, they asked Ms. Li's parents if they had any material on Falun Gong. If they did, they should take them out and burn them. Her parents said they did not have any, but the street committee members then pushed her father aside, causing him to fall to the ground. They started to search the house, turning things upside down and breaking their tape recorder along the way. When they discovered a book that Mr. Li had hidden in the rice barrel, they became incensed. They summoned the police and wanted to know if he was against the government. Ms. Li said her parents were taken to the Street Committee Office and were questioned again. Ms. Li said her father took the blame for having hidden the book in the rice barrel and was sent to a detention center for a week. During the week at the detention center, her father continued to mention the benefits of Falun Gong, so the police punished him through more questioning, kicking, pushing, and beating. They sent him to "intense education" where he was deprived of sleep, food, and water, which was knocked over and spilled by the guard. Ms. Li said her father had fainted from the conditions. The Detention Center called the family and forced the family to sign as guarantor that her father would not practice Falun Gong again, and also forced the family to pay a 6,000 yuan fine. Ms. Li said her father spent the next ten days in the hospital. They had to borrow 15,000 yuan for his medical bills.

After her father was released from the hospital, Ms. Li said she apologized to her father. She blamed herself for her father's pain and suffering. Her father said he understood, nonetheless. He said after all, he was the one who introduced her to Falun Gong.

After Ms. Li's father was released, he too was under the Street Committee's surveillance. They came to his house two to three times a week for six months and later, once a week for the rest of the year. After her father was able to walk again, they told him not to practice Falun Gong and blamed him for getting himself into trouble. Ms. Li said, after a year, when no one was at home, her parents would exercise with Falun Gong again, without music, and pretended that they were doing other things in case someone walked in unannounced.

MS. LI WAS FORCED OUT BY HER IN-LAWS AFTER HER ARREST

After Ms. Li's husband had left for the United States during the fall of 2000, her mother-in-law brought her thirteen-year-old grandson to live in Ms. Li's house while he attended school in the city. Later, her husband's three sisters moved in, too. As a result, there were at least six people in a house built for three or four people. According to custom, Ms. Li must cook for her in-laws, especially her mother-in-law who expected breakfast by 5 a.m.

To support the family, Ms. Li found a job as a laborer at a wet market that sells fresh fish, meat, and vegetable. The laborers are responsible for keeping the market clean by constantly washing down the floors with water. A wet market is not considered a desirable place to work compared to a supermarket which sells dry and prepackaged food. She said "My employer knew of my police record but hired me anyway because I was willing to accept the low wages. I did not have a choice. With the little money I received from work, I was also supporting my in-law's family!"

"Unfortunately, one of my mother-in-law's friends saw me working in the market and asked my in-laws why I was there." Li's mother-in-law was angry at Li for having "lost face" for the family and told her to find another job so she would not be seen in public. However, given her police record, no one would hire her. As a result, almost overnight, Li had gone from a respectable engineer at a government company—a model citizen—to one unemployable even as a laborer at a wet market.

Li knew her in-law's family blamed her. They told her if she had not practiced Falun Gong to begin with, she would not have brought all the trouble to the family. They were afraid the police would come to the house and ask them questions, too. The police have been known to ransack the homes of Falun Gong suspects in search of evidence of Falun Gong material, arresting suspected practitioners and relatives. She emphasized the impact of the arrest on her family: "Other friends and relatives of my mother-in-law stopped coming to visit them. My in-laws also started to complain that my husband was not repaying the money his siblings had spent helping him go to America. I was then forced to leave the house."

Li's brother saw the situation and came to help his sister. He bought her a small house in 2001 near his parents' house so that Li could also look after their parents more easily. His job in Guangzhou prevented him from looking after their parents, even though it was his duty as a son. The duty of caring for their parents now fell on Li.

During our interview, Li reflected on the chain of events that had led her to the United States. It all started with her practice of Falun Gong to improve her health, followed by the arrest, the interrogation and beating, being fired from her good engineering job, her inability to gain employment, her ostracism by her in-laws, not to mention what had happened to her father because of her arrest. She said "The only consolation was, being in my own home, away from my in-laws, I could begin to do some Falun Gong exercises in the privacy of my own little house again." Once in a while, she would also practice with a group in her city.

MS. LI'S FALUN GONG TEACHER, MS. JING, WAS ARRESTED AND IMPRISONED AGAIN

In July of 2002, Li heard that Ms. Jing, her former Falun Gong teacher who was arrested with her in 1999, was arrested again and sent to a prison in the

Northwest. Alarmed, Li felt that she was also in danger because her name was on the same list as Ms. Jing. She, too, could end up in jail. She had heard that the guards in jail were especially abusive: "not only do they beat you, even if you die in jail, no one would care." Any new arrest would not be the same as her first arrest in July 1999. Li planned to escape from this cycle of constant persecution.

PLANNING HER ESCAPE

In the Dongbei area near the North Korean and Russian border, many of Ms. Li's neighbors worked in Korea and Japan, about an hour's flight away. To control the borders, Korea and Japan reject visa applicants who had previously overstayed. To circumvent the restriction, many residents in the Dongbei area apply for the visa again under new identities, changing their name and date of birth with the help of local operators. With the goal of evading government control, Li, too, used local operators to change her name and date of birth on her documents as a first step toward escaping China. In early 2002, Li applied for a new passport under her new name after the situation for Falun Gong and its practitioners had become increasingly dangerous.

After Ms. Jing's arrest, Ms. Li knew that she must leave the country immediately. Her parents and her friends were all helping her find a way to get out of China. Because of her father's personal experience in jail, he encouraged her to leave China. He was afraid that given her poor health she might not be able to withstand the condition of jail. Li found her opportunity when someone was organizing a team "to learn about business practices" in the United States, all on government account. Li "purchased" the slot when an official business visa was vacated by another Chinese who could not make the trip.

Ms. Li said, "I was so frightened thinking of the plan. I did not tell my in-laws. I told my daughter I was visiting my brother in Guangzhou. I told my parents not to go to the airport." She took only a small piece of carry-on luggage containing a few clothing items. She did not leave from the house she was living in, or the house of her parents, but instead from a friend's house where she had been staying. She bought additional clothes and luggage from the market and left without taking anything from her own or her parents' house. She was afraid the street committee would know about her departure if they sensed anything was unusual.

LI'S CHANCE MEETING WITH HER HUSBAND AND EVENTUAL DIVORCE

Ms. Li arrived in the United States in August, 2002. She found a place to stay in Koreatown, Los Angeles, through a friend of a friend from Dongbei. She did not contact her husband, who had already gone to California, because she did not know where he was all these years. She also did not inform him of her plan to escape. By chance, her roommate's boyfriend knew her husband. Li told me about her meeting with her husband and their attempt to reconcile. "I couldn't believe I was meeting my husband in California! And we talked about getting back together." I tried to steer the conversation away from details on their relationship as it did not pertain to her asylum application and there was no reason for me to know. I did not include her chance meeting with her husband and other details in the asylum report. They filed for divorce in December of 2007.

MISSING THE ONE-YEAR DEADLINE AFTER ARRIVING ON AUGUST 31, 2002

Of particular concern to me was the reason for her delay in applying for asylum after she arrived in August 2002. It would be difficult to argue her case without some reasonable explanation. Li and I spent many hours talking about how she learned about asylum in order to reconstruct the reasons for her delay. There were many reasons for missing the deadline by several years: her fears, the rumors, her personal problems, and local obstacles. In the end, I chronologically sorted all her reasons in my report for the judge.

After Ms. Li arrived in the United States on a one-month visa, she planned to eventually return to China, disregarding the dates stamped on her passport because she had heard that the United States does not detain departing visitors who have overstayed their visa. Without a penalty for overstaying her allotted time in the United States, she would wait out the Falun Gong crisis ongoing in China so she could return to her parents and daughter. Ms. Li told me the Chinese government has a history of enacting policies in the past, only to reverse the course after a few years. She was hoping the same thing would happen with the government's Falun Gong policies.

Ms. Li had not heard of asylum protection until a Christmas gathering in 2002, a few months after her arrival. Among the fellow countrymen from her city in Dongbei, a man everyone referred to as Old Kim, became drunk at the party, and started to talk about his problems with Falun Gong. He had applied for asylum but the Chinese government knew about it and arrested his parents. The people around him told him to be quiet because it was a sensitive subject. Ms. Li asked people at the gathering what it was all about. They told her that if you apply for asylum protection, you cannot go back to China. This meant that she would never see her parents or her daughter again. Besides the rumor she had heard at the Christmas party, her husband gave her the same warning: “If you apply for asylum, you might as well forget about ever seeing your parents again.”

The following year, in 2003, while on the phone with her parents in China, she learned that they too had heard that the Chinese government was arresting and jailing people whose relatives had applied for asylum in the United States. It had happened to the daughter-in-law of the Wang family, who was not even a Falun Gong practitioner herself. Still, her family was punished when she applied for asylum. Ms. Li said, “I was really afraid the punishment against my parents would be far more severe because they were Falun Gong practitioners.” Moreover, her father had already been detained once before in August of 1999. If the government should hear about it, “I do not know what will happen to my parents. And there will be no one to look after my daughter if they were arrested.”

It was in 2006 that Ms. Li began to suspect that a person within the immigration service agencies was informing the Chinese government in the Dongbei area about Old Kim and other asylum applicants in California. Out of fear of retaliation against her parents, she abstained from applying for asylum.

The condition in China did not get better, and practitioners of Falun Gong continued to be arrested. In the summer of 2007, Ms. Li learned that a woman she knew in Koreatown from the Dongbei area had applied for asylum and was granted a green card. But when she returned to China to visit her sick parents, the woman was detained by the police at the airport and sent to jail for 8 years. The woman never saw her parents as they passed away while she was serving her time in jail. Hearing this, Ms. Li gave up the thought of applying for asylum.

Her one month stay turned into a year; a year into several years. It wasn’t until after she had gained some experience with the American legal system because of her divorce application process in 2007 and its approval in the following year that Ms. Li became less afraid of the law. She was actually surprised at her ability to negotiate the legal system in the United States to successfully obtain a divorce from her husband.

By 2008, she had heard that more Chinese were applying for asylum and that the applicants’ relatives were not facing the same threat of arrest in China. She said she was also encouraged by a compatriot whose asylum application was successful. It was only at this time that she learned about the one-year rule for asylum application.

"FALUN GONG IS NOT A KOREAN ISSUE"

By the time she had sorted out her fears regarding the Chinese government's action against the family members of asylum applicants, and contacted some Korean-speaking attorneys in Koreatown where she worked, no attorney would handle the case. They were either not familiar with Falun Gong issues or had no interest in helping her. They told her, "Falun Gong is not a Korean issue."

Asian immigrants to the United States often stay within their linguistic and ethnic community. Even though Ms. Li was a Chinese national and bilingual in Mandarin Chinese and Korean, she is ethnically Korean from an area bordering Korea where language and culture overlap. Through her co-ethnics, she landed in Los Angeles, found a place to stay, and obtained a job working in a Korean restaurant. Early in her stay in Los Angeles, she was not aware of San Gabriel Valley, to the east of Los Angeles, which has a burgeoning concentration of recent Chinese immigrants from the People's Republic of China, and has services geared toward the specific needs of the Chinese immigrant community. With advice from her friends, Ms. Li visited four separate immigration agencies in the San Gabriel Valley over the following two years. But, by the time she found Chinese-speaking attorneys familiar with Falun Gong issues, no one would take her case. They all told her: "too late, you have waited for too long to apply."

Refusing to give up the idea that she could never see her parents or daughter again, she started to learn the process of applying for asylum. She began by writing down her story, getting it translated, filling out the required forms, preparing the supporting documents, and getting friends to take her to the Immigration Office in Anaheim. While preparing her documents, she found getting a letter of support from her father was the most terrifying. All the years Ms. Li was in the United States; she had suspected she was still under the Chinese government's surveillance. The mail she sent home, and those she had received, had all been tampered with. Packages of clothes she sent her daughter had been opened and repacked. A Fed Express mailer her father had sent her had been opened and resealed. To circumvent the surveillance of the Chinese government, her father's letter of support for her asylum application was sewn into the lining of a jacket, and sent in a box containing other clothing items as well. Ms. Li said, "If the government should discover the letter, the whole family would all die." Ms. Li also used her friend's address to receive her mail in Los Angeles.

With Ms. Li's permission to share her story, I decided to include an excerpt from her father's letter, translated from Chinese:

Respectful Immigration Judge of the United States,

> I am XXX and Li's father. My wife and I initially influenced our daughter to practice Falun Gong. . . . When we started, we had no idea that simply practicing Falun Gong for health reasons could get us into that kind of trouble in 1999 . . . I was jailed for a week and beaten by police just because I kept a Falun Dafa book. My wife and I feared that I could not make it out alive.
>
> Our daughter Li was arrested by the police at XX Park with her friends in XX 1999. . . . When her group instructor, with whom she practiced a lot, was sent to a labor camp, we had to make her leave China. It was so sad that she had to leave her daughter behind. But we believe that it was better than the alternative—to be in jail.
>
> Li mentioned she wanted to apply for asylum in the United States due to her Falun Gong practice. The plan horrified my wife and me at the beginning. I made her promise not to do that. I told her that her mother and I as well as her daughter wanted to live, and not to be put in prison and die there. Her mother cried and begged her. Although she promised that she would respect our opinion, this thing is a shadow that has hung over our heads for years. It was not until a year ago, I was somewhat enlightened. I told her that maybe she was old enough to do what was right, as long as she could be certain the Chinese government would not know, as long as there would be a possibility that she and my granddaughter would be reunited soon. My granddaughter has not seen her mother for nearly 8 years. It made us heart-broken when she asked why her mom and dad never came back to see her. She was so young when Li left. We made up all kinds of excuses, but we never dare to mention "Falun Gong."
>
> Thank you very much for spending time reading my letter. Your favorable decision to Li's application will be deeply appreciated. My wife and I are very grateful that Li has been able to stay in the United States and being safe.
>
> Respectfully yours,
> XXX
> April 5, 2010

Ms. Li said everyone she had talked to about preparing and gathering the documents necessary for the asylum application had urged her to give up, because it was impossible to obtain asylum.

Ms. Li refused to give up because there was a slim chance she might see her parents and daughter if she could get asylum. Along the way, someone told her about Attorney Ken Goodsell, who had a reputation for success in Chinese asylum cases. By the time Ms. Li contacted Mr. Goodsell in 2007, she had missed the one-year rule by five years.

After completing her story, I thought to myself, if Ms. Li had to tell her whole story in court, without interruptions and without challenges from the Government Counsel, it would take at least five hearings for these details to come out. Given the extremely busy court schedule, I wondered if the adjudicators would have the patience for such details to emerge in court.

PERSECUTION BASED ON RELIGION? OR POLITICAL OPINION?

Based on Ms. Li's story, I was struggling to determine on which ground the government would grant her asylum so that I could prepare her report accordingly. Is Falun Gong considered a religion? Does Ms. Li's opposition to the government's prohibition of Falun Gong's practices constitute political opinion? Based on a dozen or so articles and books I had examined, I felt that my knowledge on Falun Gong was insufficient to assess Ms. Li's "theological" understanding of a new religion that combined meditation, qigong exercises, and spiritual improvement. In court, I would be challenged for lacking knowledge on Falun Gong, given my lack of professional expertise in the subject. If I were to argue that Ms. Li was persecuted based on her religious beliefs of Falun Gong, it would contradict what Ms. Li herself had told the police: that she practiced Falun Gong for health reasons. To explore the relationship between her health improvement and her spirituality would be an argument quite removed from revealing an understanding on how she was persecuted on account of religion.

I had reflected on the government's arrest and detention of Ms. Li as her opposition to the government's Falun Gong policy, since it was her opposition to those policies that led to her arrest. The reports on the Chinese government's treatment towards its practitioners was unbelievably inhumane, with the Falun Gong website carrying graphic pictures of the Chinese government's methods of torturing Falun Gong practitioners. Would the United States Government Counsel consider Ms. Li's arrest and detention—a comparatively mild treatment compared to the treatment of other Falun Gong practitioners—rise to the level of persecution? In addition, when news stories of refugees and asylum seekers from around the world seem to experience so much more trauma and violence, would the government be sympathetic toward Ms. Li's un-newsworthy four-day detention?

I reassessed what I had learned from Ms. Li and decided to focus on her role as a filial daughter and the delay in her asylum application given the Chinese government's harsh treatment of Falun Gong practitioners, including the vengeful actions toward the relatives of those who had escaped the government's reach and applied for asylum protection in the United States.

Even though the Chinese government's policy on Falun Gong did not specifically target women, women asylum petitioners face particular issues that men do not encounter. Their roles as mothers, wives, and daughters often interfere with their asylum application, especially within the one-year rule.

As a filial daughter, she would not put her own interest in applying for asylum for personal safety above her parents' safety. To think of her own safety and interest first would make her an unfilial daughter and she would be scorned if this was known to others. In societies with a strong sense of filial piety, unquestioned devotion to one's parents is a moral obligation.

Through her socialization as a filial daughter, she was already feeling guilty and blaming herself for her father's arrest: If she had not been arrested, the authorities probably would not have gone to his house and arrested him. The arrest and imprisonment of her parents would also mean the loss of the only caregivers her daughter has. If the judge had denied her application due to the missing deadline, the attrition from a successful asylum application was the result of her role as a woman.

It was probably the tenth time we had seen each other to go over details of her story. On that day, she gave me a check for $500.00 as payment for helping her on the case. I gave it back to her. Ms. Li told me the money she paid me was not enough to compensate me for my time. I apologized for the difficult times she had gone through and the uncertainty of her future. I told her the interviews had given me the opportunity to learn about FLG practitioners and aspects of China that I would otherwise not know.

After completing my write-up on Ms. Li's accounts, I did one more thing. Drawing on the help of a librarian colleague, Mr. Yongyi Song, with expertise on Chinese language newspaper sources, I examined accounts of torture and deaths of FLG practitioners in China to verify the accounts Ms. Li had heard from her friends and family regarding the continued arrests of FLG practitioners. Some of the information included documented deaths of individuals from Ms. Li's province (Clearwisdom 2011). I added this information to my analysis in support of Ms. Li's contention of the persecution she had suffered in China, and submitted my report to Mr. Goodsell, who included it as part of the documents supporting Ms. Li's asylum application.

MERIT HEARING

Ms. Li's Merit Hearing, which had been postponed a number of times due to conflicts with the judge's calendar, finally came. On that occasion, Ms. Li introduced me to a Master Kung, a Falun Gong master who happened to be in Los Angeles for a Falun Gong convention. Master Kung agreed to testify as a lay witness for Ms. Li. After chatting briefly while waiting for the court hearing to begin, Master Kung returned to sitting erect with his back against the wall in the corridor of the courtroom, meditating serenely among the shuffling feet in front of him as immigrants from all over the world and their attorneys jockeyed to be on time in the right courtroom for their appearance in front of judges.

I was not involved in the decision or the selection of bringing in a Falun Gong Master as a witness. But I learned that Mr. Goodsell had another Falun Gong Master as witness before. Just before he went to court for the hearing, Mr. Goodsell double checked the name of his witness and recognized that the supposed "Falun Gong master" had actually been a charlatan in another case. Mr. Goodsell said he was glad he weeded out a charlatan among the people he called on to testify.

During Master Kung's testimony, I was sequestered. Perhaps he spoke on the experience of torture and persecution of the Falun Gong practitioners in China, or the continued practice of those in the United States. By bringing a Falun Gong master as a witness, it lends credibility to Ms. Li's claim that she, too, was a Falun Gong practitioner. Master Kung's testimony would also support my mostly library and newspaper accounts.

On this particular day when the Judge was available to hear Ms. Li's case, this time, Mr. Goodsell had to attend to another case at the same time in the same court building but on a different floor. Mr. Goodsell had asked Ms. Joann Yeh, an immigration attorney, to cover for him. As usual, I made my presence known and then went to the waiting room in case the attorney or judge decided to call me. Around noon, the court broke for lunch. I returned to the courtroom, eager to hear the outcome of the morning session. When I entered the courtroom, the judge and the counsel for the government had already left. Ms. Yeh, holding a copy of my report, approached me and asked, "I have never seen anything like this before? How did you do this?" I knew Ms. Yeh had already read my report and seen my accompanying resume submitted to the court. I couldn't be happier for the opportunity for any conversations and feedback on my mostly individual endeavor.

ASYLUM LAWFARE

Ms. Yeh told me she had read my report quickly in the morning when Mr. Goodsell had to be called away. She used my argument that Ms. Li was a filial daughter who did not want to jeopardize her parents' safety by selfishly thinking only of her own well-being when applying for asylum. To ensure no harm would come to her parents, Ms. Li missed the one-year rule. It was at this point that the Government Counsel seized the opportunity to steer the court hearing into a discussion of whether Asians are filial to their parents as a way to discredit Ms. Li's application. Ms. Yeh told me the Government Counsel asked, "If Ms. Li claims filial piety towards her parents as an excuse for her application delay, wouldn't all Asian Americans use that same excuse to gain asylum?"

Ms. Yeh said she was furious at the Government Counsel's confusion of Asians with Asian Americans and snapped back at the Government Counsel, "If they [the asylum seekers] are Americans they won't be in the courtroom right now!" "It shut her up," Ms. Yeh told me.

One of the topics covered in Asian American Studies is America's ignorance of the Asians in the United States. They often confuse Asians from Asia with Asians in the United States, of which many are citizens and have been in the United States for generations. Asian Americans must constantly explain the difference between themselves as citizens and descendants of a long history of struggle to claim their legitimate and rightful place in American society from Asians who are nationals of countries in Asia.

Many Asian Americans, even if they have been in the United States for generations, are constantly asked questions such as "Where are you from?" or "Where did you learn to speak English so well?" Without accusing the questioner of ignorance, Asian Americans, sensitized to these issues often answer the latter question with the tongue in cheek response, "The same high school where you learned your English."

To Ms. Yeh, it was unbelievable that she would actually encounter and confront a Government Counsel who had so much power to affect people's lives, yet exhibited such fundamental ignorance toward Asian Americans.

If Ms. Yeh as an immigration attorney possessed such enlightened knowledge, I did not attribute it to her Asian origin. Because, in court, some of the most ferocious questioning I have encountered has come from Government Counsel who are Asians. Ms. Yeh told me her own education about issues pertaining to Asians and Asian Americans came from a course in Asian American Studies taken while she was an undergraduate in engineering at Massachusetts Institute of Technology, prior to obtaining a law degree. She argued that every Government Counsel should take such a course. I told her I couldn't agree with her more. In fact, I had founded a BA Degree in Asian and Asian American Studies at a major public university to encourage greater literacy on Asia and Asian America.

"THE JUDGE GRANTED HER ASYLUM"

A month after the Merit Hearing, Mr. Goodsell sent me a text informing me that the Judge had granted Ms. Li asylum. I called Ms. Li to congratulate her. She said she wanted to see me again to celebrate her gaining asylum. Ms. Li took me to a Chinese Korean restaurant and ordered special Korean dishes she said I had never tasted before. She insisted on paying for lunch. Then she took out an envelope containing a check for $500.00, the payment I had refused to accept earlier. Ms. Li told me that if I had not helped her with the case, she would have been deported. Once in China, she would be sent to jail to face an uncertain fate, like other asylum seekers from Dongbei in the northeast region of China. If Ms. Li had allowed the fear of a mole in the asylum system that may have reported on applicants for asylum in the United States, inaction would have a different outcome for her: she may never ever be able to see her parents again.

If she had remained as an illegal immigrant in America, she would not be able to leave the United States and return again. Without the asylum protection that will also give her the freedom to travel, she would not be able to see her parents ever again, either. "Because they are too old to travel to America." Ms. Li added, "My daughter might have a chance. That is, when she grows up, if she does well in school, she could apply to attend colleges in America. And perhaps, we would have a chance to see each other many years in the future." She thanked me. I thanked her for allowing me to write her story. I told her I see her courage in challenging a totalitarian and brutal policy. Her belief matters. Her love for her parents matter even more. As a filial daughter, their freedom from arrest and jail were more important than her own well-being. In the end, I am thankful Judge Dorfman granted her asylum. Ms. Li's love for her parents and daughter triumphs. As we dined on Korean delicacies while reflecting on the highlights of her good fortune, Ms. Li added, "Without the corruption that allowed me to escape with a business visa, I would have been dead."

Chapter 12

Her Forced Abortion was a Frivolous Claim

Mr. Goodsell called me with an intriguing and troubling case about a woman who was forced to undergo an abortion. Mr. Goodsell cited that the judge's contention was whether or not the woman had seen the fetus, if it was male or female, and from which side it had been shown to her. Curious, I had many questions prior to meeting Ms. Chun. First, if it was a forced abortion, why would it matter to the Judge whether the woman saw the fetus? Second, the sex of the fetus may be of concern to the parents, but why was it an issue in an asylum decision? Would the judge grant her asylum if the fetus was of one sex or the other?

Mr. Goodsell had shown me Ms. Chun's file on her asylum petition. She was forced to abort a much-wanted pregnancy under China's one-child policy. Reading the dense legalese, one line said she had filed a "frivolous claim."

According to several sources, "frivolous claim in legal terms refers to a lawsuit, or motion in a lawsuit motivated by an intent merely to harass, delay, or embarrass the opposition. In order to be found frivolous, the claim must have no arguable basis in law or fact." If Ms. Chun's case was about her forcibly aborted pregnancy, why would it be a "frivolous claim"? And why would she file a lawsuit with "an intent merely to harass, delay, or embarrass" the American asylum system?

In trying to decipher the rationality behind this case, I felt as if I was stepping into a Kafkaesque scene that defies explanation. Mr. Goodsell interrupted my concerns: "I want corroborative evidence that she had an abortion." With such a request, my immediate thought was a report on abortion which states that when women are forced to have unsafe abortions underground, when safe and therapeutic abortions are restricted or unavailable, the evidence of the tragic consequences is death itself (Girard and Nowicka 2002).

In 1948, the International Bill of Human Rights was created to ensure basic rights for all human beings, regardless of one's continent of residence. Included in this Universal Declaration is: "Freedom from torture or cruel, inhumane, and degrading treatment or punishment" (Cardenas 2010, 5). Forcing someone to abort a fetus without consent should be considered torturous and inhumane, therefore making it an international human rights violation. So, in what way is Ms. Chun's abortion claim frivolous? Ms. Chun's abortion was not done by some unsafe underground illegal operation. Her abortion was performed at a hospital, on the command of the Chinese government. Feminist scholars affirm that in China, "while the birth control policy has been 'relaxed' since the 2000s, the state's imposition of control over female fertility is still very intrusive and even violent" (Cao 2015, 20).

In the evidence for forced abortion, is it not a question for the doctor or the hospital that performs the abortion? I assumed Ms. Chun must not have been given a letter from the hospital showing they had forcibly aborted her pregnancy. Without some kind of documentation from the government, I wondered how Ms. Chun should prove her forced abortion. My medical consultant told me there are no physical scars from an early-term abortion performed at a hospital. However, there may be scars from late-term abortions and if surgical instruments were used. I wondered if Mr. Goodsell would send Ms. Chun to consult with a US Government–approved surgeon to attest that an abortion had actually happened, and whether or not it was forced. And how much would the cost be? For Ms. Chun, and most asylum seekers with few resources, these options are inconceivable.

Ms. Chun is a fair-skinned woman with medium build and height, and deep suffering in her eyes. She is of Korean origin, from an area near the town of Peaceful Dragon, bordering North Korea, near the Russian border in China's Dongbei (Northeast) province. We spoke in Mandarin Chinese about her situation. In recounting her case to me, Ms. Chun was upset at the attorney—"the one with the bushy beard," she said. "He was so unprofessional. He looked like a hippie with dirty clothes. He did not get dressed properly in the morning before he went to court. He did not read my files beforehand. He even made a mistake in stating my situation in court."

That is, the attorney she trusted had failed in her expectation of what an attorney should look like, how he should prepare her case, and how he should represent her. I could not give her an answer or a justification for his behavior as I did not have the details, and it was beyond my ability to find out. Saying "I am sorry" for his misconduct or for her great misfortune would seem insincere. I kept quiet. It was under the "bushy beard" attorney's representation in court that the question of whether she was actually shown the fetus came up: whether it was a male or a female fetus and whether it was shown to her from the left-hand side or the right-hand side of the hospital bed. The

Immigration Judge had already ruled against granting her asylum. The more she spoke, the more tragic the case became. To focus on the contested details at that moment would be counterproductive. Perhaps by focusing on Mr. Goodsell's request for corroborative evidence—that is, for her to tell me her story from the beginning—the evidence would emerge as we sifted through the details of her experience. Expecting to require a lot of work for the case, I told her we would need to meet a few times. From Koreatown on the west of the city of Los Angeles across town to my office in East Los Angeles is only a twenty-minute drive without traffic. She agreed to see me on her days off.

WANTING A SON

Ms. Chun was a thirty-four-year-old, married Korean woman and the eldest of five siblings. Though all of her siblings were married, none of them had sons. Even the siblings of Ms. Chun's husband had no sons. After the birth of Ms. Chun's daughter, everyone on both sides of the family were very disappointed. There was no jubilation and no celebration. In a patrilineal society where descent is based on the male line, a son is important to carry on the family name, to inherit the family wealth, and to assist his parents in their old age. A girl only brings disappointment. Ms. Chun said her husband wanted a son. She herself wanted a son too, for her own reasons.

She said life for a woman in the *Dongbei* border area is extremely difficult. She said she was brought up to believe that she was powerless. She wanted a son precisely because she felt so powerless. In observing her mother and her aunts, she explained, "It is the women who do all the work while the men sit around and drink and talk. They never helped the women with the work in the house. That was why I want a son. My desire for a son is stronger than my husband. I do not want another daughter because the girl will suffer the same fate as other women." Ms. Chun said she was very unhappy after her daughter's birth, despite her mother's loving and attentive help with her post-partum recovery.

Ms. Chun wanted a second child badly, especially a son, but China's one-child policy closed that possibility. Ms. Chun was aware of China's one-child policy, but she wanted a second child despite the risk of the child being "undocumented" after birth. The child would not be included in the country's "household registration" system, and would not benefit from the government's social services given to its citizens. She was willing to spend her own money to raise the second child.

Ms. Chun said she had discussed with her family how to have a second child without government detection, despite being in violation of the government's policy. Finally, the family decided Ms. Chun should remove her intrauterine device (IUD), which was inserted by the government after the birth of her daughter. To avoid detection, she went to a private physician in another city, complaining of bleeding from the IUD. After she became pregnant, she took a leave of absence from the government-run company where she worked and went to live with a relative in a remote mountainous village thirty kilometers away. Ms. Chun said to have a baby in a remote village would not be comfortable and she would miss the prenatal care and postpartum *zuo yue zi* customs her mother did for her after the birth of her daughter. Still, it was a sacrifice she had to make in order to have another child.

When Ms. Chun was telling me her *zuo yue zi* customs, I realized she had just given me the much needed corroborative evidence for her asylum case. *Zuo yue zi*, or literally "sitting the month" which Barbara Pillsbury (1978) has translated as "Doing the Month," is a common postpartum practice recognized by Chinese women.

Earlier in my anthropological career, while conducting research among Chinese women on reproductive decisions and the use of indigenous fertility regulations, the subject of *zuo yue zi* was very familiar to me. However, I had never had the occasion to consider whether Korean women share a similar custom until Ms. Chun told me about her experience. She revealed that, during the first month after birth, women are required to follow dietary guidelines, following loosely the principles of "hot" and "cold." That is, they must avoid "cold" foods and drinks. If these *zuo yue zi* practices are found after the birth of a child, are they carried out for an abortion too? If Ms. Chun had actually observed her post-abortion customs, I would be able to provide cultural evidence that an abortion had actually taken place. So, I encouraged Ms. Chun to tell me more about her cultural practices regarding pregnancy and birth.

PRENATAL BELIEFS AND PRACTICES

When Ms. Chun was pregnant with her daughter, her mother prepared special dishes for her. These nutritious foods were consumed by the pregnant woman to *bu tai*, or to "protect the fetus." This diet includes more meat, which is not consumed regularly by poor families. An especially important dish, eaten by only pregnant woman, is black-skin chicken made with jujube and glutinous rice. Other dishes include pork with Napa cabbage, and beef ("it must have bone on it") cooked for two to three hours and then flavored with spices, ginger, cilantro and onion. In addition, she ate two eggs daily, which she cooked herself. She emphasized that these foods were eaten to protect the pregnancy. She made a distinction between ordinary food and food for a pregnant mother. Normal diets for ordinary people consisted of rice and "small (side) dishes" of salted vegetables, commonly seen in Korean restaurants as "side dishes" accompanying the main course.

During her pregnancy, she also observed pregnancy taboos: she avoided squid because "it had no bone" and "it had eight legs"; she avoided heavy physical work because it could lead to a miscarriage, and she avoided sitting on a place with a crack to avoid having a baby born with cleft palate.

"DOING THE MONTH": *ZUO YE ZI* PRACTICES DURING POSTPARTUM

After Ms. Chun's daughter was born, in accordance with the custom of "doing the month," her mother came to live with her. During the whole month after delivery, Ms. Chun could not wash in cold water, eat cold food, or be exposed to anything cold. During the month of confinement, her mother made special food and drinks for her to encourage milk production and help her with a speedy recovery from the pregnancy and delivery. Ms. Chun provided me with a list of special "doing the month" dishes, the foods to avoid, and the taboos to observe.

HAVING AN "ILLEGAL PREGNANCY"

When Ms. Chun was three months pregnant with her "illegal pregnancy," she left her daughter under the care of her mother and went into hiding. In the remote mountain village where her mother's sister lived, there were about two dozen families and only one small store. It was inaccessible by car and without bus service. She said, even then, she stayed inside her aunt's house most of the time to avoid being discovered.

"KIDNAPPING" MS. CHUN FOR THE FORCED ABORTION

Unfortunately for Ms. Chun, during the end of her sixth month of pregnancy, her company became aware of it and sent security personnel, along with the director of the family planning unit of the government factory where she worked, to bring her back to the city. They told her they were taking her back to Peaceful Dragon, the major city close to where she came from. She refused to go. They told her "There is a matter you must deal with. You will find out when you get there." Ms. Chun again refused, but was pushed into a van, essentially kidnapped. Ms. Chun suspected their intention all along, and in the end chose to go along, feeling that resisting was futile. She also worried that if she did not cooperate, she might be beaten and killed.

MS. CHUN SUFFERING THE PAIN AND TRAUMA OF FORCED ABORTION

The van took her directly to the hospital. A nurse asked questions about her weight and height and other medical history and filled out a form. Then they wheeled her to the maternity ward where Ms. Chun said she heard the cries of women in labor. She knew they were going to force her to have an abortion. She wanted to protest, but she could not. She said they gave her an injection and then another several hours later. She said the drug from the first injection had already determined the fate of her baby. After a while, Ms. Chun said she began to feel the effect of the drug, as it forced her to abort the baby. She said the pain was more horrendous than the labor pain when birthing of her daughter: "the baby inside me was dying and it was kicking me violently here and there" as she pointed to her abdomen. "I was in so much pain I thought I was going to die. When the baby died inside me, I was dying too." Later when the nurse said she was dilated, the doctor came. "They came to my private genital area and violently pulled out the dead baby. I lost a lot of blood. I almost passed out. I knew later that they had to give me 400cc of blood. I might as well be dead because I knew my baby was already dead," she repeated. "I was so traumatized I did not care about anything in the world. Later they told me and my husband it was a boy. But what is the point? The boy was already dead. What can I say? It was hopeless."

In Ms. Chun's affidavit, she described the powerlessness against her company's security officers. She described in great details the excruciating physical pain and psychological stress during the ordeal of the forced abortion—the injections to induce the abortion, the labor pain, and the forced abortion. When she recounted for me the violent forced abortion, she described with sadness the physical pain and the emotional trauma of seeing a much desired male fetus being shown to her and her husband, who was called and waited outside in the waiting room. The point of contention in her case was whether the aborted fetus was shown from her right or left side. As a result, she had to account for the discrepancy between her statement and the attorney's account of her experience given in court.

After the forced abortion, Ms. Chun returned to her mother's house. She said her mother prepared nutritious food to protect her health; not to nurture a growing pregnancy. She lost her appetite. She had lost 8.4 kilograms of weight. She remembered one day where her mother gave her some milk because it was thought to be nutritious and Ms. Chun became violently ill. She said she almost died.

After Ms. Chun had some rest at her mother's home, she returned to her own home for the first time since she went into hiding in the mountain village. After Ms. Chun became pregnant, she had envisioned bringing home a new baby, but with the abortion, there was no baby to bring home. Ms. Chun said she was inconsolable after the trauma of the forced abortion. She felt so violated, that she became a *fong zi*—a crazy person. Knowing the intensity of her desire for a boy, the family planning committee from her street doubled its surveillance efforts on her.

In having spoken to victims of sexual assault over the years, I found Ms. Chun's suffering to be similar to victims of rape. She expressed hatred and anger over the ordeal, often taking it out on her husband. Indeed, in the opinion of the authors for the article on forced sterilization and asylum in the USA, published in the *Lancet,* and written by a team of gynecologists at New York Hospital-Cornell Medical Center and NYU Downtown Hospital, professors of law at Harvard University, and members of the US House of Representatives, "forced sterilization is an assault, and its emotional sequelae may be profound, particularly in societies where women's status is closely tied to motherhood and procreation." They opined that such patients should be invited to express their anxieties . . . , and psychiatric referral may be indicated . . . , and "political asylum may be the only resources." (Sills, et al 1998: 1729).

Given that Ms. Chun's pain was brutal and sustained, she was voiceless and suffered alone. She said her husband was kind to her. He would prepare for her nutritious slow-cooked *dun*, chicken, beef, and pork—the same as her mother's preparation for postpartum food—but she had no appetite. After a day or two, they threw away the food because they had no refrigeration, and ended up eating rice and salted vegetables. She said she was depressed and always in a bad mood. She complained that the food was not good, the house was not clean, and her husband was no longer attractive to her. She fought over little things with her husband every day. Her husband was fired from his job. Without work, he was home. She said she hated seeing him and eventually stopped talking to him. She said, "We slept on the same bed but under different blankets because I could not stand any intimacy. I quarreled with him every day. I blamed my husband for not protecting me and protecting the pregnancy to save our baby. I even asked him to leave the house to go find another woman and hope the other woman does not suffer the same fate as I have." For months she cried every day. "I was becoming insane from the forced abortion."

She divorced her husband after a few months. "In the divorce, I fought over the daughter. I told him if he took our daughter I would commit suicide.

My husband did not want the divorce and my parents objected to the divorce but I wanted my husband out of my life. I blamed him for not being assertive enough and provide the leadership to protect me from the abortion. After the divorce, I kept only my own clothes and went back to my mother's house. I did not want anything from the old house. My mother was crying every day. I was angry at her for being kind to my husband, for accepting food when he brings them to the house."

Now thinking back, Ms. Chun recognized her own irrationality, saying that if she did not have the forced abortion, she might not have divorced her husband.

CORROBORATIVE EVIDENCE

After Ms. Chun had met with me a couple of times, I was already quite confident a report could be written on Ms. Chun's tragic story—the abuse she suffered at the hands of the Chinese government's one-child policy was very extreme. The report would include a very detailed analysis embedding Ms. Chun's experience of forced abortion within her cultural practices of prenatal care, postpartum "doing the month" *zuo yue zi* practices, her pregnancy history, the detailed description of the forced abortion, and the post-abortion dietary practices. Through careful documentation of these intricate narratives as corroborative evidence, it would be difficult for the Government to deny the forced abortion never took place.

APPLYING FOR ASYLUM

Unable to face members of the street committee, Ms. Chun found a way to escape to the United States, ending up in Koreatown, Los Angeles. In 2006, her friend from the same village, who was also living in Koreatown with asylum experience, gave her the address and telephone number of an attorney and told her to apply for protection from the United States government. She went to the recommended attorney to ask for help. She said a young man interviewed her. She said it was so embarrassing telling a young man about a woman's private issues, especially a problem like abortion. Even more painful was remembering that her aborted baby was a boy. She had to relive the whole experience while writing it out in order to apply for asylum in the attorney's office. She said she did not know the words in Chinese to write her asylum application. The young man in the attorney's office would supply the words for her in Chinese and then she would write them down in her own handwriting. It took three days to complete her application. After that, she went with the young man to the city of Anaheim in Orange County to apply for asylum. A few months later, she learned the Immigration Officer had rejected her asylum application. She was referred to another attorney. She said she had no idea why all the changes with attorneys occurred. She also had to pay legal fees along the way with every attorney she met. When she went to court for the Merit Hearing in front of an immigration judge to decide her fate, the "bushy beard" attorney was not the same attorney as the one who had worked with her before. He botched her Merit Hearing by misstating a detail of her forced abortion.

Mr. Goodsell, in helping her appeal the case, had argued minor mistakes should not be an issue legally. He argued that the hospital violated Ms. Chun's rights by violently entering into her private areas and forcibly inducing a much-wanted pregnancy. He also argued the difficulty for a traumatized woman to recall details in court, inter alia.

ASYLUM ATTRITION

In continuing my interviews with Ms. Chun, I was interested in learning details on the government's surveillance on her, how she evaded their detection, and how she might be forced to have another abortion on her return to China, so I could complete the report for her appeal. Most intriguing to me was the actual sequence of events after the abortion that had taken place. Ms. Chun seemed to suggest that the nurse performing the abortion actually showed her the dead male fetus to spite her for her violation of the government's policy. Otherwise, why would the nurse present the aborted male fetus to her as if it was their collective accomplishment in delivering a healthy baby boy? However, Ms. Chun had missed her appointments. She did not return my repeated calls. Her report, near completion, sits in my computer. We have come so far, but the work is left unfinished. It leaves me wondering why. The asylum system denied what was most painfully profound to Ms. Chun—that she had lost a much wanted male child; the loss was simply too traumatic. Instead of acknowledging her loss, the focus was on the technicalities, that is, at what point she became aware of the fetus's sex. I believe she lost faith in the system and dropped out of the asylum application process, not wanting to pursue the appeals. In her mind, there was no reason why an anthropologist's additional report would help in her appeal.

Mr. Goodsell did not call me to request my report with corroborative evidence. Perhaps Mr. Goodsell's office had called her but got no response from her either. There was no need for his office to inform me of cases of men and women who do not intend to pursue their case further. There are many reasons why asylum seekers do not pursue their cases. Sometimes they run out of money. Sometimes the shame still haunts them. Ms. Chun had already been traumatized by the forced abortion of a much-wanted son, devastated by the rejection of the Immigration Officer, followed by another rejection from the Immigration Judge; perhaps she is afraid of facing yet another rejection by the Board of Immigration Appeals.

I called the number of the "young man" who had helped Ms. Chun prepare her asylum application, but nothing much came out of it. I called Ms. Chun's number again, after other leads failed to reach her. I wanted to tell her that the small check she had given me for my professional services had bounced. I wanted her to know that she did not have to pay me, and it was alright with me.

I imagine what could have been if there were better anthropological and legal cooperation from the beginning of her case. For something so important to a woman who has gone through so much pain, how could the "bushy beard" attorney have messed up? When her sanity depends on having the affirmation that the traumatic forced abortion itself was wrong, how could the Immigration Judge called it a "frivolous claim?" I was not present when Ms. Chun was told of the Immigrant Judge's asylum rejection. I wondered how "frivolous claim" was translated into a lay person's Chinese. Did the translator convey the commonsense notion of the word frivolous in English, or the legal term "with an intent to harass, delay or embarrass the opposition?" Regardless of the translation, I doubted anyone had told Ms. Chun of the larger context of the politics of asylum protection and the near impossibility of gaining protection. In reviewing Ms. Chun's case, I wondered if the Immigration Judge was ignorant of the depth of Ms. Chun's trauma and grief, or if she deliberately chose to coldly ignore her emotional devastation? One cannot help but wonder if the Judge is another bureaucrat obeying orders from above, much like the van drivers, security personnel, doctors, and nurses in China who were also obeying their own orders from above. How is this so different from the blind obedience of orders at other times and places?

Ms. Chun's case now represents another casualty of the asylum attrition. It is a double tragedy: the tragedy she suffered in China and the tragedy she suffered in the United States asylum system. In the case of the human rights violations against men and women who were forced into sterilizations, the immigration judges are merely the last in a string of misguided men and women responsible for the shameful human tragedy of Ms. Chun.

I have considered using "Double Tragedy" as the title of this chapter to capture the tragedy of Ms. Chun in the context of traditional rites of passage: the marriage of a couple and the birth of child. The marriage of a couple is supreme happiness to a man's family, as well as to the woman's family. To have a child soon after marriage is another happiness to each family, hence "happiness" all around. At Chinese weddings, the symbol of Double Happiness, 双喜, is rendered into 囍, which is ubiquitously displayed at restaurant wedding banquets, on wedding invitations, gift wrappings, wedding cakes, and is embroidered on pillows and bedsheets in the bridal chamber. In the modern popular take on it as an auspicious word in the West, it is found in designs on necklace pendants, earrings, and tattooed onto bodies. The unintended consequence of China's one-child policy has turned its country's traditional emphasis on the happiness of births into a compulsory tragic sacrifice for the state. In the execution of the asylum laws in this case there was no sanctuary for the asylum seeker. To Ms. Chun, it was a double tragedy.

Chapter 13

Mr. Sung's Embarrassment or Humiliation?

Mr. Sung came from China to the United States in 2005 on a B-1 visa and filed an I-589 Application for Asylum in 2006, more than twelve months after his entry. Even though an immigration judge granted Mr. Sung asylum due to a forced vasectomy in China, the US government overturned the immigration judge's decision and initiated procedures to remove him from the country. Mr. Sung contacted Mr. Goodsell for help with his appeal to the Bureau of Immigration Appeals. At the recommendation of Mr. Goodsell, Mr. Sung met me in my office, clutching a folder of documents. Mr. Goodsell had faxed me some pertinent documents from his file to help me understand his case before the meeting.

Most asylum seekers do not know what an anthropologist does or how we can be of help to them throughout the asylum application process. In Mr. Sung's case, he had been rejected twice before by the immigration system and was hesitant to trust me. If he were to consider me anything other than another obstacle in the American asylum system, it was important that I establish rapport with him. Mr. Sung had no reason to trust me, especially not on the recommendation of an attorney he barely knew; convincing him otherwise was awkward.

Mr. Sung was a tall, quiet, dignified-looking Chinese man in his forties, from a province in northern central China. I am an older woman of Chinese origin from "overseas." Though we shared a common ancestry, it did not guarantee a sense of kinship, familiarity, or trust. I was hopeful, but not sure that the gray hair of my age would convince him that I knew more. The task of establishing rapport takes on special importance, especially as a woman talking to him, in his native language, about his most intimate matters.

I told Mr. Sung my expertise with family planning methods, based on the research I conducted for my doctoral dissertation, as well as the World

Health Organization (WHO), which felt like eons ago. I also assured him of my familiarity with China based on my four official World Bank missions to four provinces on the Involuntary Resettlement of Populations affected by the construction of hydroelectric dam projects. In fact, I told him, I had visited regions close to his province in China while working on the resettlement of rural populations affected by the Xiaolandi Hydroelectric dam along the Yellow River. I had to convince him that I had been to more places in China than most Chinese on official visits and I had gone past the boundaries of most "foreign" visitors there for tourism or to visit relatives.

Being an anthropologist or a professor with research experience does not instantiate an automatic authority on an asylum seeker's problems. An asylum seeker has already gone through so much trauma and persecution by the authorities in his or her homeland. My expertise was not the only matter being questioned; there was also the question of whether I represented another authority. Could he trust me? I spoke, hoping to convince him that he should trust me with his story, but at the same time mentioned how difficult it would be to gain asylum. I did not want to give him false hopes. Despite having helped Mr. Goodsell and other attorneys gain asylum for their clients, I cannot always be confident that the next case I work on will ensure the same result. Aware that so few appeals are able to reverse the fate of the petitioner, I am always fearful of the consequences of a failed appeal.

Finally, he said, "I am so ashamed. I was fired from my job. I have lost face. I did not mention to anyone, except in court when the judge asked me. It was unavoidable." Often times, survivors have never told anyone what they have been through, with their interview or court hearing being the first time they are telling their story. This, in combination with intimidation and language barriers, leaves asylum applicants "unprepared for the harsh reality of the legal system in which reciting the narrative once is never sufficient" (Marton 2015). Conroy (2009) argues that it is crucial for lawyers and clients to be aware that gendered notions can still be at work in adjudicating [rape] cases. Particularly, with respect to credibility, judgments may "penalize those who do not fit within the normative male, heterosexual, American cultural expectations for testimonial behavior" (Conroy 2009, 13).

I tried to find a way to ease him into his painful story, but I could not think of what to say that would not sound hollow and insincere: Apologize on behalf of the Chinese government? The United States government? Blame it on fate? I broke his painful silence by telling him that, as an anthropologist, I was interested in his customs and cultures: where he grew up and what life was like in China to put his case in perspective. Mr. Sung put his bundle of documents on the table. We began the interview.

Mr. Sung grew up in a rural community of three hundred thousand in a province along the Yellow River, several hundred kilometers from Beijing.

Most people are farmers, and having children is important to help on the farm and for old-age support. Pensions do not exist and infant mortality is not far from their memory, not to mention the disruption of life under various government programs during the last few decades in China. He is the youngest of three children. His older brother and sister were both married and each had two children. The Chinese government's one-child policy makes exceptions to couples in the rural areas. Because of the need for help on the farm, if the firstborn is a daughter, a couple is allowed to have a second child. The government also makes exceptions for a few other conditions, but Mr. Sung did not qualify for any of them. Mr. Sung's married sister had a daughter. Even though she could legitimately have a second child, she hid her second pregnancy by staying with relatives in another part of the country. Her rationale was that if she had a girl again, she could either abort the unwanted female fetus or give the girl away without the government's knowledge. If the pregnancy was a secret, regardless of how she got rid of the unwanted female pregnancy, it would not count toward her limit of two children. But the pregnancy turned out to be a boy, so she could either come out from her hiding and stop at two, or she could keep it a secret and try her chances of having a another boy.

When she did not report her "illegal" pregnancy to the neighborhood birth planning committee, the government discovered this and she was forced to undergo an abortion. A few years later, she tried to "illegally" get pregnant again. She succeeded by having a son without detection. His brother's wife, who already had a son, had become pregnant without "permission" from the government. When her pregnancy was discovered, she paid a fine of 1,000 yuan and was allowed to keep the pregnancy. Mr. Sung and his wife wanted a second child after the birth of their first. His reason was that if the first child failed to survive, there would be a second one. He said they both love children, and that they would also act as their old age insurance.

In the rural areas, Chinese cultural traditions of worshipping ancestors remains strong even under communism. Mr. Sung's family honored the memories of his paternal grandparents and three generations above them with their names inscribed on strips of white paper and placed on the home altar. The family held special memorials for their dead ancestors with offerings of food, wine, the burning of incense, candles and joss papers during the spring festival, on the death anniversary of the deceased, and on *chingming,* a day the family gathers to clean the graves of their ancestors. On these occasions, Mr. Sung's parents prepared the offerings but the whole family took turns paying respect to their ancestors through praying, bowing, and the burning of incense. Besides honoring the four ascending generations of the deceased, the Sung family also keeps a genealogy of the more remote Sung ancestors in the village's clan temple. In this Chinese practice of "ancestor worship," only the male line is kept. Daughters marry out and they belong to the lines of their husbands. The female figures on the Sung family altars and clan temple were those who married in and had given birth to children. In this traditional culture, to have a place in the family, male or female, is defined by one's ability to have children. According to such a tradition, the epitome of a good man is to be virile and to sire children. The culture emphasizes male virility and the importance of having children through the male line. Family names are passed down from father to son to grandson. So for a woman, her place is established by having children for her husband's lineage.

FORCED CONFESSION AND FORCED VASECTOMY

After Mr. Sung and his wife had their first child, the family planning cadre at his wife's work forced Mrs. Sung to have an IUD inserted. Mrs. Sung wanted another child, just like her husband's siblings. Complaining of bleeding and discomfort, Mrs. Sung secretly asked a private doctor to help her remove the IUD. She became pregnant soon after its removal. When her work unit discovered her pregnancy, they wanted her to have an abortion immediately. Unwilling to lose the baby, Mrs. Sung went into hiding, living with relatives in the countryside, where she carried the pregnancy to full term and secretly delivered the baby.

Mr. Sung said his horrible nightmare began when his wife tried to have a second child. Mr. Sung worked as a doctor at a major hospital in his city along the Yellow River. When his employer learned that his wife had an illegal second child, the hospital used him as an example to warn other hospital employees, so they would not consider any attempts of future violations against China's one-child policy. The hospital first summoned Mr. Sung to an office, locked him up, denied him food and water, and told him to reflect on his action and write down his "crime." This went on for three days. As further punishment, the hospital shamed Mr. Sung in front of his colleagues, where seventy to eighty employees were gathered for a meeting with the sole purpose of listening to Mr. Sung's confession. After that, Mr. Sung was told to go home to wait for the hospital's decision. After a few days, the hospital fired Mr. Sung. A few days later, the family planning unit at the hospital returned to take him to the hospital for a vasectomy. Mr. Sung said that despite his begging for them not to do it, the doctor ignored him. During the operation, Mr. Sung said the anesthesia failed to work and he felt tremendous pain; he wondered how he survived it. Mr. Sung said, "Even if they had used anesthesia, I wouldn't have known. It was so painful." Mr. Sung said he got an infection from the operation. He endured pain to his lower back and abdomen and could not walk straight for six months afterwards.

In the early 1970s, the Chinese government promoted birth-planning programs emphasizing *wan, xi, shao*, or later marriage, longer birth intervals, and fewer children (Greenhalgh and Winckler 2005). The program eventually became one to reduce fertility, ultimately limiting all couples to one child with the exception of minorities, rural residents whose firstborn were daughters, the parents of the disabled, and a few other instances. However, once the government apparatus was put in place, even though it varied from place to place, it became required to have a childbearing permit. The policy became linked to birth quotas allotted to various locations.

In the local communities, Birth Control Committee members track women's menstrual cycles to monitor their reproductive profile, force women to insert intrauterine devices, have an abortion, or to have surgeries on tubal ligation, depending on the state's approved birth quotas status. (Hesketh, Lu, and Xing 2005). I was unaware of the Chinese government forcing men to have vasectomies until Mr. Sung told me his story and made sure to take careful notes on his terrible experience.

The Immigration Judge had rejected Mr. Sung's asylum application by suggesting that Mr. Sung was only embarrassed about his forced vasectomy and embarrassment is not grounds for asylum. Mr. Sung felt the Chinese government had humiliated him and took away his manhood, but the Judge discounted his traumatic experience by denying him asylum. This careful ethnographic attempt is done to anticipate other adjudicators who might think Chinese asylum seekers are bogus. As a matter of fact, American medical doctors have examined women who were forcibly sterilized in China and sought asylum protection in the United States. The doctors emphasized meticulous history-taking to differentiate a "sham" tubal ligation, in which "a local practitioner merely inches the abdomen." Noting "the 'sham' tubal ligation in the medical record is particularly important because such documentation could support the patient's assertion that a reasonable probability of future sterilization exists, on return to China." (Sills et al 1998, 1729).

Mr. Sung said the vasectomy was like a castration. He felt shameful. He did not feel like "a whole man." He no longer felt normal. He did not mention the operation to anyone, because he did not want people to know. It was a closely-held secret that he had not mentioned until he applied for asylum in the United States. He said the whole experience felt like a nightmare that would not go away.

After losing his job at the hospital, Mr. Sung said he could not find employment elsewhere. To get a job anywhere requires an "introduction letter." No employer would hire someone who had confessed to a "crime" against the State. For years, Mr. Sung tried to come to the United States, finally succeeding in 2005.

COMMUNITY IN CALIFORNIA AFTER ARRIVING IN THE UNITED STATES

After Mr. Sung arrived in the United States, he lived with friends at a cheap motel and worked in a Chinese restaurant in San Fernando Valley, to the north of Los Angeles. Aware that the Government Counsel had denied Mr. Sung's asylum application because he had missed the one-year rule, I specifically asked why he did not apply earlier.

Mr. Sung said there were few Chinese in the community where he landed in California. Among the few Chinese he came into contact with, going to America has always carried the myths that if you can afford to go you must have made it, or that America is the place of the Gold Mountain where one makes one's fortune. Few ordinary people know about asylum protection, and even fewer know about how to access the system. Mr. Sung said he did not know he could apply for asylum or that he should apply within one year of his arrival. Living in a remote rural suburb of Los Angeles, there were few Chinese, and even fewer Mandarin speakers. His visits to Chinatown in Los Angeles or to the Chinese communities in Monterey Park and Alhambra, where he could have obtained legal assistance, were infrequent. He did not disclose to anyone his closely held secret for leaving China. It was not until about six months after his arrival that he met another motel resident with whom he disclosed his fear of return to China. His knowledge about applying for asylum came only years later.

HUMILIATION OR EMBARRASSMENT?

He said, he could not possibly have confessed to the few Chinese he came into contact with by asking, "Could you recommend me a lawyer? I want to apply for asylum." He said, "I was a doctor at the hospital. I was too ashamed to mention that the Chinese government forced me to confess to a "crime" of my wife having a second child, fired me from my job, and forced me to have a vasectomy." He wrote two words *xiu ru* (羞辱) on my yellow notepad which I used to take notes. He said, "The thought of confessing to having my tubes tied was too *xiu ru* (羞辱)," which translates into "humiliation, shame, dishonor."

The Government, in a written summary of the case after Mr. Sung's hearing in front of an Immigration Judge, had written:

> Respondent stated that the reason he waited so long to file his I-589 Application was that he was too *embarrassed* to talk about what happened to him in China, namely that he had a forced vasectomy. The Immigration Judge did

> not make a finding as to whether this qualifies as an exception to the one-year deadline. In failing to decide whether this was a valid exception to the deadline, the Immigration Judge erred in granting Respondent asylum. Even if the Immigration Judge found Respondent's reasons valid to excuse the late filing, the Government would argue that *embarrassment* neither qualifies for "changed" nor "extraordinary circumstances." (my italics)

Embarrassment is 難堪 (*Nánkān*) in Chinese. Mr. Sung does not speak English. The word "embarrassment" probably came up during his testimony in court. Mr. Sung could have used the word *xiu ru* (羞辱), or shame and humiliation, when telling his story, which the interpreter then translated into English as "embarrassment." Mr. Sung might have been embarrassed to talk about his vasectomy to others, in the common understanding that most Americans would use as the word "embarrassed." He applied for asylum to escape the humiliation and punishment for wanting a second child; not because of an "embarrassment" in talking about the forced vasectomy.

Perhaps it is the job of the Government Counsel to ignore, oppose, and deny an asylum seeker as a default policy. Without taking into account the context of Mr. Sung's asylum application, the Government parsed words by focusing on Mr. Sung's "embarrassment" in talking about what had happened to him rather than the public shaming and humiliation he had endured. There is a big difference between the two. One is the Chinese government's use of forced vasectomy as a way to shame and humiliate him as a man. The other is the embarrassment of talking about the forced vasectomy. Perhaps it is a matter of the degree of intensity in how Mr. Sung feels. I would feel embarrassed about being late in completing a report to the attorney, and I would feel more ashamed in failing to perform my best when someone's future depends on it. This is a prime example of the difficulty of translation in court and across cultures.

I wanted to tell Mr. Sung that his "fall from grace" was not his fault, but was caused by the control and surveillance of the Chinese government on its subject. I wanted to tell him that his asylum rejection was not his fault, but was perhaps caused by the United States government deliberately parsing words to keep out unwanted immigrants and asylum seekers, rather than accepting the significance of a forced vasectomy to Mr. Sung's social role as a man in a strong patrilineal society with descent based on the male line. I did not say any of the above. Mr. Sung was in pain. The interview went on for more than two hours, and he looked emotionally drained. Instead, I told him I would call him for more details as I began to write his story up for Mr. Goodsell's appeal.

Mr. Sung stood up. He picked up the bundle of documents he had brought. He thanked me. I thanked him. Then Mr. Sung said, with a tone of finality, "*ke yi le*. . . . It is ok. . . . Could you please keep my paper for me?" He handed his pile of documents to me with both hands with a certain formality. I accepted his papers with both hands while standing straight up, reciprocating his formal gesture.

The papers contained "EXHIBITS" that his counsel had prepared as evidence of his asylum application. It includes the following:

1. EXHIBIT 1: A Letter from a CIS designated Civil Surgeon.
2. EXHIBIT 2: Application for Asylum and for Withholding of Removal.
3. EXHIBIT 3: An Affidavit of Asylum Application

The package also contained the following important documents, in their original form, issued by the government to Mr. Sung:

1. "Notice of Appeal from a Decision of an Immigration Judge"
2. DHS BRIEF ON APPEAL FROM THE DECISION OF THE IMMIGRATION JUDGE from the Assistant Chief Counsel from the Department of Homeland Security, U.S. Department of Justice
3. ORDER OF THE IMMIGRATION JUDGE: IN REMOVAL PROCEEDINGS
4. FILING RECEIPT FOR APPEAL from Office of the District Counsel/LOS, U.S. Department of Justice
5. NOTICE—BRIEFING SCHEDULE from the Office of the District Counsel/LOS, U.S. Department of Justice

One final document, and the only one in Chinese, was his Asylum Application (庇护申请, *Bìhù shēnqǐng*), written and signed by Mr. Sung. It detailed his pain of public humiliation by the Chinese government, the physical pain of the forced vasectomy, and the "mental" pain of his trauma.

These items were the personal copies and originals of his whole application process. Most asylum seekers keep them. There was no reason for Mr. Sung to give them to me; his attorney had already faxed over the pertinent papers to help me prepare his case. Indeed, there was no reason for him to keep those documents either. His attorney, Mr. Goodsell, would submit an appeal. My report supported Mr. Sung with an argument that he deserved a second chance through provisions in the social, cultural, and political contexts of his forced vasectomy. If his appeal was successful, they would inform his attorney, and his attorney would inform him. I would not be automatically informed. After submitting the report to his attorney, my obligation would be complete.

I did not ask Mr. Sung why he gave his papers to me. But I had an image of him going from one small town Chinese restaurant to another, working illegally, carrying around the papers that reminded him of the humiliation, and his shame. Where did he normally keep his documents? In a suitcase which he never unpacked, while living in small cheap motels or in a shared quarter with other immigrants from China? Perhaps giving away the papers would lessen his psychological burden of thinking of the past.

I prepared his case, and gave my report to Mr. Goodsell. Then, Mr. Sung and Mr. Goodsell waited. The asylum system demands absolute certainties, while the asylum seekers are expected to live with constant uncertainties.

MR. SUNG'S SHAME AND HIS MEMBERSHIP IN A PARTICULAR SOCIAL GROUP

In preparing the report on Mr. Sung, I wrote about the stigma and the shame and humiliation he had endured.

Vasectomies may have been developed as a male method of birth control, but the Chinese government imposed it on a man with strong cultural traditions and made him publicly confess that he had disobeyed the one-child policy. This resulted in a deep cultural, societal, and politically-based shame. As a man from a rural background, Mr. Sung was culturally motivated to have a second child as old-age insurance and for extra help for the difficulties of everyday life. Using the one-child policy, the Chinese government makes these cultural motivations a violation of the government's policy. The Chinese government shamed him into forceful submission by surgery, public confession, and humiliation. To Mr. Sung, the forced vasectomy was so unspeakable, he did not mention it to anyone until he had to apply for asylum. Shame delayed his application, leading him to miss the one-year rule.

One often associates gender roles and shame with women, as told by the story of Mrs. Harianto, in part III, chapter 9, who was shamed and silenced by the stigma of rape through her gendered social role as a wife, mother, and an outstanding Catholic Chinese woman in her community. Mr. Sung, from the story he has revealed, played a male gendered role, and was shamed as well. Male shame is not frequently discussed, but in the case of Mr. Sung, his shame was undeniably true.

Examining his situation from the criteria for qualification under the ground of Membership in a Particular Social Group, the attack is against his gendered roles as a man. If Mr. Sung's case had been prepared with due diligence from the beginning, he could have been qualified under Membership in a Particular Social Group.

A WELL-FOUNDED FEAR OF RETURN TO CHINA

While reading over the CIS-designated Civil Surgeon's letter corroborating Mr. Sung's forced vasectomy, it clearly certified that the applicant's status was "post Vasectomy, a procedure for sterilization in men." In my closer examination, the letter also contained the following:

> But apparently, the surgery of vasectomy that this applicant had back to more than ten years ago might not be very successful per lab report of semen analysis of this applicant. He should not be completely sterile, because his ejaculates are not sperm-free based on the semen analysis result.

I am not sure if Mr. Sung was given a close translation of the letter except to prove positively that he had a vasectomy. A careful examination of the report might have assured him he might still be able to sire another child of his own. The condition in China, however, would not allow him to have another child, regardless of his ability to have one.

Having a child within the permitted system means receiving access to various state benefits. Having a child outside the allocation, especially for state employees and those in the urban areas, means facing sanctions that range from reduction of salaries to loss of work. Under China's one-child policy, zealous birth control committees compete regionally and nationally to meet allotted quotas by monitoring women's menstrual cycle, their every pregnancy, and every contraceptive pill taken (Zhang 2017). Matters previously considered private and personal have become public and national concerns of the government. Issues which were previously cultural taboos became topics of discussion at confession sessions. In the hands of some fanatical and highly efficient birth control committee members, China's birth-planning programs became a coercive population control program, leading many to leave the country to seek asylum.

In October 2015, the Chinese government changed its policy from a one-child policy to a two-children policy. However, this change would not benefit Mr. Sung as he already had two children. The second child came with the price of enduring public humiliation, the loss of his job, a forced vasectomy, escaping from the country, separation from his family, and the huge financial cost of applying for asylum. If he should return to China, he would not be allowed to have another child even under the new policy. If Mr. Sung should impregnate his wife accidently, since he may not know he is not "sperm free," his wife will be forced to abort the next pregnancy, given they have already reached the new quota of two children under China's new two-children policy.

Part V

LAW AND ANTHROPOLOGY

Chapter 14

Article I Court in a World of Uncertainties

Coauthored with Joann Yeh

When I first met Joann Yeh in court, she was representing Ms. Li, whose case I had begun working on with Mr. Goodsell. In preparing the case, Joann Yeh was able to read my carefully crafted report on the persecution against Ms. Li rather than having to go through her several-inch-thick files. Joann Yeh said it was the first time she encountered an anthropologist's account of an asylum petition. She was interested in learning how I had prepared my report.

In my own struggle to navigate the unfamiliar terrain of figuring out the anthropological figures for the asylum courts, I was only too eager for any conversation to learn about legal expectations and to account for my own difficulty in preparing the cases. Over the years, I found no anthropological model or test that could verify a person's identity with certainty, no scientific test on a person's "race," no checklist that could verify a person's religion, or to substantiate if a rape had actually occurred long after the incident.

Joann Yeh and I met and discussed the differences between law and anthropology through our presentations at the annual American Anthropological Association and Society for Applied Anthropology conferences. Joann Yeh examined the legal system affecting asylum hearings and I tried to imagine the Government Counsel and Judges' adjudication of asylum cases given their legal structural constraints. Eager to gain insights in the difficulty of obtaining asylum from the perspectives of the asylum seekers, we conducted fieldwork in Los Angeles, where most Chinese-speaking asylum seekers came from. We also examined the asylum petitioners' encounter with the legal system by focusing on the encounters between the asylum seekers and the asylum adjudicators. In the simplest terms, we considered questions from three perspectives: the asylum seekers, the anthropological expert witness, and the asylum adjudicators.

With regard to the asylum seekers, we were interested in how applicants found ways to make their status legal when they are in a strange land without relatives, resources, or fluency in the language after they fled persecution in their homeland. In the case of the anthropological expert witness, to navigate an unfamiliar terrain, it was important to know the requirements and expectations for proving persecution on account of the grounds of the 1951 Refugee Convention: race, religion, nationality, membership in a particular social group, and political opinion; that is, to provide expert knowledge on the social science canons of race, religion, and gender with certainties. But, the question remained, how do we do it?

In the case of the asylum adjudicators, from the initial request from the Immigration Officer who rejected Dewi's asylum application and sent her to an anthropologist to "prove" her "Chinese race" (see chapters 1 to 3) to a private attorney in solo practice and to Seyfarth Shaw's attempt to find an anthropologist who could help Rani's claim of domestic abuse, it is clear that sociocultural expertise is crucial for a fair and accurate assessment of the *identities* of the petitioner as well as the *conditions* of the country from where they have escaped from. But is it possible to do so?

As we considered these questions, foremost on our minds was the perception in the Chinese community that obtaining asylum is easy. In the community, there are oftentimes many who know personally, or know of, someone who has sought asylum. Based on our involvement with the asylum seekers we have worked with, however, we knew that their experiences in their pursuit of asylum was not so simple. To determine the extent of the difficulty, we decided to examine a subset of the asylum-seeking population familiar to both of us: Chinese asylum seekers in Los Angeles.

We wanted to know what it was like when an asylum seeker with limited means, speaking only Mandarin Chinese, decides to apply for asylum protection in the United States. How do they access the legal system? Are they coming to the United States with the intention to cheat the system, as the legal system and public seem to think?

OUR FIELDWORK AND OUR FINDINGS

In understanding this asylum-seeking process, we limited ourselves to the likely resources available to those who knew only Chinese. Often without friends, families, the English language, or the familiarity of the local communities, we believed the asylum seekers found information through those in the same linguistic community. We did not contact high profile NGOs such as Public Council and the Program for Tortured Victims, because they would not be on the radar for a new asylum seeker from Asia. Instead, we explored law offices and social service agencies in and around the Chinese communities with advertisements in the Chinese Consumer Yellow Pages and the free vernacular tabloids available at local Chinese supermarkets and Chinese restaurants.

Two major centers that we thought would provide legal assistance to asylum seekers were the Asian Pacific Legal Center in Los Angeles, and the Chinatown Social Service Center, but this was not the case. The Asian Pacific American Legal Center made its name fighting for the rights of illegal garment workers more than a decade ago, and in the community it is well known for helping with citizenship applications. Chinatown Social Service Center was set up to provide services for new immigrants, from employment training to learning English. We called the center regarding services for asylum seekers but were told to contact a similar office in the San Gabriel Valley. We were unsuccessful at reaching anyone at the second office. We were equally unsuccessful with law offices in Chinatown. There were few advertisements about law offices in Chinatown in English on the internet and those few we found and visited were closed.

Our most successful research result came from the advertisements in the Chinese newspapers and the Chinese Consumer Yellow Pages. We found law offices advertised in the greater Los Angeles area, most of them concentrated in San Gabriel Valley, a region east of Los Angeles, hugged between two major freeways. Over the last few decades, San Gabriel Valley has become home to a burgeoning Asian population, some of them from Los Angeles' old Chinatown and others directly from Asia, to create new "ethnoburbs," (Li 1997) or communities with ethnic concentrations in the suburbs. Following the advertisements in Chinese vernacular newspapers on law offices providing immigration services, we visited six law offices in the suburban Chinatowns of Monterey Park and Alhambra.

In our visit to these law offices, known as *lüshilou* in Mandarin Chinese, whether talking to the attorney or the person at the front desk, we were informed of the many services they provided. For the new and old immigrants with limited English and unfamiliarity with American government institutions, they include disability benefits, food stamps, social security, medical and welfare benefits, setting up trusts, and translation services.

In legal services, the *lüshilou* provide green card renewal, application for citizenship, H1-B Visa, Visa for China, and consultation on investment for obtaining permanent residency. In our interviews at the *lüshilou*, we were told there were three major ways to obtain legal residency in the United States: marry a citizen, start a company if one had a million dollars, or apply for asylum. In probing for details on how one obtains asylum protection, we were also told: "We will do everything including driving the asylum seekers" by one receptionist at a *lüshilou*. While the statement can be taken as questionable in the operation of the enterprise, it could also point to the needs of the asylum seekers who must depend on others for all aspects of help in applying for asylum. To understand asylum seekers' search for legal representation, we were interested in how asylum seekers end up selecting a particular attorney. Anecdotal evidence from the asylum seekers we have worked with suggested service providers' use of cultural and ethnic cues in the ethnic media to attract potential asylum seekers.

IDENTITY-MAKING AND COMMODIFICATION OF ETHNICITY AND CULTURE

A page from an advertisement of a free Chinese newspaper in Los Angeles in January, 2011 shows *lüshilou*'s attempts to appeal to the potential Chinese-speaking clients through the languages and dialects they speak: Mandarin, Cantonese, Taiwanese, and Fujianese. They also showed traditional good business practices such as "free consultations," "guaranteed success," and "rapid results." In reviewing these advertisements of the *lüshilou*, we were surprised at the use of the *ethnicities* of the attorneys to attract potential customers. One firm advertises its attorney's twenty-eight years of experience and *Jewish* background. Another *lüshilou* proclaims a team of "white attorneys" will personally appear in court for the client.

Evidently, Jewish and "white" ethnic identities are considered appealing to the potential Chinese clients who may view Jewish and white lawyers as more capable in court than their own Chinese ethnicities. In this asylum market, not only is ethnic language and culture employed to attract potential asylum clients, ethnicities of the attorneys are commodified for profit as well.

In this commodification of the ethnicity for profit in asylum cases, cultural and ethnic information are being repackaged to communicate with the potential asylum applicants. Through the asylum marketplace, the seller and buyer of the asylum services are able to use common cultural and ethnic assumptions, and common language, through the ethnic media, to eventually locate needed services.

ASYLUM PROTECTION: A CHOICE AMONG MANY OPTIONS

To understand the asylum seeker's search for legal representation, we were interested in how they end up selecting asylum as a way to remain in the country.

From the *lüshilou* advertisements, there are many avenues for legal residence in the United States. In a smorgasbord of options for one to remain in the United States, potential asylum seekers can also choose to be a student, marry a citizen, invest a million dollars in a business to gain permanent residency, or apply for an H1-B visa if one has special skills.

Given these advertised choices, submitting an asylum petition is only one among the many options to legally remain in the United States. If a person wishes to remain in the United States and does not qualify due to a lack of special skills, enormous wealth, qualification to be a student, or is not willing to commit to marrying a citizen to gain residency, applying for asylum is considered an attractive option. That is, the asylum petitioners did not intentionally arrive in the United States to defraud the asylum system. They apply for asylum because they do not fit into all other categories of remaining in the United States.

For instance, we know of people who are here while on a tourist visa and find themselves helping relatives in a business or caring for an aging parent, but currently there is no existing visa category that fits this laboring class of visitors, who wish to remain for a year or two, working in a low level laborer's job. Thus, while their intention was for a short-term stay, the lack of opportunities makes asylum an attractive option to remain in a country. To apply, they exaggerate their experiences that seem to fit the stories most likely to be granted asylum at the moment, leading to the potential for fraud. For example, a woman from China may have had an abortion as a part of China's one-child policy. When she wanted to remain in the United States but was ineligible for any of the legal means or categories, she applied for asylum by using the experience of her abortion as a coercive element.

It is interesting that the advertisements in the Chinese newspapers do not list visas available for farm workers, presumably because people who have the intention to migrate to a new country would not consider laboring in the fields as an attractive option. If there is an additional category for the nonfarm laborers, in addition to those categories available to potential migrants, it would be applicable to many of those who apply for asylum as a way to remain in the United States, but may not have suffered persecution.

IMMIGRATION COURT AS A QUASI-JUDICIAL INSTITUTION

Even though the tribunal where asylum as well as other immigration decisions are made, is referred to as "immigration court," these proceedings do not take place in what most people in the United States would consider a legitimate court of law. When most people think of a court of law, they refer to something they've seen depicted on television or the movies. For the most part, the courts portrayed are criminal or civil courts and are what legal scholars would call "Article III" courts. This definition applies to all the trial or appellate courts in the federal or state court systems. Specifically, federal courts (including the district courts, the circuit courts of appeal, and the Supreme Court) were established by Article III of the US Constitution to adjudicate, among other things, all "controversies to which the United States shall be a party; controversies between two or more states; between a state and citizens of another state; between citizens of different states; between citizens of the same state claiming lands under grants of different states, and between a state, or the citizens thereof, and foreign states, citizens or subjects." (U.S. Const. art. III, § 2.) The fifty states, through their own state constitutions, have set up their own court systems in roughly the same manner to adjudicate all state-level criminal and civil matters.

In addition to Article III courts, the Constitution also established what are known as administrative law courts under Article I, which authorizes Congress as the legislative branch to establish tribunals to review decisions made by the various administrative agencies as well as the military courts. (U.S. Const. art. I, § 8, cl. 9.) Examples of administrative law courts include the U.S. Tax Court and the U.S. Bankruptcy Courts, among many others. While the immigration court system was indeed created by acts of Congress, unlike most other administrative law tribunals, immigration courts are not covered by the Administrative Procedure Act ("APA"), which assures the neutrality and independence of administrative law courts even though they operate within the Executive Branch of government. In fact, Congress intentionally kept immigration courts out of the jurisdiction of the APA, because forcing them to comply with the statute would be too "cumbersome" (Marks 2012, 28–29).

Thus, technically, immigration courts are not administrative law courts either. In fact, immigration judges are classified and employed as *attorneys* under the US Department of Justice. This is extremely important to note, because it means that they are beholden to the ethics and standards of attorneys—*not* judges. Specifically, they are not subject to the Code of Conduct for United States Judges or the Code of Judicial Ethics of the states, both of which, above all else, emphasize the importance of impartiality, appearance of impartiality or impropriety, and judicial independence. That is why generally judges rarely speak during trial, other than to rule on a motion or objection made by an attorney, to give jury instructions, or to render a verdict if there is no jury.

In contrast, in immigration "court," the immigration "judge" is allowed, if not encouraged, to question the witness or asylum seeker, often creating the appearance that they are continuing the work of the government attorney. In a crucial way, they are, because they are technically attorneys instead of judges; they must have a client to whom they are beholden. In this case, it is the US government in its efforts to deport an alien if that alien is found to be removable, which is the same client the government attorney from Immigration and Customs Enforcement (ICE) is representing. It is extremely interesting to note that in the Department of Justice's (2018) own job posting for immigration judges, under "Duties," it specifically states: "Immigration Judges preside in formal, *quasi-judicial* hearings" (para. 6).

REAL ID ACT

Because immigration courts are not traditional judicial tribunals, the rules of evidence have been softened to accommodate the particular bind that asylum seekers are in of simply not having the "right" kind of admissible evidence. Of particular note is the fact that hearsay evidence is not only allowed in immigration court but is often the *entire basis* of the asylum seeker's case. His or her entire direct testimony is a retelling of what was done and said to him/her outside of the courtroom in a different country. If hearsay evidence were barred as it is in traditional courts, virtually every single asylum case would be denied as the asylum seeker would not be able to present their story at all.

If asylum proceedings were allowed to continue in this evidentiary grey area, asylum seekers would have been able to maintain a reasonable chance in the removal hearing process. Prior to the enactment of the REAL ID Act on May 11, 2005, people applying for asylum in the United States were only required to truthfully provide a statement under oath about the events that were proof of their persecution. If and when their cases were referred to immigration court for further review before a decision was rendered, the main purpose was for a judge to ascertain their credibility and be questioned in depth about their persecution.

With the REAL ID Act, however, immigration judges could for the first time ask for corroborating evidence from the asylum seeker. (See 8 U.S.C. § 1229a(c)(4)(B).) In fact, the immigration officer who first examines the case can now also request supporting documents to substantiate the applicant's claims. (See 8 U.S.C. § 1252(b)(4).) In addition, the immigration judge, in his/her assessment of the asylum applicant's credibility, could now take the applicant's "demeanor" into account, thereby adding even more subjective discretion into the already amorphous process of determining the applicant's credibility.

Passage of the REAL ID Act was achieved with little scrutiny at the time, because it was attached to an emergency appropriations bill to fund the Iraq War as well as disaster relief. All discussions were dominated by the Republicans in charge of Congress who prevented any Democrats from attending or voicing their concerns over the bill.

LEGAL CURRICULUM

Most attorneys, even those with immigration law as a specialty, do not have in-depth training about the five grounds of the Refugee Convention. Law schools do not teach students about "race," culture, religion, or what it means when a person is a member of a particular social group, much less investigating the intricacies of how to interpret the five grounds. Their understanding of the identity of the asylum seeker is based on common sense assumptions formed by the culture of the adjudicators as members of an elite North American community. The idea that "race" is socially constructed rarely enters the legal lexicon. The attorneys and judges (and everyone else) assume they and everyone knows what "race" is, which means that a white is a white, a black is a black, and a Latino is a Latino. At most, they know about diversity in the United States.

To determine whether or not an asylum seeker qualifies for protection on account of a particular criterion, the attorney examines legal precedents based on cases that have been determined. For instance, arguing that the Chinese Indonesians were persecuted on account of "race"; the case referred to was *Lolong v. Gonzalez*. After *Lolong v. Gonzalez* was overturned, however, attorneys referred instead to *Sael v. Gonzalez*, an earlier case on a Chinese Indonesian woman who claimed persecution on account of her "race." But it is problematic when it comes down to actually verifying whether a Chinese Indonesian asylum seeker, or any asylum seeker for that matter, is indeed of a particular "race" as we have seen in Dewi's case in part I, chapter 1.

Even more difficult, is to articulate why a rape victim is a "member of a particular social group," as we have seen in Mrs. Harianto's case in part III, chapter 9.

There is a dissonance between the practice of law and social reality. Joann Yeh suspects that the inability to make decisions on the merit of a case makes asylum adjudicators skirt these issues and focus instead on credibility. Critical legal studies scholars have attempted to address these new challenges through their publications in law reviews. Joann Yeh contends that few lawyers in actual practices deal with issues of change. Furthermore, an asylum seeker is unlikely to contact a legal scholar for his or her asylum petition.

ANTHROPOLOGICAL CONCEPTS AS THEY RELATE TO CONVENTION GROUNDS

If concepts such as "race," culture, identity, and social change are not everyday parlance of law, they are, in contrast, the staple of anthropological theorizing, the subjects of critical cultural and ethnic studies, and are the fundamentals of scholarship in the social sciences. If anthropologists work with these concepts, why can't we state unambiguously for the public and the adjudicators whether an asylum seeker is of one race or culture or the other? To answer the question, I explore the emergence of the study of anthropology and suggest examining the ideas of race and culture by employing Lavie and Swedenburg's (2001) ideas of "Old Certainties" in a world of uncertainties.

Anthropology, which emerged as a North American and European study of the inhabitants of the world, focuses on humans in their interaction with others in the environment—both natural and biological. Major concepts associated with anthropology that are covered in an undergraduate's socio-cultural anthropology curriculum typically include the study of culture, language, economics, social stratification based on "race" and class, sex and gender, marriage, kinship and family, political life, religion and magic, and the application of anthropology in an age of globalization. Through the study of cultures and peoples of the world far and near, the discipline of anthropology has come to play a significant role in describing for the public the diversity of humanity in other places and other times.

"Culture," as understood by anthropologists means "the learned behaviors and ideas which humans acquire, create, and contest as a member of a society, and which they interpret as in some way defining the characteristics and parameters of that society and unifying the people who live within it." (Traphagan 2004, 12). Bourdieu, a French anthropologist, posited that culture is not simply a set of rules or codes but rather is "actively constructed by social actors from cultural dispositions and structured by previous events" (as cited in Moore 2009, 326). Culture is not a set of rules, rather it is a "dynamic outcome of interactions" (330). Bourdieu (1977) coined the term "habitus" which consists of "systems of durable, transposable *dispositions*" (72). Habitus refers to a collection of dispositions of people in a particular group, and these dispositions are seen as natural to them (78–79). These dispositions are acquired through social interaction (Samuelsen and Steffen 2004, 5). Habitus guides our everyday practices and actions. The people within a habitus cannot see it because they are inside of it (Bourdieu 1977, 78–79). Habitus influences practice; for example, in gift-giving exchanges, what is seen as a strategy based on a particular situation is actually influenced by habitus (Bourdieu 1977, 73). Bourdieu states that anthropologists can see both the objective and the subjective, and as such they can perceive practices that people embedded within cannot see (1977, 3–9).

Anthropology, given the nature of the discipline, is comparative and holistic. It studies subject matters both local and global. It takes into account definitions and interpretations of the meanings of its subject matters that are generated locally, and are not the same across different societies. In the life of anthropology and the social sciences, "race" and culture have become the labels when representing others. Both have been used as an analytical concept to help us view others as belonging in one culture or other. The "natives" in anthropology studied in the "field," became "the Other," and were at once different from the "Self" in terms of time and space. The world came to be understood as divided into a world of "Here" (the West) and the world "Out There" (the non-West). In this conceptualization of the world, pervasive throughout the humanities and the social sciences, there is a notion that a permanent link exists between cultures, peoples, and identities and specific places. In this sense of inseparability of identity from place, culture is seen as fixed, and encapsulated. One culture can be compared and contrasted with another. That is, a certain people as inhabitants of a particular terrain, possesses a particular culture. Culture is seen as internally homogeneous, and distinguishes members of one society from another: Chinese live in China and possess Chinese culture; whereas the French live in France and possess French culture. Culture distinguishes members of one society from another. This association between a particular culture and a stable terrain has served to ground our modern governing concepts of nations and cultures (Lavie and Swedenburg 2001, 1). As such, identities of a person based on "race" and culture used to be unproblematic.

OLD CERTAINTIES AND NEW UNCERTAINTIES

Over the years, the notion of an immutable link between culture and place is disrupted by massive migrations of subjects into the heart of the former colonial powers, challenging the binary between the "center" and the "margin." The former "natives" we used to define as distant and distinct who are supposed to be "there" are no longer "out there" but are now "here" as migrants, tourists, investors, students, refugees and asylum seekers. Tourists, students, and investors return home, but the refugees and asylum seekers knock on the doors of the Western democracies seeking protection. Their identities are now questioned and credibility challenged.

Faced with the forces of globalization and confronted with its own positivism, anthropology, like other disciplines in the social sciences, was confronted with the intellectual upheaval caused by a postmodernist condition, requiring a rethinking of its theoretical premises. Innovations and self-critique in anthropology and in the social sciences took place by drawing theories from feminist studies, cultural studies, postmodernism, and began to deconstruct the old ideas of "race," culture, and identities. Culture, at its root, is a result of invention and reinvention of previous ideas interacting with available resources. With the displacement and diaspora of peoples, cultures change. With migration to a new environment, people draw on old ideas and borrow from new resources available to them to produce an understanding of (about) themselves.

In *Identity and Agency in Cultural Worlds*, Holland (1998) pictures ourselves, and other individuals and groups as always engaged in forming identities, in processing objectifications of self—an understanding that may guide subsequent behavior (4). Major structural features in society are ideas on "race," ethnicity, gender, sexual orientation and nationality. Our lived world is also constituted by power, status, wealth, and privilege. People care about and care for what is going on around them. Their identities are social products formed "by one's position in relation to socially identified others, one's sense of social place, and entitlements" (125). They are important bases from which people conceptualized as imaginings of self which then direct new attitude, new worlds, and new ways of being" (5).

When the old concept of culture is used as an analytical concept, it makes us view people as belonging to one or the other culture, unchanging, and fixed to a place. When required to verify if a person belongs to a particular "race" and its related idea of culture is to assume that the ideas of "race" and culture are stable, and the verity of a person's identity can be compared, contrasted, and verified against an imagined and commonsensical standard.

Anthropological contribution in helping asylum adjudicators is to argue against a narrow use of cultural categories and labels in defining a people. Instead, it takes a social constructivist approach by drawing on innovative ideas on identity and agency in a cultural world, and cautions against assumptions of these concepts when old certainties are no longer certain. It provides the asylum adjudicators the contexts, nuances, and cautions against reifying "race" and essentializing culture. The focus should be on whether or not the person was persecuted based on local understanding of the grounds of the Refugee Convention.

For example, while identity based on "race"/culture is evident and significant in some societies, the assumption upon which "race" is defined is very different. As seen in part I on Race, the Indonesian Chinese view on "race" is particularly appropriate for challenging preconceptions about the relationship between "race" and identity precisely because Indonesian Chinese, in general, do not recognize their identity around notions of racialized groups of black, white, Hispanic and Asian Pacific Islander common in North America—the categories employed by asylum adjudicators. When these American categories are applied to the asylum seekers from around the world, it forces asylum adjudicators to fit a person's culture into a set of beliefs or learned behavior, particular to a location but subjected to tremendous influences and changes. The strength of anthropology is its ability to incorporate the local with the global in understanding an asylum seeker's perspective.

In the anthropological study of human suffering, Liisa Malkki's (2007) commentary on the politics of trauma and asylum points to the fact that "although it might be accepted in receiving countries that rape was widespread in Rwanda in 1994, e.g., the individual asylum seeker claiming to have survived rape there has to be examined by experts for her story to be accepted as factually 'true'" (337). However, if the anthropological expert puts the individual and the particular, specific claims of an asylum seeker into a generalized form of the claim, the asylum seeker's veracity can be elevated.

Asylum adjudicators, not trained in sociocultural anthropology (and even sociocultural anthropologists who have not taken into account the globalization, identity formation, and culture change), are likely to misjudge the asylum seekers who are lacking certain "requisite" cultural values as fraud. The asylum adjudicators' identities themselves are social products of their own cultural milieu structured by a different environment and its own assemblage of resources. Without a reflexivity of their own social position as immigration officers, attorneys, and judges growing up in different places and times, and their social positions formed by different sources of education and wealth, power, and political orientation, making judgements on asylum seekers using the standards of their own cultural values would present a precarious cultural trap of erroneous judgements.

Chapter 15

There is an Anthropologist in the Courtroom

Coauthored with Joann Yeh

Mr. Goodsell had two cases scheduled on the same Monday morning in April 2014 and asked Joann Yeh to represent Ms. Huang in court during her Merit Hearing. Yeh had requested the files on the client during the week. Yeh felt uncomfortable representing an asylum petitioner without preparation as she had not received the file on her client until the night before the Merit Hearing. She immediately requested to meet the client to review the testimony and go over how the court proceeding would go forth so the client would not be surprised by how the Government Counsel would attack her testimony, the type of questions that would be asked, and so on. The client was not scheduled to arrive until early on the morning of the hearing as she was coming in from out of town.

Before the court hearing began, Yeh finally met and spoke to Ms. Huang regarding her case. Speaking in Mandarin Chinese, Ms. Huang said she flew down from Northern California where she had been working as a babysitter. She said she was applying for asylum because she had been forced to have two abortions in China. Yeh informed Ms. Huang that she would be asking her a series of questions to help her tell her story and suggested they go over it. After reviewing the initial questions about her identity and where she was from, Yeh began asking about the two forced abortions. As the questions got more detailed, Ms. Huang seemed to get more nervous, especially when pressed for details about the second forced abortion. Just before the Judge entered the courtroom, Ms. Huang blurted out in Mandarin, "The second abortion did not happen!" Yeh was stunned. Ms. Huang had clearly lied in her petition. For an attorney to know the truth but to knowingly allow a client to lie under oath in court is to suborn perjury and her whole petition would have to be abandoned due to her lie.

Yeh speculated that Ms. Huang might have had a single forced abortion, or perhaps just a miscarriage, in China. She probably went to the doctor and had some kind of written proof of her visit. If she was trying to remain in United States, she could have used her legal visa to enter the country and then applied for asylum. She had probably been told along the way to embellish the story to make it sound more compelling.

Further complicating this issue was the fact that forced abortion was not formally and statutorily considered a ground for seeking asylum or refugee status until 1996 when Congress passed the Illegal Immigration Reform and Immigrant Responsibility Act of 1996 (IRRIRA), which amended section 1101 (a) (42) of the Immigration and Nationality Act. Specifically, Congress broadened the definition of refugee under the statute to automatically grant asylum and/or refugee status to victims of forced abortion or involuntary sterilizations—victims of a "coercive population control program." (8 U.S.C.§ 1101 (a) (42) (B) (2006). This led to an influx of Chinese applications claiming that because they already had one child, they feared forced sterilization if they were sent back to China. Without further clarification by Congress, USCIS (United States Citizenship and Immigration Services, formerly INS, or Immigration and Naturalization Services) has thus been left to evaluate each case individually on the facts but without much guidance as to how much fear of coercive reproductive control one must have to have a successful asylum case. Ms. Huang was also a bad liar, which would make her a bad witness. The Judge would not find her credible and she would not be granted asylum.

The Judge called the court to order. Yeh had no time to sort out the details of Ms. Huang's lies, and was worried about her own potential complicity if she put forth the fraudulent testimony of Ms. Huang's abortions. Yet, she also had an obligation to protect and advocate for her client and could not simply withdraw her representation without arousing suspicion or break attorney-client privilege to reveal to the court what the client had revealed to her in the course of the representation. The Hearing began with the Government Counsel requesting Ms. Huang's current address and the places she had lived before. Pinning Ms. Huang down on the precise chronology and locations of her places of residence and whereabouts since arriving in the United States started to consume a significant amount of time. The Judge became impatient. After thirty minutes with no end in sight, he told Ms. Huang to sort out details of her whereabouts since arriving in the United States before the next hearing and to provide the court with an extensive and detailed list of her addresses and the dates she had lived at each one. His next step was to reschedule her Merit Hearing to a later date.

Yeh felt thankful she had been spared the need to represent Ms. Huang, under oath, regarding the topic of her forced abortions. Later, in consultation with Mr. Goodsell on how to handle the case without perjuring herself, Mr. Goodsell suggested that Yeh go with Ms. Huang's asylum petition, which she had initially filed with another attorney and which Goodsell had subsequently inherited. Ms. Huang had already established a paper trail and for her to retell her story would be to dismantle whatever she had said before—her whole petition would have to be abandoned due to her lie.

This was the closest Joann Yeh came to encountering a fraudulent case.

THE FEAR OF FRAUD

In the context of media coverage of refugees and asylum seekers pushing across the borders in Europe, Australia, and through South America up to the US-Mexico border, one debate on illegal immigration in the United States concerns those who view "asylum as a 'loophole' in immigration laws that undocumented aliens can use to gain legal status" (Einolf 2001, xvii).

Each time a "criminal" is unveiled that he is also a former refugee or asylum seeker, the news only adds fuel to the flame of the argument or belief that asylum is a backdoor which immigrants use to enter the United States. Two cases that received repeated coverage are Amadou Diallo, who was shot forty-one times in New York City in 1999 and whose illegal status was revealed after his death, and Nafissatou Diallo (no relation to Amadou Diallo), the hotel maid who accused Dominique Strauss-Kahn of sexual assault and attempted rape at a New York hotel and whose identity as an illegal immigrant was revealed after she had filed charges in 2011.

Other high profile asylum fraud cases on the United States government website also remind the readers that these were operated by ethnic community service agencies and attorney "middlemen" of fraud rings, ranging from Russians to Chinese, and from Albanians to Indonesians, who have been "coaching" their clients on how to file false asylum claims. The most notorious case of the misuse of identity for legal defense is one involving Hans Gauw who was charged with asylum fraud by the US government in his assistance given to Indonesian Chinese asylum seekers in Virginia by claiming that they were targeted because of their Chinese ethnic identity during the May 1998 anti-Chinese riots in Indonesia. It is unclear how many of these assisted by Hans Gauw were genuine asylum seekers who were persecuted and those who were not. But when the case was in the news, Dr. Nauman and I were concerned that the courts could view our expertise with suspicion. We believe these fraudulent cases represent only a tiny percentage of the number of asylum cases overall.

In the opinion of those who were arrested for fraud, based on an article on New York City's Chinatown, some said they were "motivated by a compulsion to help Chinese immigrants make a better life for themselves [because they] had worked so hard to flee authoritarian rule in China, they should be able to stay in the United States" (Semple, Goldstein, and Singer 2014, 7). They knew they were breaking the law, but they believe their actions were righteous.

At the core of the concern of fraud is, of course, fairness. Generally, the public disapproves of situations where it appears one type of immigrant group is queue-jumping to get ahead of applicants who have to wait or have already waited for years to be reunited with their families under the categories of family unification or immigration through employment-based visa processes.

If some migrants are perceived as using asylum petitions as a "backdoor" to gain legal residency in the United States, the fear of fraud has perhaps created an asylum system that focuses on checking the credibility of the asylum seeker. Because the asylum seekers' refugee status that allows them to gain permanent legal status is determined by the asylum courts, the crisis of border control is being managed in the courts. The moral panic over a perceived "asylum factory" or "asylum loophole" is a conflation of asylum with immigration and the fear of the loss of control over the border. The courts are asked to discern the genuine asylum seeker from the fraudulent, and to adjudicate an increasing number of cases with little resources, all the while operating in an adjudicatory system without "real" judges and without the normal, established, constitutionally tested rules of the game. That is, the immigration courts must take on the failure of the immigration policies in the country.

The fear of fraud presents particular challenges to the asylum seeking process. Asylum seekers are asked to *do the impossible of proving their identities*. A genuine asylum seeker's last defense against deportation is a Merit Hearing that is fair, with immigration judges and government counsel who are informed, and attorneys who are determined. With the fear of fraud, an undue burden has been shifted onto the genuine asylum seekers. Their identities have been on trial; their fate is fraught with uncertainties.

In all practicality, the asylum seekers' words on their own do not count anymore even though the law requires that they are to be believed. Because each individual immigration judge can apply the laws as they feel are appropriate in an Article I court, the result is that current asylum seekers must produce evidentiary proof even when the law does not require them to do so. When judges are uncertain if the evidentiary proofs provided are credible, the focus is on their demeanor: Are they lying? Do they appear honest?

In helping attorneys as an anthropological expert witness, the burden on me has shifted too. In earlier cases with the Indonesian asylum seekers, I only had to speak on my expertise on the "race" and culture of the asylum seekers of Chinese origin from Indonesia; or the identity of the asylum seeker, whether he is a Muslim from Indonesia, a homosexual from China, or a victim of domestic abuse from Malaysia. In recent years, the questions from the Government Counsel became aggressive and downright nasty.

With much at stake for the fate of the asylum seekers, my response was to conduct even more research on the country conditions of the asylum seekers, spend ever more time interviewing them for details they may not have even considered for their application, and write each report under enormous pressure because it could determine their chance for a better life or a fate that could include imprisonment or even death if they were not granted asylum.

In the stories we have recounted in this volume, some of the asylum seekers were granted asylum. To examine the incredible fortune that some asylum seekers had actually received asylum protection, we conducted a postmortem on the twenty-seven cases I had worked on as an expert witness. This postmortem examination was done to bring to light what makes asylum success possible with anthropological input, to demystify the process, and to argue that these successful cases are as important in the final analysis as those that were denied asylum in understanding the asylum seeking process.

A POSTMORTEM OF TWENTY-SEVEN ASYLUM CASES

It is impossible to know the combination of factors that lead to the approval or denial of an asylum case. The immigration judge's decisions are communicated to the attorney and the petitioner. When a judge grants a favorable decision, the government may appeal and overturn the decision. If an asylum petition has been rejected, the petitioner may appeal to the next level adjudicator—the Bureau of Immigration Appeals—which may take several years before a case is decided. The anthropologists are not privy to this information unless they conduct research to track down the decision of the higher court. The decisions of the higher court are selectively published and inaccessible to the public.

However, in analyzing the asylum outcome of the twenty-seven cases I had worked on between 2002 and 2016, it is possible to compare the successful cases with those that were not successful. Of the twenty-seven cases, three were appeals to the higher court. That is, the attorneys requested my help as an anthropological consultant only *after* the cases were already rejected by the immigration officers and the immigration judges. Two of the cases were requested by Mr. Goodsell with the understanding that perhaps there was evidence missed by the first attorney, or, perhaps, the petitioner possessed new information that needed to be re-examined. The success of gaining asylum at the appeals level is extremely difficult. The panel of Judges may accept certain aspects of the case, and then send the case back to the lower court for reconsideration. The three appeals cases are elaborated in the earlier chapters, Ms. Jeni in chapter 8 under Membership in a Particular Social Group, and Ms. Chun in chapter 12 and Mr. Sung in chapter 13 under Political Opinion. Of the remaining twenty-four cases, two were "incomplete": one asylum seeker returned home and one asylum seeker married, which changed his legal status. As of September 2017, the status of three of the twenty-seven cases are pending. Of the three, only Khun Yaw's case, where the Judge is still waiting on his final piece of evidence before making a decision, is included here (see part I chapter 4).The result on another case was unknown and there was no follow-up. By removing from the analysis the appeals (3), incomplete (2), unknown (1), and those pending (3), I had completed eighteen cases where the asylum decision had been determined. Of these eighteen completed cases, fifteen cases were either granted asylum or granted the status of "withholding from withdrawal." The latter refers to a decision that allows asylum seekers to remain in the United States and not be forced to be deported. Of these fifteen successful cases, eleven were based on collaboration with a single attorney, Mr. Kenneth Goodsell, resulting in a 100 percent success rate.

Based on this analysis, I theorize that the ethnographic information constructed by the anthropologist for an attorney has made a significant difference in the asylum outcome. My role as a social scientist in the courtroom and my positive asylum results confirms Wilson's (2016) opinion that, "The prominence of social researchers as experts runs counter to the general trend in favor of material-object science, and within the category of social research, qualitative social research is more likely than quantitative research to influence a judgement" (734).

Second, in reflecting on the success of the cases, I propose the idea of "asylum lawfare" to speculate on the strategies and tactics of two attorneys in two case studies to account for the success and failure of some asylum cases. And third, I recommend Attorney Joann Yeh's position on the importance of having anthropological input in a case.

ASYLUM LAWFARE

In reflecting on these cases, it has become clear that, despite the difficulty of gaining asylum, some petitioners are, in fact, granted asylum. It is also clear that some attorneys are more successful in gaining asylum than others. To understand this difference, the idea of "going to war" is an appropriate analogy to understand the differences in approaches taken by attorneys working on asylum cases.

In *Primitive War*, Reyna and Downs (1994) suggested that social scientists have a tendency to view war as a crime against humanity rather than as a

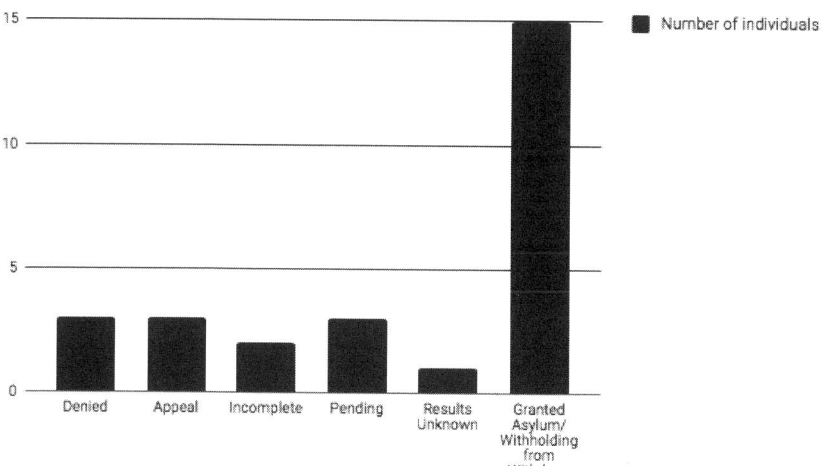

Figure 15.1 A Post-Mortem of 27 Asylum Cases between 2002–2016.

feature of human society, and have therefore shied away from analyzing war. War, as defined by Malinowski, who had devoted considerable effort to study war, is "the use of organized force between two politically independent units, in pursuit of tribal [or national] policy" (quoted in Reyna and Downs 1994, 6). In calling the process by which attorneys handle an asylum petition as a process analogous to going to war, I attempt to understand the attorney's behavior which has played an important role in gaining asylum for their clients, just as warfare "has played a tremendous role in human affairs" (H.H. Turney-High 1949, *Primitive War*, quoted in Reyna and Downs 1994, 4).

War is something that occurs between groups and not individuals. Therefore, in the discussion of attorneys, judges and government counsels, it is not about individual personality, but about the positions they represent, and the processes within the structures of the institutions governing asylum cases. This "asylum lawfare" refers to the restrictions and the possibilities within this prescription.

The work of an attorney and his "asylum lawfare" team is to defend against the "opposing force" comprised of the immigration judge and the government counsel whose decisions dictate the outcome of the asylum cases.

The cast of those involved in the "asylum lawfare," therefore, includes the judges, the government counsel attorneys, the attorneys representing the asylum petitioners and the asylum seekers themselves. Under the laws and regulations set up by the United States government, the asylum petitioner who has been rejected (now, technically termed "referred for further findings") by immigration officers at USCIS gets a hearing for the first time in what is known as a "Merit Hearing." Immigration judges are hired as regular employees of the US Department of Justice and thus, are not allocated funding to call upon experts. Therefore, like the immigration officers, they must learn about the world of asylum seekers very quickly and adjudicate accordingly.

It is not unusual for an immigration judge to take out a world map to try to locate the asylee's country of origin during the Merit Hearing, as I had observed when Judge Rose Peters took out a National Geographic map to locate Mongolia during a hearing at the San Pedro Detention Center on Terminal Island in California; or as filmmakers Shari Robertson notes in the documentary *Well-Founded Fear,* a world map is in the tool kit of the Immigration Office in Anaheim, California; or as Judge Daw has expressed, (when the recording device was turned off during the hearing) that she knew the meaning of "apostasy" in the case of a Muslim convert to Catholicism (part II, chapter 7).

JUDGES

Immigration judges are assigned cases randomly. But one of the first questions the attorney has on a claimant is "Who is the immigration judge on the case?" Given a rejection rate range of between 10 percent to 90 percent among immigration judges (TRAC figures), and given that some judges have certain reputations in the courtroom, both positive and negative, the asylum seekers undoubtedly hope for a reasonable, experienced, and fair immigration judge who will rule in their favor.

Does the ethnic background of the immigration judge play a role in the decision in an asylum case? Are government counsels of minority background tougher because they must prove that they are for "law and order" and "tough on crime" to serve the narratives of the government? While it is difficult to know if ethnicity plays a role, when an asylum petitioner's life depends on the immigration judge's decision, the speculation on whether the judge (including government counsel, and interpreters) would play the "ethnic/race card" from their ethnicized positions is important. Immigration judges' reputations in the courtroom are well-known. Joann Yeh has personally worked on cases with an Immigration Judge who has a reputation for publicly saying, "I hate Chinese Christian cases," when presiding over Chinese cases. The Immigration Judge on the Burmese case requiring Khun Yaw to produce a High School Leaving Certificate to prove his identity was reported to have a bad reputation and was moved from San Francisco to Los Angeles. An attending attorney on a case I have worked on had wondered whether the presiding Immigration Judge, who was African American, would be sympathetic to yet one more asylum seeker coming to Los Angeles when "within five miles of the court house there are many unemployed African Americans." With varying opinions on the potential influence of the personal opinion of the Judges based on their ethnicized and cultural background (and their education, political and ideological orientation, etc.), what remains is for the attorney and the expert witness to work even harder to decipher the meanings of every word uttered and every action taken by the government counsel, the interpreter, and the immigration judge, to speculate on their implication for an asylum case.

GOVERNMENT COUNSEL

The government counsel (GC) sits facing the immigration judge and acts as a functionary of the system. The GC checks on the claimant's eligibility, uncovers any inconsistencies in the asylum petition, questions the witnesses' credibility, and asks leading questions to test if the asylum claimant gives answers that contradicts other information in the asylum petition.

The attorney representing the asylum applicant has no control over the choice of the government's counsel and there is also a severe turnover of government attorneys. One never knows who the government counsel will be on a case. As an expert witness sitting in the back of the gallery, I often do not have a good look at the government counsel unless I am called to testify. When that happens, I am seated at an angle from the judge and facing the government counsel.

Dr. Nauman has been at the receiving end of some of the meanest government counsels' nasty remarks. He derisively refers to the counsel as "TA"—not as in "Trial Attorney" but as in the "Teaching Assistant" of his big undergraduate classes. Depending on the government counsel, the courtroom atmosphere can range from professional to extremely adversarial. Many try to confuse and entrap the respondent so that they can use any inconsistency to reject the case. A less than vigilant expert witness or attorney for the asylum claimant could easily fall into that trap. Sitting on hard, uncomfortable, benches in the windowless waiting room of the Federal Court while being sequestered during Merit Hearing, Dr. Nauman tutored me with stories of his experience as an expert witness giving "smart answers" in response to the Government Counsel:

GC: How do you know she was not pretending to be her sister?

Expert Witness should say: I did not know she has a sister.

GC: How do you know she was not lying?

Expert Witness should say: I have no control over someone's lies.

GC: How much are you paid to do this work?

Expert Witness should say: I was not paid. I was compensated for this work.

GC: So, you said you were in the US Navy?

Dr. Nauman: Yes, I was.

GC: What was your Navy number?

Dr. Nauman: Gee. So you think I should carry around my US Navy number in my pocket?

GC: What makes you an expert?

Dr. Nauman: I have published a few books on the subject.

Dr. Nauman said when he mentioned the number of books he had published as evidence of his expertise, "the TA sneered at me, as if writing a book was as easy as sneezing." I was not sure if Dr. Nauman actually replied this way to the last question. My concern was if his rhetorical "talking back" would incur the wrath of the Government Counsel and hurt the asylum seeker.

THE INTERPRETER

When an asylum petitioner requires an interpreter, the attorney can request one. In fact, this is the only support the government provides in an asylum case. The interpreter is supposed to be neutral, but the interpreter's ethnicity and ethnic allegiance are the subject of speculation by the asylum petitioners and their attorneys. With the Indonesian Chinese cases, the Indonesian Chinese asylum seekers often wonder if the interpreters are native *pribumi* or ethnic Indonesian Chinese; and what would the native *pribumi* interpreter think of them giving accounts of their persecution in the hands of the interpreters' co-ethnics in Indonesia? Dr. Nauman, who has testified as an expert witness on many Indonesian cases appeared to be familiar with the Indonesian interpreters and did not have objections to their role in the cases we were involved in.

Joann Yeh, who speaks fluent Mandarin Chinese, however, had encountered interpreters whose Chinese language skills were deficient in the courtroom. In a case involving a Chinese Christian asylum seeker, the interpreter repeatedly mistranslated the immigration judge's questions. When the claimant did not exactly answer the questions asked, it caused the judge to think that the asylum seeker had been purposefully "evasive" and therefore was not credible. In a situation where the success in a case rests on a judge's perception of an asylum seeker's credibility, a bad interpreter can easily derail a case.

THE ASYLUM SEEKER

The major difficulties faced by asylum seekers include differences in cultural norms, language barriers, their inability to recall persecution and flight due to trauma, limited access to counsel, and the adjudicators' inadequate and inaccurate knowledge of foreign cultures related to issues of ethnic and religious conflict, gender, and sexual orientation. In my interviews with asylum seekers, I have focused on their decision to apply for asylum to learn about the persecution they had encountered. The research on their decision directs my attention on their interests and actions. In fact, the decision to apply for asylum is not always deliberate and premeditated. It can also be unplanned and is often a last resort in the course of escaping difficult conditions in their home country. Examining the motivations of asylees helps refute the commonsense assumption that all asylum seekers are economic refugees. Mr. Harianto, the husband of the asylum seeker whose story was mentioned in part III, chapter 9 provides such an example. Mr. Harianto was a successful factory owner in Indonesia. After his wife was raped by the military during the anti-Chinese riot in Indonesia in 1998, they left the country in desperation. When his wife applied for asylum, he applied as a family member on her case. His wife was granted "Withholding from Withdrawal," which meant she did not have to be deported, but it was not a pathway to permanent residency and citizenship for her and her husband. It also meant that he would not be able to return to Indonesia. If he were to return, he would not be able to enter the United States again, because he would have triggered a lifetime bar. For the sake of his wife of more than thirty years, he made the difficult decision to leave behind the wealth he had accumulated and the life he had built for himself in Jakarta without looking back. He literally lost his life's fortune by being on his wife's application.

THE ATTORNEY

Attorneys vary in experience, skills, styles, and effort. There are competing demands on the attorney's time. An asylum case is only one among many other cases. Some attorneys absolutely have no knowledge of what to do with an asylum case, as Rani's case had shown when her search for an attorney took her through more than a dozen law offices in a Midwestern city (chapter 10). Even among attorneys who are familiar with the work of an anthropological expert witness, it remains uncertain whether their clients even knew how an anthropologist would be able to help them. The attorneys must consult with their clients on the decision when hiring an anthropological expert witness. Without the certainty of a positive asylum outcome, the asylum seeker must weigh the costs involved unless the attorney can advocate for the potential contribution of an anthropologist. In my encounters with attorneys, I have learned to expect their ignorance of the advantage of having an anthropologist on board.

An attorney's overall strategy for the client is pivotal to improving the chances of winning an asylum case. Having a strategy can mean working hard lining up witnesses such as the petitioner's family members, if they are available, or a letter of support or affidavit from them, written, translated, and notarized. It could also mean making sure that the asylee dresses appropriately for the Merit Hearing, is punctual, knows where to find parking, locate the correct courtroom, and make sure biometric requirements and change-of-address information are filed with the court. In addition, an attorney with an awareness that anthropological expertise could be of help in an asylum case, as documented by the cases in this book, is armed with resources that could be strategically deployed, if needed.

In short, the attorney as the commander-in-chief, must ensure that all aspects of the case are in place, with the sole purpose of winning asylum for the petitioner. Without an overall strategy, and the willingness to explore additional expertise, the challenges of deciphering the human condition to account for persecution resulting from a person's "race," religion, membership in a particular group, political opinion, and nationality can be particularly challenging. Extraordinary difficulty in winning an asylum case demands extraordinary effort.

In positioning my argument that preparing asylum cases is analogous to going war, in a legal sense, I am responding to the opportunity to reflect critically on the potential resources and strategies that could bring about a positive asylum outcome.

To win an asylum case, the attorney must maximize the opportunities through all levels of logistical preparation and support, to strategize within existing constraints and resources, and must desire victory. This premise directs attention to the interests, the financial means, and the actions of the potential asylum seeker, the community and all those supporting the asylum seeker, and the attorney. If an asylum seeker has the means to afford an attorney, the attorney may call witnesses and consider other resources to support the asylum petitioner, such as consulting an expert witness or obtaining a medical opinion on a scar left behind. That is, only if the asylum seeker is able and willing to pay for the services above and beyond consulting an attorney for the asylum case. An NGO, or a major law firm accepting pro bono cases, is able to employ resources at their disposal to support an asylum petitioner, but not the average attorney in solo practice.

As I became more confident in my own ability as an expert witness, every encounter I had with the attorney and the asylum seeker became an opportunity to consider how to increase the petitioners' chances of gaining asylum for survival. Not all asylum seekers are frauds. Not all attorneys are equal. To win a case, it had become a game of strategies. It was war. It was an asylum lawfare. As in a war, victories are possible at times. The two cases below are examples of the winning and the losing asylum cases.

CASE #1: MY ATTORNEY DID NOT TELL MY STORY IN COURT

Dr. Nauman had introduced me to Ms. Joy Batang, her husband, and two children. Ms. Batang is ethnic Indonesian of the Batak tribe from Sumatra. Her husband is Indonesian Chinese and was in Jakarta during the May 1998 anti-Chinese riot.

Ms. Joy Batang was afraid to return to Indonesia because she feared for the fate of her husband and especially her two children, whom I met, because "they look very Chinese." Her two boys, in fact, perhaps due to recessive genes, looked like two typical pupils in one of the Mandarin Chinese classes for youngsters in the East San Gabriel Valley area of Los Angeles.

When I finished my report on the Batang family's fear of persecution against the Chinese in Indonesia, I sent it to the attorney representing them in court. We met at a coffee shop in front of the courthouse before the Merit Hearing. We chatted over coffee, but the Attorney did not ask me questions regarding the case, or invite me to testify, even though I was willing and prepared to do so.

A month later, Ms. Batang called to say she was not granted asylum. She thanked me for helping her and her family tell their story. I asked her what had happened in court. She said the attorney did not try to be persuasive in arguing her case the way I had represented her fears and her husband's suffering during the May 1998 riot. Stunned by Ms. Batang's loss, I thought perhaps her attorney felt it was all written in her report and there was no need for the oral argument during the Merit Hearing; or perhaps she did not believe Ms. Batang's story to begin with and went through the motions without pressing the case for her client; or perhaps she did not know what an anthropologist does and how to use her skills in court. That is, Batang's attorney might not even have had a strategy for winning an asylum case and did not fight for Ms. Batang and her family even with some of the resources at her disposal.

Mr. Goodsell, on the other hand, exemplifies an attorney who has an overall strategy of helping his clients win their asylum petition. He prepares his cases as if he was fighting for his client's life. He is open to the ideas of learning about the skills of an anthropologist. Indeed, he was the one who reminded me a number of times that "There are things you can say as an anthropologist but I cannot say as an attorney."

In this "asylum lawfare," if an attorney does not embrace a mentality of "going to war" for his asylum claimant, he may not seek out additional potential resources, or be open to what might help win a case. The story, "The Woman in a Burka," below demonstrates an opportunity that presents itself during a Merit Hearing that Mr. Goodsell seized upon as a tactic for winning a case.

CASE #2: THE WOMAN IN A BURKA

In 2005, Dr. Nauman, Mr. Goodsell, and I had flown to Phoenix, Arizona, for Ms. Lu's Merit Hearing. Ms. Lu was an Indonesian Chinese whose asylum petition was based on claims that she was targeted and sexually assaulted by native Muslim men in Central Java. Unlike Los Angeles, the Phoenix courtroom did not have the throngs of lawyers and immigrant families negotiating traffic, urban parking, multiple floors of a federal court in a high rise, security checks, and endless rooms along long corridors. Instead, the quiet Phoenix courtroom was situated in a calm neighborhood, inside a single-story government building. Ms. Lu, who had flown in from New York City, was already waiting for us. Sitting in the back of the empty wood-paneled gallery was another woman in a flowing black burka, revealing only her face. The young woman, probably of African American origin, was likely a legal intern who had been granted permission to sit in the hearing. Mr. Goodsell and I exchanged a couple of words noting her presence. After the Immigration Judge had arrived and taken his seat, Mr. Goodsell approached the bench and requested the removal of the woman in a burka.

Mr. Goodsell had argued that given the persecution and trauma the asylum claimant had experienced in Indonesia, the court should not subject her to a re-traumatization with another Muslim in the audience while she testified about her persecution by other Muslims. The Judge granted the attorney's request. Ms. Lu had her Merit Hearing in court and won the case.

Did the removal of the Muslim woman in a burka help the claimant's composure and retelling of persecution by the Muslims in Indonesia during the court hearing? Was the claimant able to differentiate an Indonesian Muslim from an American Muslim? These academic questions were not part of the courtroom drama. But through Mr. Goodsell's tactic of intervention, he was able to highlight the trauma experienced by the claimant by acting to minimize a re-traumatization in his request for the removal of the Muslim woman from the American courtroom. In this example of the deployment of commonsense ideas of culture and anti-Muslim sentiment current in the United States in the courtroom, Mr. Goodsell had signified that the burka worn by the American Muslim woman was representative of Islam. He then magnified the burka and conflated the burka with the terror perpetrated by the native Muslims against the Chinese in Indonesia that had struck at the heart of his client. The courtroom was not the place for the anthropologist's academic intervention of the attorney's stereotyping of the burka-wearing American Muslim. But it was a case study of the attorney's careful deployment of a commonsense fear of the Muslim in the United States in the courtroom, put to strategic use in an asylum case. The attorney may not personally harbor any anti-Muslim sentiment, and may also be inclusive in his professional practice, having indeed represented Muslim asylum seekers, but given the contentious and extreme difficulty of obtaining asylum, every tactic counts and must be available. The utilization of culture and identity to paint a sharper image of his client's persecution was ammunition he had successfully deployed.

In August 2010, I had flown to Edinburgh to meet with Dr. Anthony Good, the only anthropologist who had completed a book on the anthropologist as an expert witness in asylum cases. I was under tremendous pressure to help the asylum seekers win their cases, and I needed help from other professionals doing similar work. Dr. Good had read a couple of my chapters. He explained to me that the story of the woman in a burka is especially interesting as there is a lot of debate all over Europe (though initiated in France) over whether burkas can be worn in public contexts. Indeed, over the years in Germany and other European countries, politicians are backing a ban on burka in schools, courts and other state buildings (BBC 2017).

In November 2016, when I mentioned to Mr. Goodsell I was including in my book the case where we encountered the woman in a burka in the Phoenix, Arizona courtroom, he merely brushed it off by saying it was important to ensure the comfort of the asylum seeker. Another example of Mr. Goodsell's use of this kind of "asylum lawfare ammunition" occurred when an asylum seeker was several months pregnant when her Merit Hearing came up. Mr. Goodsell requested a postponement so as not to cause her a miscarriage. Mr. Goodsell did add that some attorneys are afraid of the immigration judges and attorneys frequently cave in to their aggressive questioning.

ATTORNEY YEH: "THERE IS AN ANTHROPOLOGIST IN THE COURTROOM!"

The men and women who come to the United States to flee persecution need to know that such a legal system exists to protect them. But by the time they learn about asylum protection, they have often missed the one-year deadline. Asylum is not granted unless they can prove exceptional circumstances for a waiver of that requirement. The asylum petition forms are available online, but few are aware of it or are internet savvy enough to access and navigate such a process. Through the ethnic media, or a chance learning of an immigration NGO, some asylum seekers learn of legal help. Without legal help, the task is insurmountable. With an NGO working with the resources of major law firms' pro bono legal representation, the chances of gaining asylum improve significantly.

But there are few NGOs, and even fewer that are culturally and linguistically specific and accessible to the myriad of needs of the asylum seekers. If an asylum seeker looks for legal help, it is first and foremost the immigration services in the ethnic community. In places without ethnic enclaves, and without asylum seekers, there are few lawyers who know the asylum legal system, as Rani had encountered in her saga looking for an attorney in a Midwest city in the United States (part V, chapter 13).

When the fear of fraud poses an outright challenge on an asylum seeker's credibility, the chance of obtaining asylum is zero. They are presumed liars, economic migrants, or one who uses the asylum process as a way to gain legal status in the United States. They are required to remember events that had happened many years before. Any minor discrepancy, even though allowed by law, is erroneously challenged by asylum judges.

Therefore, to prove they are a genuine asylum seeker persecuted on account of the grounds of the Refugee Convention, they must document everything by bringing evidentiary proof such as medical certificates or newspaper accounts of events that had happened. But, as the stories of the asylum seekers show, sometimes it is impossible to provide evidence—as in the case of a rape kit—when physical evidence disappears and witnesses disappear.

The National Immigration and Justice Center advises potential asylum seekers of the following five points: (1) know that asylum protection exists, (2) find a lawyer who knows the system, (3) establish credibility, (4) document everything, and (5) get the right immigration judge.

But how does an asylum seeker find a lawyer who knows the system and can get the right immigration judge? According to Transactional Records Clearing House (2012; 2017), the granting rates of Immigration Judges can vary from 10 percent to 90 percent, even in the same city. Attorneys do not select the immigration judges. Presumably, if an attorney has done his research, and learned that his client has been assigned a difficult immigration judge, it is possible for him to petition his client to a different date or a different courtroom if he could produce exceptional excuses. But, for the most part, it is impossible to change the assigned government counsel or the assigned immigration judge.

What, then, can be done to improve the asylum seeker's chance of gaining asylum approval? In the expert opinion of Joann Yeh, if an attorney brings in an expert witness, it indicates that the professor with established credibility from a major university is willing to risk his or her reputation to work on a case. Joann Yeh believes that probably less than half of a percent (0.005 percent) of asylum cases are supported by expert witness reports and/or testimony. In addition, the written testimony of the anthropological expert witness is very specific to the evidence to the case, which gives the case legitimacy. When an anthropologist is called in to testify in court, the expert's presence shows that there is a real person willing to testify on the facts of a case under oath. Even if the government counsel appears to challenge the credibility of the expert witness in court, the counsel and judges know that, at the very least, the case is not a fraud. That is, aside from the research and writing as an expert witness, the mere presence of an anthropologist in the courtroom can change the outcome of a case.

SOCIAL SCIENCE EXPERTISE WANTED

While helping attorneys with their clients on asylum cases, it is evident that the credibility of the asylee's identity itself is also on trial. The asylum adjudicators' inability to ascertain their identity can be traced, in part, to the asylum seekers' hybridized identity in the diaspora which has been transformed by forced assimilation, localization, migration, and acculturation into American society and culture, as their case goes through the legal system. While the world we live in has undergone tremendous transformation, the grounds for determining persecution, codified since 1951, remain unchanged. A major hurdle of the asylum seeker points to a lack of "fit" between their life in a globalized postmodern world and the adjudicators' strict adherence to the meaning of Convention grounds.

When the asylum seekers' rejection letters and documents become available for examination, the adjudicators' reasoning for rejection become even clearer. Their ignorance of the country's condition and local knowledge, or refusal to take into account the social and cultural changes in the world of the asylum seekers, leads to faulty, and sometimes perverse, arguments given of their rejections of the asylum seeker's petition. Indeed, some scholars are suggesting that the "cloistered life of the law" is now gone (Einhorn and Berhold 2015, 46). Instead, the multicultural world we live in today demands judges and lawyers "to end their intellectual isolation and matriculate with other professionals who have different and helpful worldviews" (46).

The fortuitous initial request from Meiji Sopoto to help Dewi, and the subsequent requests on other cases, had presented me the opportunity to verify the asylum seekers' identity based on the grounds of the 1951 Refugee Convention.

It provided the opportunity not only to verify on the grounds of the Convention using anthropological concepts, but also provide a valuable service to those in need, in a system suspicious of their intention and their identities.

The anthropological assistance provided to Mr. Ken Goodsell and other attorneys, and the collaboration with the attorneys of Seyfarth Shaw, have all shown that by regarding an asylum seeker as an *anthropological figure*, each case is amenable to the advantages of a systematic anthropological inquiry. The positive asylum outcomes are concrete evidence of Mr. Goodsell's mantra: "There are things an anthropologist can say that a lawyer can't," as well as the relevance of Seyfarth Shaw lawyers' requests for social science input. The latter's requests for anthropological research on gender and labor relations, caste cultures, and civil and religious laws on marriage on a domestic abuse case all point to the breadth of the potential for social science contribution. The successful outcome of utilizing social science input echoes Wilson's (2016) point on the importance of the value of social science expertise. Indeed, over the past decade, judges and adjudicators have demonstrated sensitivity to evidence by incorporating external expertise and testimony (Good 2006; Haas 2017; Lawrance and Ruffer 2015) from experts including cultural anthropologists.

Besides employing the substantive staples of the social sciences to support an asylum case, the collaboration with Attorney Joann Yeh also points to an unexpected finding: government attorneys and judges must decide, among the thousands of cases they face, whether a particular asylum seeker, whose petition is supported by an anthropologist's research, and its author is ready to testify in court, is still a fraud. She believes that given the fact that most immigration cases are not even represented by an attorney, any anthropological support given to an asylum case will likely be of help compared to those without it.

As the world faces the greatest numbers of refugees and asylum seekers to date, the political impulses towards greater surveillance of immigrants, and the closing of borders among the signatory nations of the Refugee Convention, the greatest hope for asylum seekers under the current conditions may come from the collaboration between law and the social sciences.

References

Agamben, Giorgio. 1999. *Remnants of Auschwitz: The Witness and the Archive*. Translated by Daniel Heller-Roazen. New York: Zone Books.

Aguilar, F.V., Jr. 2001. "Citizenship, Inheritance, and the Indigenizing of 'Orang Chinese' in Indonesia." *Positions: East Asia Cultures Critique* 9 (3):501–33.

Aleinikoff, T. Alexander 1991. "The Meaning of 'Persecution' in United States Asylum Law." *International Journal Refugee Law* 3 (1):5–29.

American Anthropological Association. 2017. "Race: Are We So Different?" American Anthropological Association, Last Modified 2007, accessed July 1, 2017. http://www.understandingrace.org/history/science/early_class.html.

Amnesty International. 2005. "Amnesty International Report 2005: The State of the World's Human Rights." Accessed November 11, 2007. https://www.amnesty.org/download/Documents/POL1000012005ENGLISH.PDF.

———. 2007. "Amnesty International Position on the Return of Christian Converts to Iran." Amnesty International New Zealand. Accessed November 11, 2007. http://www.amnesty.org.nz/web/pages/home.nsf/dd5cab6801f1723585256470053277c8/.

Anderson, Benedict R. 1991. *Imagined Communities: Reflections on the Origin and Spread of Nationalism*. London: Verso.

Anderson, Margo J., and Stephen E. Fienberg. 1999. *Who Counts?: The Politics of Census-Taking in Contemporary America*. New York: Russell Sage Foundation Publications.

Arbel, Efrat, Catherine Dauvergne, and Jenni Millbank. 2014. *Gender in Refugee Law: From the Margins to the Centre*. London: Routledge.

Arendt, H. 2004. *The Origins of Totalitarianism*. New York: Schocken Books.

Bailey, Benjamin, and Sunny Lie. 2013. "The Politics of Names among Chinese Indonesians in Jakarta." *Journal of Linguistic Anthropology* 23 (1):21–40.

Bailey, Garrick, and James Peoples. 2013. *Essentials of Cultural Anthropology*. 3rd ed. Boston, MA: Cengage Learning.

Baker, Beth, and ChorSwang Ngin. 2017. "Making Space: Ethnic Towns and the Racing of Public Space in Los Angeles." In *Anthropology of Los Angeles: Place and Agency in an Urban Setting*, edited by Jenny Bahn, 177–193. Lanham, MD: Lexington Books.

Banton, Michael. 1998. *Racial Theories*. Cambridge: Cambridge University Press.

Barth, Fredrik, ed. 1969. *Ethnic Groups and Boundaries: The Social Organization of Culture Difference*. Results of a symposium held at the University of Bergen, 23rd to 26th February 1967. Oslo, Norway: Universitetsforlaget.

BBC News. 2017. "The Islamic Veil across Europe." January 31, 2017. http://www.bbc.com/news/world-europe-13038095.

Beyond Rangoon. 1995. Directed by John Boorman. Culver City, CA: Columbia TriStar Home Video. Videocassette (VHS).

Blommaert, J. 2009. "Language, Asylum, and the National Order." In *Current Anthropology* 50, (1):415–41.

Bohmer, Carol, and Amy Shuman. 2008. *Rejecting Refugees: Political Asylum in the 21st Century*. London; New York: Routledge.

Bourdieu, Pierre. 1977. *Outline of a Theory of Practice*. Translated by Richard Nice. *Cambridge Studies in Social and Cultural Anthropology*, edited by Jack Goody. Cambridge, MA: Cambridge University Press.

Bostom, Andrew G. 2005. *The Legacy of Jihad: Islamic Holy War and the Fate of Non-Muslims*. Amherst, NY: Prometheus Books.

———. 2006. "Under the Scimitar of Damocles." *American Thinker*. March 26, 2006. https://www.americanthinker.com/articles/2006/03/under_the_scimitar_of_damocles.html

———. 2008. *The Legacy of Islamic Anti-Semitism: From Sacred Texts to Solemn History*. Amherst, NY: Prometheus Books.

Brace, C. Loring. 2005. *"Race" is a Four-Letter Word: The Genesis of the Concept*. Oxford, U.K.: Oxford University Press.

Brace, C. Loring, and George W. Gill. (2000). "Does Race Exist?" *NOVA*, February 15, 2000. http://www.pbs.org/wgbh/nova/evolution/does-race-exist.html

Briggs, Charles L., and Richard Bauman. 1992. "Genre, Intertextuality, and Social Power." *Journal of Linguistic Anthropology* 2, no. 2 (December): 131–72. http://www.jstor.org/stable/43102167.

Buss, Doris E. 2009. "Rethinking 'Rape as a Weapon of War'." *Feminist Legal Studies* 17:145–63.

Buettner-Janusch, John. 1966. *The Origins of Man*. New York: John Wiley & Sons, Inc.

Cao, Weiwei. 2015. "Exploring 'Glorious Motherhood' in Chinese Abortion Law and Policy." *Feminist Legal Studies* 23 (3):295–318. doi: 10.1007/s10691-015-9291-7.

Cardenas, Sonia. 2010. *Human Rights in Latin America: A Politics of Terror and Hope*. Philadelphia, PA: University of Pennsylvania Press.

Chang, Kwang-chih. 1977. *The Archaeology of Ancient China*. New Haven: Yale University Press.

Cheng, Vincent J. 2004. *Inauthentic: The Anxiety over Culture and Identity*. New Brunswick, NJ: Rutgers University Press.

Clearwisdom. 2011. "Recent Persecution of Falun Gong Practitioners in Yanbian Autonomous Prefecture, Jilin Province." *Falun Dafa Minghui,* June 9. http://

en.minghui.org/html/articles/2011/6/9/125904.html.Cohen, Abner. 1969. *Custom and Politics in Urban Africa: A Study of Hausa Migrants in Yoruba Towns*. Campus 43. Berkeley, CA: University of California Press.

Conroy, Melanie A. 2009. "Real Bias: How REAL ID's Credibility and Corroboration Requirements Impair Sexual Minority Asylum Applicants." *Berkeley Journal of Gender Law & Justice* 24 (1):1–47. doi: 10.15779/Z38J96086D.

Coombe, Rosemary J. 1991. "Encountering the Postmodern: New Directions in Cultural Anthropology." *Canadian Review of Sociology and Anthropology/ Revue canadienne de sociologie* 28 (2):188–205. doi: 10.1111/j.1755-618X.1991.tb00151.x.

Coppel, Charles A. 2005. "Introduction: Researching the Margins." In *Chinese Indonesians: Remembering, Distorting, Forgetting*, edited by Timothy Lindsey, Helen Pausacker and Charles A. Coppel, 1–13. Singapore; Clayton: Institute of Southeast Asian Studies; Monash Asia Institute.

Dawis, Aimee. 2008. "I am Chinese Indonesian." *The Jakarta Post*, February 6, 2008. http://www.thejakartapost.com/news/2008/02/06/i-am-chineseindonesian.html

De Certeau, Michel. 1997. *Culture in the Plural*. Translated by Tom Conley. Minneapolis: University of Minnesota Press.

Dow, James. 2005. "The Expansion of Protestantism in Mexico: An Anthropological View." *Anthropological Quarterly* 78 (4):23.

Dube, Clayton. 2003. "Workshop: Islam in China." University of California, Los Angeles, Last Modified March 1, 2003. http://international.ucla.edu/institute/article/3175.

Eastwood, Brent M. 2007. "'Citizen Diplomacy'—A Very Democratic Idea." *The American*.

Edwin. 2008. *Blind Pig Who Wants to Fly* (*Babi Buta Yang Ingin Terbang*). Indonesian ed. Amsterdam: Filmfreak Distributie.

Einhorn, Bruce J. and Megan Berthold. 2015. "Reconstruction Babel: Bridging Cultural Dissonance between Asylum Seekers and Adjudicators." In *Adjudicating Refugee and Asylum Status: The Role of Witness, Expertise, and Testimony*, edited by Benjamin N. Lawrance and Gayla Ruffer, 27–53. New York: Cambridge University Press.

Einolf, Christopher J. 2001. *The Mercy Factory: Refugees and the American Asylum System*. Chicago: Ivan R. Dee.

Ember, Carol R., and Melvin Ember. 2009. *Cross-Cultural Research Methods* [in English]. 2nd ed. Lanham, MD: AltaMira Press.

Fassin, D. 2013. "The Precarious Truth of Asylum." In *Public Culture 25*, 1. Durham, NC: Duke University Press.

Fassin, D., and E. d'Halluin. 2005. "The Truth from the Body: Medical Certificates as Ultimate Evidence for Asylum Seekers." *American Anthropologist 107*, 4: 597–608.

Firth, Raymond. 1968. *We, the Tikopia: Kinship in Primitive Polynesia*. Boston: Beacon Press.

Foster, Michelle. 2012. "The 'Ground with the Least Clarity': A Comparative Study of Jurisprudential Developments relating to 'Membership of a Particular Social Group.'" Geneva, Switzerland: UN High Commissioner for Refugees (UNHCR).

Geertz, Clifford. 1973. *The Interpretation of Cultures: Selected Essays* [in English]. New York: Basic Books.

Girard, Francoise, and Wanda Nowicka. 2002. "Clear and Compelling Evidence: The Polish Tribunal on Abortion Rights." *Reproductive Health Matters* 10 (19):22–30. doi: 10.1016/S0968-8080(02)00023-X.

Gladney, Dru C. 1998. *Ethnic Identity in China: The Making of a Muslim Minority Nationality*. Fort Worth. TX: Harcourt Brace & Company.

Goldberg, David Theo. 1990. *Anatomy of Racism*. Minneapolis: University of Minnesota Press.

Good, Anthony. 2006. *Anthropology and Expertise in the Asylum Courts*. Abingdon, Oxon: Routledge-Cavendish.

Goodman, Alan H. 2001. "Biological Diversity and Cultural Diversity: From Race to Radical Bioculturalism." In *Cultural Diversity in the United States: A Critical Reader*, edited by Thomas C. Patterson Ida Susser. Wiley-Blackwell.

Goodman, Alan H., Yolanda T. Moses, and Joseph L. Jones. 2012. *Race: Are We So Different?* Malden, MA: Wiley-Blackwell.

Green, Jennifer L. 2004. "Uncovering Rape: A Comparative Study of Political Sexual Violence." *International Journal of Sociology* 34 (1):97–116.

Greenhalgh, Susan, and Edwin Winckler. 2005. *Governing China's Population: From Leninist to Neoliberal Biopolitics*. Stanford, CA: Stanford University Press.

Gunn, T. Jeremy. 2002. "The Complexity of Religion in Determining Refugee Status." In *Roundtable on Religion-Based Refugee Claims*. Washington D.C.: Emory University.

Haas, Bridget M. 2017. "Citizens-in-Waiting, Deportees-in-Waiting: Power, Temporality, and Suffering in the U.S. Asylum System." *Ethos* 45 (1):75–97. doi: 10.1111/etho.12150.

Hacker, Andrew. 2003. *Two Nations: Black and White, Separate, Hostile, Unequal*. New York: Scribner.

Heinz, Carolyn Brown. 1999. *Asian Cultural Traditions*. Prospect Heights, IL: Waveland Press.

Henry, Nicola. 2010. "The Impossibility of Bearing Witness: Wartime Rape and the Promise of Justice." *Violence Against Women* 16 (10):1098–119.

Hesketh, Therese, Lu Li, and Wei Xing Zhu. 2005. "The Effect of China's One-Child Family Policy after 25 Years." *New England Journal of Medicine* 35, 11: 1171–1176.

Holland, Dorothy. 1998. *Identity and Agency in Cultural Worlds*. Cambridge, MA: Harvard University Press.

Hott, Lawrence R., and Claudia Levin. 1991. *Rebuilding the Temple: Cambodians in America*. Santa Monica, CA: Direct Cinema LTD.

Human Rights Watch. 2006. "Malaysia: Events of 2005." In *World Report 2006*: *Events of 2005*. Accessed August 20, 2006. https://www.hrw.org/world-report/2006/country-chapters/malaysia.

———. 2007. "Indonesia: Events of 2006." In *World Report 2007: Events of 2006*. Accessed January 20, 2008. https://www.hrw.org/world-report/2007/country-chapters/indonesia.

———. 2017. "Burma: Landmines Deadly for Fleeing Rohingya: Military Lays Internationally Banned Weapon." Human Rights Watch, Last Modified September 23, 2017, accessed September 23, 2017. https://www.hrw.org/news/2017/09/23/burma-landmines-deadly-fleeing-rohingya.

Hustings, Erin. 2010. "PHR Statement to U.S. Senate in Support of Refugee Protection Act of 2010." New York: Physicians for Human Rights. Last modified June 19, 2010. Accessed July 1, 2010. http://physiciansforhumanrights.org/blog/phr-statement-of-support-of-refugee-protection-act.html.

Islamic Tourism Centre of Malaysia. 2017. "Islam in Malaysia." Accessed September 19, 2017. http://www.itc.gov.my/tourists/discover-the-muslim-friendly-malaysia/islam-in-malaysia/.

Jakarta Post. 2006. "Sect Leader Lia Jailed for Blasphemy." *Jakarta Post*, June 30, 2006. https://strategypage.com/militaryforums/512-29900.aspx#startofcomments.

Jesudason, James V. 2001. "State Legitimacy, Minority Political Participation, and Ethnic Conflict in Indonesia and Malaysia." In *Social Cohesion and Conflict Prevention in Asia: Managing Diversity through Development*, edited by Nat J. Colletta, Teck Ghee Lim, and Anita Kelles-Viitanen. Washington, D.C.: World Bank.

Junaidi, Ahmad. 2007. "Democracy and Religion." *Jakarta Post*. July 17, 2007.

Kamus.net. 2017. *The Web's Largest Dictionary*. STANDS4 LLC. http://www.kamus.net/

Kelly, Nancy. 1997. "Political Rape as Persecution: A Legal Perspective." *Journal of the American Medical Women's Association* 52 (4):188–90.

Khan, Mizhan, and Deepa Khosla. 1999. "Minorities at Risk Dataset." Minorities At Risk Project (MAR). College Park, MD: Center for International Development and Conflict Management. http://www.mar.umd.edu/

Koptiuch, Kristin. 1996. "'Cultural Defense' and Criminological Displacements: Gender, Race, and (Trans) Nation in the Legal Surveillance of US Diaspora Asians." In *Displacement, Diaspora, and Geographies of Identity*, edited by Smadar Lavie and Ted Swedenburg, 215–33. Durham, NC: Duke University Press.

Koss, M. P. 2006. "Restoring Rape Survivors." *Annals of the New York Academy of Sciences* 1087 (1):206–34.

Kottak, Conrad P. 1996. *Mirror for Humanity: A Concise Introduction to Cultural Anthropology*. Boston: McGraw-Hill.

Lavie, Smadar, and Ted Swedenburg. 2001. *Displacement, diaspora and geographies of identity*. Durham, NC: Duke University Press.

Lawrance, Benjamin N., and Galya Ruffer, eds. 2015. *Adjudicating Refugee and Asylum Status: The Role of Witness, Expertise, and Testimony*. New York: Cambridge University Press.

Leach, Edmond R. 1967. *Political Systems of Highland Burma*. 2nd ed. Boston: Beacon Press.

Lee, Michelle Y. H. 2015. "The viral claim that 'not one' refugee resettled since 9/11 has been 'arrested on domestic terrorism charges.'" In *Washington Post*. Retrieved from https://www.washingtonpost.com/news/fact-checker/wp/2015/11/19/the-viral-claim-that-not-one-refugee-resettled-since-911-has-been-arrested-on-domestic-terrorism-charges/

Lessa, William A. 1966. *Ulithi: A Micronesian Design for Living*. Edited by George and Louise Spindler. *Case Studies in Cultural Anthropology*. New York: Holt, Rinehart and Winston.

Li, Wei. 1997. "Spatial Transformation of an Urban Ethnic Community from Chinatown to Chinese Ethnoburb in Los Angeles." PhD Dissertation, Philosophy, University of Southern California.

Linnaei [Linnaeus], Caroli. 1758. *Systema Naturae*. 10th ed. Stockholm: Laurentius Salvius.

Lopez, Ian Haney. 2006. *White by Law: The Legal Construction by Race*. 10th ed. New York: NYU Press.

Mahmud, Sumiya Fatima. 2017. "Origin Culture and Domestic Violence against Bangladeshi Immigrant Women in Southern California." *Migration and Development* 0 (0,0):1–16.

Makinen, J. 2015. "Taking Names, Keeping Score: China Plans to Rank Its 1.3 Billion Citizens in Social Credit System." In *Los Angeles Times*, November 22, 2015.

Malaysian Digest. 2015. "10 Countries with the Largest Muslim Population in the World." *Malaysian Digest*, May 26, 2015. Accessed September 20, 2017. http://malaysiandigest.com/features/555150–10-countries-with-the-largest-muslim-population-in-the-world.html.

Malkki, Liisa. 2007. "Commentary: The Politics of Trauma and Asylum: Universals and Their Effects." *Ethos* 35 (3):336–43. doi: 10.1525/eth.2007.35.3.336.

Marks, Dana Leigh. 2012. "Still a Legal 'Cinderella'? Why the Immigration Courts Remain an Ill-Treated Stepchild Today." *Federal Lawyer* (March 2012):25–33.

Marton, Miriam H. 2015. "Beyond Expert Witnessing: Interdisciplinary Practice in Representing Rape Survivors in Asylum Cases." In *Adjudicating Refugee and Asylum Status: The Role of Witness, Expertise, and Testimony*, edited by Benjamin N. Lawrance and Galya Ruffer. New York: Cambridge University Press.

Mathews, Gordon. 2014. "Asylum Seekers in Hong Kong: The Paradoxes of Lives Lived on Hold." In *Migration in China and Asia: Experience and Policy*, edited by Jijiao Zhang and Howard Duncan. International Perspectives on Migration, vol. 10, 73–85. Dordrecht: Springer Netherlands.

McGurn, William. 1998. "Indonesia's Kristallnacht." *Wall Street Journal*, July 10, 1998.

McKinney, Kelly. 2007. " 'Breaking the Conspiracy of Silence': Testimony, Traumatic Memory, and Psychotherapy with Survivors of Political Violence." *Ethos* 35 (3):265–99. doi: 10.1525/eth.2007.35.3.265.

Miles, Robert. 2003. *Racism*. Edited by Peter Hamilton. *Key Ideas*. London: Routledge. First published 1989.

Montagu, Ashley. 1997. *Man's Most Dangerous Myth: The Fallacy of Race*. 6th ed. London: AltaMira.

Moore, Jerry D. 2009. *Visions of Culture: An Introduction to Anthropological Theories and Theorists*. Walnut Creek, CA: AltaMira Press.

Musalo, Karen, Jennifer Moore, and Richard A. Boswell. 2007. *Refugee Law and Policy: A Comparative and International Approach*. Durham, N.C.: Carolina Academic Press.

Mydans, Seth. 1998. "Ethnic Chinese in Indonesia Still Fearful." *New York Times*. September 6, 1998, 1–3.

Newman, Lucile F., ed. 1985. *Women's Medicine: A Cross-Cultural Study of Indigenous Fertility Regulation*. Douglass Series on Women's Lives and the Meaning of Gender. New Brunswick, NJ: Rutgers University Press.

Ngin, ChorSwang. 1995 [1985]. "Indigenous Fertility-Regulating Methods among Two Chinese Communities 1995 in Malaysia." In *Women's Medicine: A Cross-Cultural Study of Indigenous Fertility Regulation*, edited by Lucile F. Newman. New Brunswick, NJ: Rutgers University Press.

———. 2001/2002. "Yesterday's Enemy Is the Friend of Today: Villain in One Location Is the Victim at Another." *Amerasia Journal* 27 (3)/28 (1):257–68.

Ngin, ChorSwang, and Rodolfo Torres. 2001. "Racialized Metropolis: Theorizing Asian Americans and Latinos in Southern California." In *Asia and Latino Immigrants in a Restructured Economy: The Metamorphosis of Los Angeles*, edited by Looez-Garza and David R. Diaz. Palo Alto, CA: Stanford University Press.

Oldenburg, Veena Talwar. 2002. *Dowry Murder: The Imperial Origins of a Cultural Crime*. New York: Oxford University Press.

Pan, Lynn. 1999. *The Encyclopedia of the Chinese Overseas*. 1st ed. Cambridge, MA: Harvard University Press.

PBS. 2003. "Race–The Power of an Illusion." Accessed June 20, 2017. http://www.pbs.org/race/000_General/000_00-Home.htm.

Permanent Mission of the People's Republic of China to the UN. 2001. "Falun Gong Cult Murderous: Chinese Ambassador to the USYang Jiechi, Chinese ambassador to the US, pointed out Tuesday that the evil Falun Gong cult has exerted all its efforts to entangle itself in various activities against China and turned out to be a political 'cat's-paw' of international anti-China forces." *Permanent Mission of the People's Republic of China to the UN* online. s.

Peters, Rudolph, and Gert J. J. De Vries. 1976–1977. "Apostasy in Islam." *Die Welt des Islams* 17 (1/4):25.

Perlez, Jane. 2006. "Once Muslim, Now Christian and Caught in the Courts." *New York Times*, August 24, 2006, A4. http://www.nytimes.com/2006/08/24/world/asia/24malaysia.html.

Pfeiffer, John E. 1969. *The Emergence of Man*. New York: Harper & Row Publishers.

Pickering, S., and Leanne Weber, eds. 2006. *Borders, Mobility and Technologies of Control*. Dordrecht: Springer.

Pillsbury, Barbara L. K. 1978. "'Doing the Month': Confinement and Convalescence of Chinese Women after Childbirth." *Social Science & Medicine. Part B: Medical Anthropology* 12:11–22. doi: 10.1016/0160-7987(78)90003-0.

———. 2003. "Workshop: Islam in China." University of California, Los Angeles. Last Modified March 1, 2003. http://international.ucla.edu/institute/article/3175.

Purdey, Jemma. 2005. *Anti-Chinese Violence and Transitions in Indonesia June 1998–October 1999*. Singapore: Institute of Southeast Asian Studies.

Ramji-Nogales, Jaya, Andrew Ian Schoenholtz, and Philip G. Schrag. 2009. Refugee Roulette: Disparities in Asylum Adjudication and Proposals for Reform. New York: New York University Press.

Ressa, Maria. 2003. *Seeds of Terror: An Eyewitness Account of Al-Qaeda's Newest Center of Operations in Southeast Asia*. New York: Free Press.

Reyna, Stephen P., and R.E. Downs, eds. 1994. "Studying War: Anthropological Perspectives." *War and Society Series 2*. Amsterdam: Gordon and Breach.

Robertson, Shari, Michael Camerini, Karen Schmeer, Christopher Osborn, Suzanne Pancrazi, and Mark Suozzo. 2006. *Well-Founded Fear*, DVD. Produced and directed by Shari Robertson and Michael Camerini. New York: Docurama, New Video.

Rowan, Carl T. 1996. *The Coming Race War in America: A Wake-Up Call*. Boston: Little, Brown.

Ruffer, Galya. 2013. "Testimony of Sexual Violence in the Democratic Republic of Congo and the Injustice of Rape: Moral Outrage, Epistemic Injustice, and the Failures of Bearing Witness." *Oregon Review of International Law* 15:101–47.

———. 2014. "Research and Testimony in the 'Rape Capital of the World': Experts and Evidence in Congolese Asylum Claims." In *Adjudicating Refugee and Asylum Status: The Role of Witness, Expertise, and Testimony*, edited by Benjamin N. Lawrance and Galya Ruffer, 84–101. New York: Cambridge University Press.

Saeed, Abdullah, and Hassan Saeed. 2004. *Freedom of Religion, Apostasy and Islam*. Burlington, VT: Ashgate.

Said, Edward W. 2000. *Reflections on Exile and Other Essays*. Cambridge, MA: Harvard University Press.

Samuelsen, Helle, and Vibeke Steffen. 2004. "The Relevance of Foucault and Bourdieu for Medical Anthropology: Exploring New Sites." *Anthropology & Medicine* 11 (1):3–10. doi: 10.1080/1364847042000204951.

Sanjek, Roger, and Steven Gregory, eds. 1994. *Race*. New Brunswick, NJ: Rutgers University Press.

Semple, Kirk, Joseph Goldstein, and Jeffrey E. Singer. 2014. "Asylum Fraud in Chinatown: An Industry of Lies." In *New York Times*, Retrieved from http://www.nytimes.com/2014/02/23/nyregion/asylum-fraud-in-chinatown-industry-of-lies.html?_r=0.

Siegel, James T. 1986. *Solo in the New Order: Language and Hierarchy in an Indonesian City*. Princeton, NJ: Princeton University Press.

Sills, E. Scott, William Strider, Henry J. Hyde, Deborah Anker, Grover Joseph Rees, Owen K. Davis. 1998. "Gynaecology, Forced Sterilization, and Asylum in the USA." *Lancet*, June 6, 1998, 351: 1729–30.

Spijkerboer, Thomas. 2000. *Gender and Refugee Status*. Burlington, VT: Ashgate/Dartmouth.

Shaw, Carolyn Martin. 2009. "The Nature of Gender: Bodies, Culture, and Performance in the Construction of Gender." *Teaching Anthropology: SACC Notes* 16 (2):12–17.

Smedley, Audrey, and Brian D. Smedley. 2011. *Race in North America: Origin and Evolution of a Worldview*: Westview Press.

Suryadinata, Leo. 2004. *Chinese Indonesian: State Policy, Monoculture and Multiculture*. Singapore: Eastern University Press.

Suwarni, Yuli Tri. 2007. "Bandung Churches Again in the Crosshair." *Jakarta Post*. June 2007.

Takaki, Ronald. 1989. *Strangers from a Different Shore: A History of Asian Americans*. New York, New York: Penguin Books.

Thompson, Laurence G. 1995. *Chinese Religion: An Introduction*. 5th ed. Belmont, CA: Wadsworth Publishing Company.

Times of India. 2013. "Dowry Deaths: One Woman Dies Every Hour." *Times of India*, September 1, 2013. https://timesofindia.indiatimes.com/india/dowry-deaths-One-woman-dies-every-hour/articleshow/22201659.cms.

Transactional Records Access Clearing House. 2012. "Judge-by-Judge Asylum Decisions in Immigration Courts FY 2007-20012." TRAC, Syracuse University Accessed June 1, 2018. http://trac.syr.edu/immigration/reports/306/include/denialrates.html.

———. 2017. "Asylum Outcome Continues to Depend on the Judge Assigned." TRAC, Syracuse University Accessed June 1, 2018. http://trac.syr.edu/immigration/reports/490/.

Traphagan, John W. 2004. *The Practice of Concern: Ritual, Well-Being, and Aging in Rural Japan*. Ethnographic Studies in Medical Anthropology, edited by Pamela J. Stewart and Andrew Strathern, Durham, NC: Carolina Academic Press.

UN High Commissioner for Refugees (UNHCR). 2016. "The 10 Point Plan in Action, 2016 Update." *UN High Commissioner for Refugees* online. http://www.refworld.org/docid/581b3bf54.html.

U.S. Census Bureau. 2017. "Race." In *United States: Population Estimates*. Population Estimates Program. Accessed May 1, 2018. https://www.census.gov/quickfacts/fact/note/US/RHI425216.

U.S. Department of Justice. 2007. "Asylum Variations in Immigration Courts." In *Fact Sheet*. Washington, DC: US Government Publishing Office. Accessed June 1, 2016. https://www.justice.gov/sites/default/files/eoir/legacy/2008/09/09/AsylumVariationsNov07.pdf.

———. 2018. "Legal Careers: Immigration Judge." *The United States Department of Justice* online. April 24. https://www.justice.gov/legal-careers/job/immigration-judge-1.

U.S. Department of State. 2005. "Indonesia." In *2005 Report on International Religious Freedom*. Washington, DC: US Government Publishing Office. Accessed July 1, 2016. http://www.state.gov/g/drl/rls/irf/2005/51512.htm.

———. 2007. "Indonesia." In *2007 Report on International Religious Freedom*. Washington, DC: US Government Publishing Office. Accessed July 1, 2016. https://www.state.gov/j/drl/rls/irf/2007/90137.htm.

U.S. Office of Management and Budget. 1997. "Revisions to the Standards for the Classification of Federal Data on Race and Ethnicity." *Federal Register*

Notice, October 30, 1997. https://obamawhitehouse.archives.gov/omb/fedreg_1997standards.

Ying, Fan. 2000. "A Classification of Chinese Culture." [In English]. *Cross Cultural Management: An International Journal* 7, 2: 3–10, https://doi.org/10.1108/13527600010797057.

Wandita, Galuh. 1998. "The Tears Have Not Stopped, the Violence Has Not Ended: Political Upheaval, Ethnicity, and Violence against Women in Indonesia." *Gender and Development* 6 (3):34–41.

Wang, L. Ling-chi, and Gungwu Wang, ed. 2003. *The Chinese Diaspora: Selected Essays*. Illustrated, Reprint ed. 2 vols. Vol. 1. London: Eastern Universities Press.

Warner, William Lloyd. (1941). *Yankee City*. New Haven, CT: Yale University Press.

Williams, Thomas Rhys. 1965. *The Dusun: A North Borneo Society*. Edited by George and Louise Spindler. *Case Studies in Cultural Anthropology*. New York: Holt, Rinehart and Winston.

Wilson, Richard Ashby. 2016. "Expert Evidence on Trial: Social researchers in the international criminal courtroom." *American Ethnologist* 43 (4):730–44. doi: 101111/amet.12387.

Wilson, William J. 1980. *The Declining Significance of Race: Blacks and Changing American Institutions*. Chicago: Universtiy of Chicago Press.

Zhang, Junsen. 2017. "The Evolution of China's One-Child Policy and Its Effects on Family Outcomes." *The Journal of Economic Perspectives* 31 (1):141–59. doi: 10.1257/jep.31.1.141.

Zheng, Tiantian. 2015. "Intimate Partner Violence, Women, and Resistance in Postsocialist China." *Wagadu* 13:155–82.

Index

About the Contributors

ChorSwang Ngin is a professor of anthropology and the founder of the BA in Asian and Asian American studies at California State University, Los Angeles (CSULA). She has conducted research on the Vietnamese Boat People in the refugee camps in Southeast Asia, served as an anthropological expert witness in asylum courts in the United States over the last decade, and recently coauthored an article on the Dreamers Resources Center at CSULA.

Joann Yeh received her BS from MIT where a course in Asian American studies inspired her to take up law. She received her JD from the University of Pennsylvania Law School and was the Law Review's executive editor. She is currently with the law firm of John Johannes in Los Angeles.

INSIGHT PUBLISHING
SEVIERVILLE, TENNESSEE

Copyright © 2009

Published in the United States by
INSIGHT PUBLISHING
647 Wall Street • Sevierville, Tennessee • 37862
www.insightpublishing.com

All rights reserved. No part of this book may be reproduced in any form or by any means without prior written permission from the publisher except for brief quotations embodied in critical essay, article, or review. These articles and/or reviews must state the correct title and contributing authors of this book by name.

Publisher's Disclaimer: This book is a compilation of ideas from numerous experts who have each contributed a chapter. As such, the views expressed in each chapter are of those who were interviewed and not necessarily of the interviewer or Insight Publishing.

ISBN 978-1-60013-292-6

10 9 8 7 6 5 4 3 2 1